Migration, Remittances, and Small Business Development

Series on Development and International Migration in Mexico, Central America, and the Caribbean Basin

Sergio Díaz-Briquets and Sidney Weintraub,
Series Editors

Volume I
Determinants of Emigration from Mexico, Central America, and the Caribbean

Volume II
Regional and Sectoral Development in Mexico as Alternatives to Migration

Volume III
Migration Impacts of Trade and Foreign Investment: Mexico and Caribbean Basin Countries

Volume IV
Migration, Remittances, and Small Business Development: Mexico and Caribbean Basin Countries

FORTHCOMING

Volume V
Small Country Development and International Labor Flows: Experiences in the Caribbean,
edited by Anthony P. Maingot

Volume VI
The Effects of Receiving Country Policies on Migration Flows

Migration, Remittances, and Small Business Development

Mexico and Caribbean Basin Countries

EDITED BY
Sergio Díaz-Briquets
and Sidney Weintraub

Routledge
Taylor & Francis Group
LONDON AND NEW YORK

First published 1991 by Westview Press

Published 2018 by Routledge
52 Vanderbilt Avenue, New York, NY 10017
2 Park Square, Milton Park, Abingdon, Oxon OX14 4RN

Routledge is an imprint of the Taylor & Francis Group, an informa business

Library of Congress Cataloging-in-Publication Data
Migration, remittances, and small business development : Mexico and Caribbean Basin countries / edited by Sergio Díaz-Briquets and Sidney Weintraub.
p. cm.—(Series on development and international migration in Mexico, Central America, and the Caribbean Basin ; no. 4)
Includes bibliographical references.
ISBN 0-8133-8340-4
1. Small business—Caribbean Area. 2. Emigrant remittances—Caribbean Area. 3. Caribbean Area—Emigration and immigration—Economic aspects. 4. United States—Emigration and immigration—Economic aspects. I. Díaz-Briquets, Sergio. II. Weintraub, Sidney, 1922– . III. Series.
HD2346.C4M54 1991
338.972—dc20 91-8691
CIP

ISBN 13: 978-0-367-01664-7 (hbk)
ISBN 13: 978-0-367-16651-9 (pbk)

Contents

Series Preface

The Immigration Reform and Control Act of 1986 (IRCA) was a manifestation of widespread public concern over the volume of undocumented immigration into the United States. The principal innovation of this legislation—the provision to impose penalties on employers who knowingly hire undocumented immigrants—was a response to this concern.

This effort at restriction was tempered in IRCA by other provisions permitting the legalization of two types of undocumented immigrants—those who had resided in the United States since January 1, 1982; and what were called special agricultural workers (SAWs), persons who had worked in perishable crop agriculture for at least 90 days during specified periods from 1983 to 1986. Approximately 3.1 million persons sought legalization (what is popularly referred to as amnesty) under these two provisions. The breakdown was roughly 1.8 million under the regular program and 1.3 million as SAWs. Mexicans made up 75 percent of the combined legalization requests.

Two elements—punishment and exoneration—were essential ingredients of the compromise that made possible the passage of IRCA, but they also had the effect of working at cross purposes, at least temporarily. For a time, many persons who might have crossed the border without papers took the opportunity to regularize their status and thus enter legally. In our research we discovered many non-farmers who had not earlier considered temporary migration but who obtained papers as SAWs to enter the United States. Officials of the U.S. Immigration and Naturalization Service (INS) asserted that there was widespread fraud under the SAWs program for applicants from Mexico and elsewhere. We verified from the Mexican side of the border that, indeed, there was fraud, but our evidence does not permit making an estimate of its magnitude. The two provisions together did not slow immigration but instead permitted some switching from undocumented to documented border crossing. During the period that legalization applications could be submitted, therefore, data showing a decline in unauthorized border crossings (apprehensions) were deceptive.

In due course, however, undocumented immigration began to pick up again, and apprehension data and other evidence now indicate that it is at a level similar to that before enactment of IRCA. There is ample proof of the production of fraudulent documents permitting immigrants to show employers that they are "legally" in the United States. It is probably impossible to end this entrepreneurial document production short of instituting a foolproof identity card, assuming the word "foolproof" is an accurate characterization of technology. The idea of Americans having to show an identity card when seeking employment has not been accepted.

It is an overstatement to say definitively that IRCA has failed to accomplish its main task, to staunch the flow of undocumented immigrants by means of penalties on employers, but that is the initial conclusion one must reach. Its failure means that the available options for reducing the inflow of undocumented immigrants—assuming this is still the U.S. goal—are reduced by the one option that was earlier considered the most promising.

An identity card is not acceptable. A high fence, patrolled by armed guards keeping persons without papers from entering the United States, would be unacceptably obtrusive and also alter the relationship with Mexico. It would be anomalous to forcefully close the border to people at the same time the United States and Mexico are planning to open the border to the free flow of goods and services.

There thus remains only one feasible option—short of leaving bad enough alone and letting those who wish to come do so—and that is to foster the economic development of those countries that send the bulk of undocumented migrants to the United States. If punishment is not the solution, then perhaps development is.

We did not know development was really the only option when this research project was started. However, IRCA had a little-noticed provision that established the Commission for the Study of International Migration and Cooperative Economic Development with the following mandate:

> The Commission, in consultation with the governments of Mexico and other sending countries in the Western Hemisphere, shall examine the conditions in Mexico and such other sending countries which contribute to unauthorized migration to the United States and [shall explore] mutually beneficial, reciprocal trade and investment programs to alleviate such conditions.

THE RESEARCH PROGRAM

The research program of the Commission focused on two broad themes: why people emigrate from their own countries to enter clandestinely into the United States, and what cooperative development measures are most appropriate to reduce the economic incentive to emigrate. More emphasis in the research was placed on the second of these two issues, particularly job creation in migrant-sending countries, because there was already ample scholarly literature on the motives for emigration. These motives are not solely economic, but evidence from years of research demonstrates clearly that the economic dominates.

We have culled the research supported by the Commission to sort out those essays that we think make valuable contributions to the literature on the relationship between development and migration. The authors of the essays are experts in this field from migrant-sending countries, Europe, and the United States. The essays selected are organized into six volumes, each dealing with a specific aspect of the development theme; each volume is therefore self-contained. In our judgment, the six volumes together make the most original contribution that exists to date on the development-migration relationship. We are gratified that Westview Press reached a similar conclusion and wished to publish the series.

Both editors were involved in the research program of the Commission: Sergio Díaz-Briquets as research director and Sidney Weintraub as senior research adviser. Our motive in bringing out the series is to provide scholars with a base of research from which they can delve further into the development-migration nexus.

As the listing of the series shows, one volume (Volume II) deals exclusively with Mexico, and three others (Volumes I, III, and IV) with Mexico and with other countries in Central America and the Caribbean. For the sake of convenience, we use the phrase Caribbean Basin to refer to the collectivity of countries in this region. The emphasis on Mexico is warranted by the evidence that Mexicans constitute about 70 percent of the unauthorized immigrants in the United States. Volume V deals with Central America and the Caribbean, and the final volume (Volume VI) with U.S. policies relating to development in and emigration from Mexico and other countries of the Caribbean Basin. Although we take responsibility as senior editors for all the volumes, the editor for Volume V is Anthony P. Maingot. The final volume contains the executive summary of the report of the Commission submitted to the Congress and the president.

The essays deal mostly with migrant-sending countries in the Western Hemisphere because that was the Commission's mandate and because the bulk of undocumented immigrants into the United States come from Mexico and other countries of the Caribbean Basin. However, the Western Hemisphere emphasis is not exclusive, and several comparative essays on receiving-country policies in Europe are included in Volume VI.

KEY OVERALL FINDINGS

Although research conclusions in the specific areas are discussed in each volume, some overall findings merit emphasis. The most important is the one already stated: that no viable alternative to economic development seems to exist that would significantly reduce undocumented immigration into the United States. It is hardly original to state that as a country becomes better developed, the economic pressure to emigrate is likely to be reduced. Historically, the development thesis has been demonstrated, particularly in Western Europe where countries of emigration became lands of immigration. Western Europe is now coping with its own undocumented, or unwanted, immigrants. Ireland, which has not enjoyed as much sustained growth as other countries in Western Europe, is still a country from which people emigrate. We observed, over time, that domestic economic well-being in European countries overcame the strength of networks in perpetuating outward migration.

Skeptics (including us) acknowledged the need for development, but they argued that it took too long to be relevant for dealing with current problems of undocumented immigration or, indeed, with anticipated migration movements over the next several decades. We do not know what income differential stimulates undocumented migration; nor do we know how much narrowing of this differential is necessary to deter emigration. We do know, however, that the difference between $1,900 and $19,000 a year—which are the respective 1990 per capita incomes in Mexico and the United States—is a stimulant to emigration. Completely closing this gap, even under wondrous estimates of Mexican economic growth, is apt to take more than 100 years. This is not the kind of assessment a policy maker likes to hear.

Yet, it is to this advice that our research leads. Sherlock Holmes was fond of saying that if all explanations but one to a conundrum must be discarded, then that one must contain the answer. This is the conclusion we reach. If emigration cannot be curtailed by other means, then the remaining viable option must be exploited; and it really does not matter if policy makers and legislators with a short-term outlook grumble at this conclusion.

The saving grace is that incomes do not have to be identical to act as a deterrent to clandestine migration. There is a natural desire of most persons to remain at home, which can be reinforced if economic hope is offered to would-be migrants and their children. We suspect, based on the research contained in the series, that absolute income differentials may matter less in the migrate-stay calculus than the direction of economic hope (that is, whether economic conditions at home are improving or deteriorating). We are not referring here to improved economic conditions for one year or two, but sustained over a decade or so.

The importance of sustaining economic growth over some unquantifiable time period must be emphasized. What we found in study after study was that a short-term increase in income, over one or two years, leads to increased emigration. We came across no study that contradicted this finding. The reason, presumably, is that a modest increase in income makes it possible for people to afford the trip. If, as in the Mexican case, income per person increases by, say, 3 percent after inflation, this adds only $57 to the annual income of the average Mexican. Even this overstates the case; the "average" Mexican, some 50 percent of the population, earns much less than $1,000 a year. An increase in income of $57 or less is not enough to deter the economic incentive to emigrate. But adding 3 percent a year, compounded over 10 or 20 years, might make a difference.

The conclusion that it requires continued economic growth to have a meaningful influence on curtailing emigration has as its corollary that the "cooperative" U.S. policy contained in the Commission's mandate must also be sustained. Although development is essentially an internal responsibility, and Mexico and other countries in the region are taking many needed steps to restructure their economies, the external environment plays a decisive role. This is not the place for a detailed discussion of U.S. economic policy except to note that if sustained economic growth is required in sending countries to reduce emigration pressures, then U.S. measures that frustrate this growth (particularly trade protectionism but also U.S. macroeconomic policy that slows U.S. growth or pushes up the interest rate that sending countries must pay on their foreign debt) will stimulate undocumented immigration. If the current push toward free trade between Mexico and the United States serves to augment the growth of income and employment in Mexico, it will also have a long-term effect of curtailing emigration pressure. Free trade between the United States and other countries of the region is a less immediate prospect, but it too may eventually help to stimulate the growth of income and employment of these nations.

One other overall conclusion that emerges from the research is that the economic development process as it has been pursued, certainly in the period since World War II, has stimulated internal migration. In country after country, the rural-urban population relationship has shifted in favor of the urban part of the ratio. Cities have burgeoned as the relative role of agriculture has diminished. Manufacturing and services have grown in importance compared with agriculture. This is the normal pattern of development, as witness the historical experience of Europe and the United States. Habits of migration have thus become commonplace in sending countries in the Western Hemisphere, as elsewhere. Although it is more traumatic to pick up stakes and leave one's own country than to shift within the country, the difference is a matter of degree. Once networks, or ethnic diasporas, have been established in the United States, as they generally have for migrant-sending countries in the Western Hemisphere, even the difference of degree between internal and external migration diminishes. Thus, the number of undocumented immigrants to the United States should not be expected to diminish for the foreseeable future; and this fact increases the importance of sustained economic growth to keep people home.

The relative importance of Mexico as a sending country may decline in coming decades because its economic prospects are more auspicious than those of other countries in the region, particularly in Central America. In addition, migrant networks in the United States have now been established for Central American countries.

Populations in the migrant-sending countries are quite young, and none of these countries is creating enough jobs to satisfy all persons entering the labor force. This situation, once more, points to the primacy of economic growth as the necessary deterrent to emigration.

We have been struck in our investigations by how extensively people in the world are on the move. Our studies concentrated on the movement of people in the Western Hemisphere to the United States, but there are large migrations within Africa and Asia, and into Western Europe from the east (the former Communist countries) and the south (such as from North Africa into France and Italy). It is easier—not easy, but easier—to control immigration into Western Europe than it is into the United States, to which migrants can come across a large land border with Mexico. Yet the West Europeans are not having much success either in dealing with their immigration problem. As with the United States, the key to control is development in the sending countries. We are dealing, in other words, with a global phenomenon. The subject presents itself as a migration issue, but at its core it is a development matter.

WHAT COMES NEXT

The proper approach to development must differ from country to country—even apart from the conceptual or ideological model that is used. Mexico is a large, populous country in which there is scope for regional differentiation. This approach is not available to any meaningful extent for other countries in the Caribbean Basin. Mexico has a substantial industrial structure on which to base export-led growth, as it is now doing. The industrial structure is more modest in Central America and hardly exists in much of the Caribbean.

Overall findings of the type set forth in this preface can take a policy maker only so far. Understanding the link between development and migration, and then making policy to influence both phenomena, requires intimate knowledge of conditions in sub-regions and in each country. This is provided in the six volumes in this series.

Our objectives in bringing out these volumes are twofold: to augment understanding of the development-migration relationship based on the extensive research that was carried out; and, much more importantly in the long run, to stimulate further scholarly research about this theme.

Sergio Díaz-Briquets
Sidney Weintraub

Introduction

Sergio Díaz-Briquets
and Sidney Weintraub

The small business sector is extremely significant in Mexico and other countries of the Caribbean Basin because of the employment that it generates. These businesses, whether in the formal or informal sector, provide employment and income for millions of persons, mostly in cities but also in rural regions. The precise economic role of small businesses varies from country to country and the nature of these businesses appears to be linked to a country's development level, the speed with which it is urbanizing, and the stage of the economic cycle. There are also links between international labor migration and the health of a country's small business sector. Migrant remittances contribute to the growth of small enterprises; this contribution could be greater, however. Better jobs in small businesses could, over time, help reduce pressures to emigrate.

There is some debate about the role of small businesses in the economies of Mexico and other Caribbean Basin countries. Some analysts regard small business—especially in the informal economy—as a low-productivity economic activity that, at best, provides only minimal incomes to persons with limited options elsewhere. Others view small businesses as a dynamic sector of the economy with substantial growth potential that would be met if unneeded regulatory burdens could be removed and if institutional and financial support could be provided. Both descriptions, we believe, are true in part. There are many small businesses in the region capable of generating only basic subsistence income. However, there are also competitive firms that create well-paying jobs.

There are many definitions of a small business. Some businesses are so small as to elude study. The distinction between formal and informal activities is conceptually straightforward, but is not as clear in practice. Many small enterprises move between these two categories.

The usual definition of a small business is based on the number of workers or gross income, but these are imperfect measures. In all Caribbean Basin countries, the vast majority of businesses are "small." Income data are notoriously inadequate, especially in the informal sector. Small firms use a variety of production arrangements to serve their customers—wholesale, retail, and subcontracting to name but three—and employ different types of labor, such as non-paid family labor, apprenticeship, and wage labor. Definitions and characterizations are not consistent across countries or even among analysts within a single country.

The small business sector, however defined, provides much employment in the migrant-sending nations of the Caribbean Basin. One constraint commonly faced by small businesses is a shortage of investment and operating capital. Thus, programs to support the growth of small firms in developing countries seek to provide loans, often at subsidized interest rates. These programs typically are underfunded and reach few businesses. Another source of funding derives from international labor migration. Many migrants utilize savings accumulated while working abroad to begin or maintain small businesses. Some of these businesses are established by the migrants themselves after they return to their home countries, and others are managed by relatives of migrants with the support of remittance income. Most of these migration-related businesses have low productivity and could not survive without a regular flow of remittances. However, only a small share of remittance income is used for productive investments; much goes to augment consumption. Nevertheless, remittances could constitute a significant development resource if they were channeled into viable small businesses. This has not been easy to accomplish and it would be unwise to be glib about the prospects.

The policy interventions to promote small business growth have had only modest impact. One reason is that the overall policy environment—such as civil wars, overvalued exchange rates, and exchange controls—does not support the growth of small business. More effective use of remittance income for development purposes also depends on a receptive policy environment. Instead, policies in most countries of the region discourage migrants from investing their savings at home.

Policies geared to increase the volume of remittances and those formulated to encourage the growth of the small business sector are potentially complementary. Remittances can, in principle, provide the capital infusions required for many small enterprises to succeed. As several of the chapters in this volume suggest, programs to assist the home-grown small entrepreneur should also consider the needs and interests of the migrant investor. Migrants may be prepared to increase investments at home if circumstances make this a good risk.

If small businesses can be developed in migrant-sending communities, they could alter local employment and income prospects, which might reduce migratory pressures over time. However, in the short term, the migratory process itself engenders a dependency on remittance income, which is necessary to start or maintain small businesses. This dilemma is implicit in the discussion in the chapters of this volume. Yet, it is clear that vibrant small businesses are necessary for economic growth in the countries examined.

This volume offers an analysis of the employment and income potential of the small business sector in a number of migrant-sending countries. Contributing authors evaluate programs that support the sector and give recommendations for improving their effectiveness. Several seek to explain why most countries in the region have not made the most of remittance income to create employment. Finally, others examine the imperfectly understood linkages between remittances and small businesses. Together, they provide an overview of how to enhance the employment potential of the small business sector and how remittances can contribute to that objective.

Half of all jobs in Central America are generated by poorly capitalized businesses with fifty employees or less. These small- and medium-sized enterprises account for 80 percent of all businesses in the region. Value added per unit of input is generally higher in small and medium industrial enterprises in Central America than in larger firms. The small firms also tend to create more jobs per unit of capital input. Francisco A. Leguizamón therefore sees the small and medium business sectors as "a valuable resource for expanding output and creating employment." He believes that helping these businesses grow would lead to retention of people in Central America; workers, he argues, would not be forced to emigrate in search of economic opportunity.

Leguizamón's chapter contains a country-by-country discussion of national institutions and the types of assistance they provide to small and medium businesses in Central America. He reviews the major impediments faced by these businesses and critically examines the strategies pursued by the countries in the region to promote their growth. Leguizamón lists major obstacles to the growth of small businesses as unstable social environments, poorly conceived macroeconomic policies, and ineffective institutions. Credit availability and technical and managerial assistance to small and medium businesses are limited. Although every country in Central America has policies intended to encourage small and medium business growth, none has created favorable conditions for promoting these activities.

Leguizamón argues that new initiatives to support the sector must move away from an almost exclusive attention on credit needs. Emphasis, he says, must shift to a support strategy that integrates financing with the provision of technical and managerial assistance. Support institutions with credibility among intended beneficiaries must be established. Costa Rica, he asserts, is the country best positioned to make such policies work, partly because it enjoys internal peace and democratic institutions, but also because the policy framework is comprehensive. Leguizamón is most pessimistic regarding small and medium business development in Nicaragua. However, many of the conditions he describes have changed since the Sandinista defeat in the 1990 elections.

Small business is an important component of the economy in the Dominican Republic, especially in commerce and services, according to Rolando Reyes. As in other countries, small businesses, formal and informal, are related to the overall business sector in various ways. There is competition as well as complementarity between the two segments. Small business growth continues due to high levels of rural-to-urban migration. There is still considerable urban unemployment in the Dominican Republic and, partially stemming from this, much emigration abroad. This connection between urban unemployment and emigration leads Reyes to postulate that emigration pressures might be reduced by raising the employment absorption capacity of the small business sector. Reyes cautions, however, that this strategy is not a panacea because emigration is driven largely by the large wage differential between the Dominican Republic and the United States—a conclusion borne out by other studies that show that most Dominican emigrants were employed at home before leaving.

Reyes provides a detailed assessment of the programs in support of the small business sector in the Dominican Republic. These include some of the most successful programs in the developing world, such as Asociación para el Desarrollo de la Pequeña Empresa (ADEMI); nevertheless, most small enterprises in the Dominican Republic still cannot obtain credit on reasonable terms, despite the fact that the focus of most assistance programs is on providing credit. The funds available for these lending programs are quite limited. A significant shortcoming of small business support programs in the Dominican Republic—as in Central America—is the inadequacy of training and technical assistance. Reyes makes a number of recommendations to strengthen support activities. These include creating a loan portfolio for intermediate and long term financing; taking employment effects into account in the evaluation of loan requests; modifying the criteria used to set loan interest rates; and assigning a portion of the loan portfolio to financing new small businesses.

Wilbert O. Bascom examines how the flow of migrant remittances in the English-speaking Caribbean could be attuned to the dramatic changes taking place in international financial markets. Bascom describes the existing mechanisms for remittance transfer, including the regulatory framework of various U.S. states. He believes that the authorities in English-speaking Caribbean countries do not fully appreciate the significance of recent financial market changes or understand how these changes can be exploited to enhance the region's development. Bascom argues that English-speaking Caribbean countries should adopt a broad definition of remittances by including accumulated stocks of wealth of emigrants and expatriates. He then advocates policies in home countries that encourage these expatriates to diversify their investment portfolios by allocating some of their holdings back home. Such allocation will not take place, he says, as long as the English-speaking Caribbean countries lack efficient financial markets or maintain overvalued exchange rates and negative real interest rates for savings. Bascom states that "the Caribbean countries are in competition with the rest of the international economy for savings, trade, and direct investment flows. They could effectively participate in this competition only if their monetary and fiscal policies are adapted to the rules of the game of international financial competition."

The next three chapters examine an issue that has received inadequate attention from the research community: How are remittances related to the establishment and growth of small businesses in migrant-sending countries? These three chapters deal with the Dominican Republic, Mexico, and El Salvador, respectively.

In their ground-breaking study, Alejandro Portes and Luis E. Guarnizo examine the interplay between Dominican enterprises in New York City and those in the Dominican Republic. The data sample included firms in both locations. The firms in the Dominican sample were located in Santo Domingo and Santiago and "were somewhat larger than the more abundant, but short-lived microenterprises." To be included, firms had to have between five and fifty permanent employees, although smaller firms were included if they had a minimum capital of or equivalent to U.S. $5,000. The firms chosen also had to meet one or more criteria that clearly linked them to emigration: "be owned by returned migrants or migrants still living abroad; be managed or staffed by returned migrants; receive transfers in cash or kind from migrants abroad; be acquired or started, partially or exclusively, with monies from migrant labor; [and] have major clients among Dominican migrants abroad."

The most important finding of the study is that a thriving Dominican business community in New York City is associated with business activities in the Dominican Republic, particularly through the capital invested in the creation of new jobs in the Dominican Republic. These emigration-related firms "appear better capitalized than the 'typical' Dominican small firm, a fact which may reflect their continuing links with outside sources of financing." Investments in these firms are not always liquid; they often involve producer goods or commodities for sale. One important finding is that the operators of the Dominican firms often travel abroad to purchase inputs or to raise investment capital, sometimes by means of their own wage work. Many small entrepreneurs indicated that they use skills acquired abroad in their businesses. These skills were often obtained while working in small Dominican-owned firms, rather than in large, technologically more advanced firms not owned by Dominicans. The continued success of many of these enterprises in the Dominican Republic depends on the ebb and flow of Dominican emigration and on the fact that the emigrants believe they can do well in their home country in the context of an emerging "binational economic community."

Portes and Guarnizo conclude that although the further development of the small business sector is unlikely to halt Dominican emigration, it can reduce emigration pressures. The authors argue that U.S. assistance policies, for example, those providing subsidized credit to the small business sector in the Dominican Republic, can reduce the attraction of emigration by reinforcing the entrepreneurial orientation of Dominicans. The Dominican authorities, they argue, "should work with, not against, the immigrant community" in order to maximize transfers to the Dominican Republic. Such policies should include ensuring the unrestricted convertibility of all financial transfers and allowing individual migrants and emigrant firms to have dollar-denominated accounts in the Dominican Republic.

Agustín Escobar Latapí and María de la O Martínez Castellanos review linkages between small-scale firms and international migration from Guadalajara. Their study is based on labor market surveys and small firm case studies conducted between 1982 and 1989. This period encompasses the years of the Mexican economic crisis, permitting an assessment of how the small business sector of Guadalajara adapted to the economic downturn.

Guadalajara has a vibrant small business sector that has learned how to live with adversity. Emigration, nonetheless, is frequently the solution for entrepreneurs and employees seeking to cope with temporary economic downturn or to sustain small ventures. According to an official 1981 survey, 17 percent of small-scale firm owners (firms with less than twenty-five employees and sales under $400,000) had worked in the United States. For many of these entrepreneurs, "migration is not undertaken because life in the United States is preferable, but because the United States offers certain things that can improve life in Mexico."

Escobar Latapí and Martínez Castellanos make a distinction between microenterprises and craft shops. The former usually require a larger capital base, and their owners shun manual labor and generally come from a higher social class than the workers. Owners of craft shops, by contrast, usually possess considerable manual skills and work side by side with their employees. Business success acts as a deterrent to emigration in both types of firms. If the owner of a craft shop were to emigrate, the shop would suffer because much of the production depends on the owner's own output. However, both in craft shops and in microenterprises, emigration often has occurred when there was a need to accumulate savings, as was the case during the economic downturn in Guadalajara.

Escobar Latapí and Martínez Castellanos found that credit programs geared to small businesses often benefit larger firms. They suggest that the Mexican government should facilitate the establishment of credit programs managed directly by distributors of modern equipment who know their local markets and who could therefore reach a greater number of small business credit users. This strategy, they suggest, could lead to a wider availability of credit sources and to the modernization of the industrial plant of many small firms. Low productivity in many of the small firms they studied was traced to obsolete and insufficient equipment. Small firms also could benefit greatly from programs to disseminate marketing opportunities.

The current socioeconomic and political context of El Salvador is far different from that of either the Dominican Republic or Mexico. José Roberto López and Mitchell A. Seligson review the linkage between remittances and small business development in a nation devastated by a decade of civil war. This situation also stimulated extremely high emigration rates during the 1980s. As a result, remittances have become the country's main source of foreign exchange in most years. A significant share of all Salvadoran families receives remittances. López and Seligson provide evidence that remittances are an important source of resources for many small businesses in the country.

Their study is based on a purposeful sample of small businesses in and around the San Salvador metropolitan area. The analysis suggests that the very existence of these businesses depends on the remittances they receive. From one-quarter to one-third of the firms in the sample were established because of the availability of remittance income. Survival of many of these businesses, most of them only a few years old, is directly linked to the continued arrival of remittances. Remittance income, on average, accounted for almost 50 percent of the gross income of these firms. Remittances have become a substitute for business income that would be generated during normal peacetime activities. These firms provide occupation for their owners and paid employment to the few workers they hire. There is understandable concern among the owners of these businesses that remittances continue. These small firms, while not now independently viable, might assist with economic recovery after peace is reestablished because they provide a business base on which to build.

Despite the significance of remittances to the Salvadoran economy, the authorities have done little to maximize benefits from the remittances.

What has been done has often been counterproductive. López and Seligson comment that "efforts devoted to taking advantage of remittance inflows from Salvadorans residing in the United States are almost nonexistent compared to official measures taken to promote nontraditional and cotton exports." Their recommendations are consistent with those made by Bascom for the English-speaking Caribbean countries, and by Portes and Guarnizo for the Dominican Republic: That the Salvadoran authorities facilitate remittances by expatriates and not frustrate them by misguided policies and red tape.

As is evident from the chapters, remittances provide substantial resources for the region. However, their contribution to small business development has been modest. In addition, governments of the region have not always adopted policies to encourage emigrants to channel a greater share of their savings to the home countries. Both types of policy change—internal, to direct remittances to small business development, and external, to encourage more remittances—could help raise levels of income in the region. Yet, in the short term, the search for remittances is likely to intensify emigration because this is one way in which small entrepreneurs are able to acquire investment and working capital. Over the long term, the employment and income effects of small business development will be indispensable in dampening pressures for emigration from the region.

1

The Small Business Sector in Central America: A Diagnosis

Francisco A. Leguizamón

I. INTRODUCTION

Before 1980, the small- and medium-sized business sector in Central America (S&MSB) was virtually ignored by decision makers and by economists. They did not consider it a viable alternative for helping the region develop. Indeed, in spite of the fact that more than 90 percent of businesses operating in the area could be classified as small- or medium-sized, only from 1980 on did national policymakers, government agencies and some private development organizations (generally with backing from international agencies) begin to show an interest in this sector. By increasing the sector's productivity, competitiveness and participation in the benefits of development, and with the backing of local supporting agencies, S&MSBs began to be thought of as a vehicle for development.

Part of the explanation for the increasing interest in S&MSBs lies in the onset of the worst depression since the 1930s. World prices for Central America's main exports—coffee, sugar, cotton, beef and bananas—have, with few exceptions, fallen. Productivity has also fallen because of increased violence and political uncertainty. For the first time in half a century, economic growth rates of the Central American countries have not kept up with that of their population, thus bringing about a drop in per capita income. In spite of government efforts backed by international organizations, changes have not been very significant. Among entrepreneurs, therefore, there is widespread dissatisfaction with official efforts.[1]

This chapter pinpoints the main factors that make S&MSBs a key component of the Central American economies. In the second section, national strategies for developing S&MSBs that seem to emerge from both government policies and the existing local institutional framework are described. They are then translated into norms, processes and programs for implementation. The third section presents the main barriers to the development of S&MSBs and what both entrepreneurs and support institutions consider the main problems with strengthening the sector. The final section presents the conclusions deriving from my analysis of the problems and national strategies. It then proposes a radical change in the institutions' approach to relations with the beneficiary entrepreneurs and the outlook for producing a tangible drive in the development of S&MSBs throughout the region.

II. RELATIVE SHARE

In Central America, businesses with fewer than 50 employees, managed by no more than three people and using relatively simple tools, machinery and technology form the category that, in this paper, I shall call small- and medium-sized businesses. These businesses generate about 50 percent of total employment,[2] represent more than 80 percent of the existing businesses and a good deal of the value-added that they generate corresponds to salaries and wages. The relative share of S&MSBs in each of the Central American countries can be seen in Table 1.

When population growth goes hand in hand with a scarcity of financial resources, reduced workable territory and limited international competitiveness, common sense suggests that the effort to create jobs should focus on activities capable of generating the greatest number of jobs per unit of output. In Central America, as can be seen from Table 2, the S&MSB sector achieves a unit of value-added with a lower proportion of inputs than does the rest of the industrial sector. The figures also indicate that S&MSBs achieve a higher proportion of employment for each unit of inputs used.

Central America's small businesses apparently offer an increasing opportunity for incorporating women into the formal economy. The Alliance for Juvenile Community Development (ALIANZA) in Guatemala has been developing a successful program for exporting handicrafts made by peasant women since 1982. A study carried out in Honduras found that two-thirds of small rural businesses were managed by women. Studies in other countries indicate a lower, but still significant, percentage of between 40 and 50.

In addition to representing a valuable resource for expanding output and creating jobs, S&MSBs can be seen as a source of other benefits, such as social cohesion and the democratization of the economy, the latter being understood as promoting a greater number of businesses throughout society. Because of the total share of S&MSBs, entrepreneurs can organize to obtain sufficient resources to maintain themselves and to regulate internal relations, relations with other sectors of the economy and with governmental institutions. This process would, in turn, lead to a more stable democracy in the countries where democracy is still in its infancy or not yet a reality. On the whole, an increase in the number of S&MSBs would tend to keep people in their own region, thereby reducing the marked tendency of people to emigrate in search of opportunities or jobs.

III. KEY FACTORS FOR THE DEVELOPMENT OF S&MSBs

The use made of the potential of S&MSBs for producing economic and social benefits depends on various factors. World Bank studies supply abundant evidence that economies that grow rapidly provide drive for the development of S&MSBs.[3] Unfortunately, in the case of Central America,

TABLE 1

SHARE OF S&MSB IN THE ECONOMY

(percentages)

Country	S&MSB Value-Added–GDP Ratio	S&MSB Value-added–Industrial Value-Added Ratio	S&MSB Employment–Industrial Employment Ratio	S&MSB Value of Assets-Value of Total Industrial Assets Ratio
Guatemala (1977)	3.5	21.7	28.4	N.D.
El Salvador (1978)	5.0	25.2	25.0	10.9
Honduras (1975)	3.2	20.0	29.4	17.2
Nicaragua (1981)	5.5	19.6	36.8	8.0
Costa Rica (1980)	5.7	33.7	46.9	12.5

Source: Francisco A. Leguizamón, John C. Ickis and Francisco J. Gómez, *El extensionista empresarial: un vínculo para el desarrollo* (Editorial Universitaria Centroamericana, 1987), p. 28.

TABLE 2

INDICATORS OF S&MSB USE OF ASSETS IN JOB CREATION AND INDUSTRIAL VALUE-ADDED

Country	Proportion of Value of Assets to Obtain 1% of Value-Added		Proportion of Value of Assets to Obtain 1% of Industrial Employment	
	S&MSB	Rest of Sector	S&MSB	Rest of Sector
Guatemala	—	—	—	—
El Salvador	0.43	1.07	0.77	1.07
Honduras	0.86	1.03	0.58	0.85
Nicaragua	0.41	1.14	0.22	1.46
Costa Rica	0.37	1.32	0.27	1.65

Source: Francisco Leguizamón, John C. Ickis and Francisco J. Gómez, *El extensionista empresarial: un vínculo para el desarollo* (Editorial Universitaria Centroamericana, 1987), p. 30.

the economic environment can be described as stagnant or, in some countries, as frankly impoverished since the late 1970s. Until 1986, as shown in Table 3, two countries in the region, El Salvador and Nicaragua, were characterized by a decline in their GNP. Per capita GDP may have declined in all of them. Gross investment in 1986, in comparison with 1977, decreased in all five countries. Exports also dropped, except in Honduras and Costa Rica. External debt increased in all of them while banking reserves diminished. Private consumption exhibited the same behavior in relation to total consumption.

A stable social climate, characterized by institutions and social groups with accepted, though not necessarily shared, interests and objectives creates the necessary environment for new enterprises to emerge and for the maintenance and progress of existing ones. The second factor is lacking; therefore, it is difficult for S&MSBs to develop in Central America. In fact, the economic crisis in which the region still finds itself goes hand in hand with a precarious social situation: the Salvadoran government has difficulty controlling or negotiating with local guerrillas; there are uncertain but improved prospects for the democratization process in Nicaragua; there is uneasiness in Honduras and Costa Rica caused by unexpected migration from neighboring countries. These circumstances taken together limit the opportunities for the development of local S&MSBs.

Another factor generally accepted as crucial for the development of S&MSBs is government macroeconomic policies and the institutional policies drawn up by organizations directly related to the sector. All the Central American countries have laws aimed at helping develop S&MSBs; however, these laws have not become an effective tool. They emphasize tax incentives that small entrepreneurs cannot necessarily take advantage of (for example, exemption from customs duties on imports). The interinstitutional committees set up to study the problems and coordinate programs for S&MSBs have not been effective in meeting their objectives.

The institutions responsible for implementing policies designed to create and provide services are also very important in strengthening and developing S&MSBs. In a study carried out by the Instituto Centroamericano de Administración de Empresas (INCAE) in 1985, we pinpointed 37 primary institutions for providing support to S&MSBs. Many others were being set up, but their success was hindered for many reasons. Some of these barriers are of an internal nature and refer to operational incapacity to carry out the programs. Other barriers are external and range from beneficiary mistrust of, and resistance to, using the institution's services, to difficulties in carrying out interinstitutional efforts in programs requiring cooperation.

Financing is widely recognized as critical for the development of S&MSBs. In Central America, credit granted to this sector is insufficient,

TABLE 3

MACRO-ECONOMIC INDICATORS

Indicators	Guatemala 1977	Guatemala 1979	Guatemala 1986	El Salvador 1977	El Salvador 1979	El Salvador 1986	Honduras 1977	Honduras 1979	Honduras 1986	Nicaragua 1977	Nicaragua 1979	Nicaragua 1986	Costa Rica 1977	Costa Rica 1979	Costa Rica 1986
Population (Million Inhabitant)	6.44	6.73	8.19	4.52	4.66	5.35	3.44	3.56	4.49	2.61	2.69	3.38	2.14	2.21	2.67
Gross National Product (Million 1970 US$) 1. 1977, 1979 2. 1986	2,983.0	3,280.0	3,105.1	1,480.0	1,548.0	1,294.9	943.0	1,120.0	1,236.6	1,136.0	790.0	835.9	1,612.0	1,692.0	1,800.9
Gross Investment (Million 1970 US$) 1. 1977, 1979 2. 1986	463.0	471.0	250.4	300.0	260.0	168.1	220.0	249.0	185.3	241.0	53.0	184.9	413.0	476.0	368.9
Exports (Million 1970 US$) 1. 1977, 1979 2. 1986	576.0	633.0	400.1	308.0	506.0	268.6	255.0	322.0	344.0	302.0	384.0	142.7	497.0	514.0	545.7
Terms of Trade Index 1. 1977, 1979 2. 1986	100.0	81.6	ND	100.0	67.7	89.0	100.0	90.9	94.0	100.0	81.3	ND	100.0	90.3	ND
International Dept (Million 1970 US$) 1. 1977, 1979 2. 1986	302.0	427.0	2,516.0	458.0	ND	2,200.0	538.0	964.0	2,880.0	874.0	1,131.0	5,773.0	812.0	1,463.0	3,739.0

International Monetary Reserves 1. 1977, 1979 2. 1986	628.0	663.0	(61.0)	206.0	126.0	102.0	111.0	116.0	(129.0)	29.0	(151.0)	(139.0)	232.0	117.0	(68.0)
Fiscal Coefficient	10.2	9.0	7.0	15.8	13.5	ND	13.7	13.1	ND	10.4	10.2	ND	12.5	11.6	ND
Fiscal Coefficient-GDP Ratio 1. 1977, 1979 2. 1986	1.8	3.7	1.9	(2.1)	1.0	4.5	6.6	6.4	7.8	8.2	7.5	17.6	4.4	8.0	3.3
Index of Private Consumption to Total Consumption 1. 1977, 1979 2. 1986	91.1	90.9	89.3	88.1	86.0	82.4	83.3	84.5	81.2	86.3	76.2	44.2	82.8	82.7	83.3
Ratio of Private Investment to Total Investment 1. 1977, 1979 2. 1986	72.3	69.2	71.7	63.0	62.6	68.1	61.6	62.6	22.5	50.4	55.7	ND	63.6	66.2	67.0
Ratio of Private Sector Credit to Total Credit 1. 1977, 1979 2. 1986	86.8	90.4	63.4	82.0	82.2	64.0	87.1	81.1	77.7	94.1	71.2	55.7	74.5	62.8	49.0

Notes: ND—No data available
M—Estimate based on figures from CEPAL. Cable Centroamericano and the Centro de Estudios Financieros, S.A. (CEFSA)

Sources: SIECA, *Estadísticas macroeconómicas de Centroamérica*; SIECA, *Estadísticas macroeconómicas de Centroamérica, 1982–1986*, September 1987; *Inforpress Centroamérica 1984–1986*, September 1984; *Inforpress Centroamérica 1988*; CEPAL, *Estudio económico de América Latina y el Caribe*, 1987.

poorly timed and difficult to access.[4]

The technical assistance required by small businesses is also insufficient and not easily available. However, there are numerous initiatives that attempt to deal with technological improvement,[5] such as the Rural Technology Program (RTP) administered by the Center for Industrial Development (CID) of Honduras,[6] similar programs carried out by the Central American Institute on Research and Industrial Technology (ICAITI) and others promoted by the Dutch and Swiss governments.

One of the few novel programs in managerial assistance (another key factor in the development of S&MSBs) is run by the Instituto Nacional de Aprendizaje (INA) of Costa Rica.[7] However, this kind of support has not been adopted as a primary means for improving small businesses; when it is offered, the training is not necessarily accompanied by other forms of assistance or support. This leads to a low level of practical application of what the trainees have learned.

In summation, all the countries of the region have made efforts to support the development of S&MSBs; however, none of them have received sufficient backing from support institutions to create favorable conditions for promoting the sector. According to a group of six researchers who analyze Central American S&MSBs, none of the countries have favorable conditions to support the key factors outlined in Table 4. Only in Costa Rica are the social factors and the capacities of the support institutions above "satisfactory." Nicaragua recorded the most precarious conditions for the development of small- and medium-sized businesses at the end of 1989.

IV. DEVELOPMENT STRATEGIES

It seems obvious that the efforts to develop S&MSBs in Central America have been insufficient. The challenge facing both policymakers and decisionmakers in the institutions supporting the sector thus begins with an examination of which comprehensive strategy alternatives each country might adopt to promote the development of S&MSBs in the 1990s.

Such a strategy might be characterized by the following: a definition of S&MSBs; the objectives that economic policies have assigned to the sector; the attention paid to the sector; the approach of support services and the incentives they provide; the number and capacity of support institutions; the importance accorded to management training and promoting self-help; the relative importance of planning production in the national territory; and the tendency to relate S&MSBs to other industrial sectors (for example, handicrafts to large-scale industry).

To identify a support strategy for S&MSBs, I have used the taxonomy proposed by Joseph E. Stepanek,[8] which distinguishes the most effective

TABLE 4

EIGHT KEY VARIABLES FOR THE DEVELOPMENT OF SMALL- AND MEDIUM-SIZED INDUSTRIAL BUSINESSES

Country	Guatemala					El Salvador					Honduras					Nicaragua					Costa Rica				
Variable	VP	P	S	F	VF	VP	P	S	F	VF	VP	P	S	F	VF	VP	P	S	F	VF	VP	P	S	F	VF
Economic Conditions		x					x						x			x							x		
Social Factors		x					x					x				x								x	
Public Policy		x						x				x				x						x			
Supporting Institutions' Installed Capacity		x						x					x						x					x	
Credit		x					x					x					x					x			
Technical Assistance		x					x						x			x							x		
Managerial Assistance	x						x					x				x						x			
Motivational Factors		x						x				x				x							x		

Notes: VP: Very precarious; P: Precarious; S: Satisfactory; F: Favorable; VF: Very favorable.

Source: Prepared using a simplified 3-round adaptation of the Delphi method. The test was made by a group of six researchers on the problems of S&MSBs in Central America, December 1985.

characteristics of a strategy to speed up the development of S&MSBs (see Table 5).

From the research carried out by INCAE to pinpoint the strategies adopted by the countries in the region, one can conclude that, except in Nicaragua, none of the local strategies contain elements that explicitly constrain sectoral development.[9] All the countries have a set of strategies that permit moderate development of S&MSBs, but none of them have a vigorous strategy of support for small industrial or agricultural producers.

Guatemala

In Guatemala, promoting small enterprises is considered a means of creating jobs and a vehicle for the decentralization of industry and the more intensive use of raw materials. The institutions supporting the sector are interested in the development of S&MSBs and this interest is part and parcel of the industrial plan prepared by the Office of the General Secretary for Planning. This plan, which covers the period 1979–2000, rests on four main strategies: (1) fostering medium-sized and large industry through financing; (2) stimulating exports; (3) fostering small rural industries; and (4) legal and institutional support.

The incorporation of small- and medium-sized industry into the government's longer-term plans has not achieved the expected goals of facilitating the industrialization process. The return to civilian government and the attempts to revive the organizations responsible for financial support and assistance have neither led to the adoption of the plan nor has it been put into practice completely. The decline in the financial health of Corporación Financiera Nacional (CORFINA), the concentration of its credits on large-scale projects and the small amount of technical assistance provided by the Instituto Técnico de Capacitación y Productividad (INTECAD) in the context of a still shaky democracy have made it impossible for S&MSBs to benefit yet from economic policy and its implicit strategy for the sector.

In practice, in Guatemala, S&MSBs are not used as a tool for creating jobs and increasing value-added. The tendency to link S&MSBs to the informal sector and to handicrafts limits even more the possibility of small businesses playing a key role in the national economy.

El Salvador

In El Salvador, a multidisciplinary group composed of representatives of both the government and private institutions prepared guidelines for a nationwide strategy for the S&MSB sector.[10] These guidelines suggest that efforts should be concentrated on the decentralization of production, more intensive use of labor, an increase in the sector's export capacity and

TABLE 5
MOST EFFECTIVE AND LEAST EFFECTIVE CHARACTERISTICS FOR DEVELOPING S&MSBs

Most Effective	Least Effective
At the strategic level: national policies	
Definition of S&MSB is complemented by notion of size according to fixed capital, by output–fixed capital ratio, to maximize productivity	Definition of S&MSB is made according to level of fixed capital, or number of employees
Strategic objective of support to S&MSBs is to raise industrial value-added from 30% to 50%	Strategic objective is to sustain employment and restrict growth in number of small- and medium-sized businesses
Central authorities pay particular attention to sector	Central authorities pay some attention to sector
Basic approach includes policies and measures tending to encourage growth, intensive training in management and direction, consulting services, and financial assistance	Basic approach consists of financial assistance and limited counseling services
Less dependence on financial incentives	Great dependence on financial incentives
Consulting services provided by wide range of public and private organizations	Consulting services provided principally by civil servants
System of support to sector depends on wide range of organizations that provide varied services	System of support to sector depends above all on organizations specializing in financing or control
Training is considered essential, above all for head of firm	General training provided
Development of entrepreneurs' capacity for self-help is strongly fostered	No importance given to developing capacity for self-help
Emphasis on good planning of industry and on providing public services	Not much emphasis on planning industry or on providing public services
Close relations between small- and large-scale industry encouraged	Tendency to link small industry to handicrafts
At the strategic level: relationship with the environment	
Agreement on which economic conditions are furthering development of S&MSBs and which are constraining them	Lack of agreement as to which economic conditions are furthering development of S&MSBs and which are constraining them
Agreement as to which social environment conditions are furthering development of S&MSBs and which are constraining them	Lack of agreement as to which social environment conditions are furthering development of S&MSBs and which are constraining them
Agreement as to which elements of public policy are encouraging S&MSBs, and which are constraining them	Lack of agreement as to which elements of public policy are encouraging S&MSBs and which are constraining them
Confidence in capacity of directors of the supporting institutions to carry out development programs	Mistrust in capacity of directors of the supporting institutions to carry out development programs

continued

TABLE 5—*continued*

Most Effective	Least Effective
Agreement that financing is critical for development of S&MSBs	Lack of agreement that financing is critical for development of S&MSBs
Agreement that technical assistance is essential for development of S&MSBs	Lack of agreement that technical assistance is essential for development of S&MSBs
Agreement that managerial assistance is key element for development of S&MSBs	Lack of agreement that managerial assistance is key element for development of S&MSBs
Agreement that entrepreneur's motivations play decisive role in development of S&MSBs	Lack of agreement that entrepreneur's motivations play decisive role in development of S&MSBs
Agreement that small- and medium-sized entrepreneurs develop a strategy for their firm that strongly influences possibility of development	Lack of agreement that small- and medium-sized entrepreneurs develop a strategy for their firm that strongly influences possibility of development
At the program level	
Institutions provide services or take corrective action on each of nine key factors for development of S&MSBs, strengthening conditions that encourage it and eliminating those that hinder it	Institutions provide services or take corrective action on only one, or very few, of nine key factors for development of S&MSBs, or even strengthen some particular condition that hinders it
Institutions provide multiple services that are complementary, in order to give comprehensive support to beneficiary	Institutions provide isolated services that overlap or duplicate efforts of other institutions, or neutralize them
Services to which the institutions give emphasis correspond to needs felt by entrepreneurs	Services to which institutions give emphasis do not correspond to needs felt by entrepreneurs
At level of predominant form of relationship between entrepreneur and supporting agency	
Beneficiary and supporting agency jointly diagnose firms' problems, work together to identify them and to prepare a program for applying corrective action	Beneficiary is passive subject. Diagnosis of the firm's problems, identification of corrective action, and selection and process of providing services are designed and implemented by supporting institutions

the creation of a national capacity for assistance and management training. To achieve these goals, the group called for a national system for pinpointing 50,000 entrepreneurs and workers each year. Technical assistance to 700 firms and financial support from 300 agencies of the existing financial institutions would grant 25,000 loans every six months. At the beginning of 1986, the pilot project for the new strategy had still not been developed. The participating institutions continued to provide their services in the same way as they had formerly.

Since 1984, the executive branch has tried to make laws that encourage S&MSBs. Training programs, annual awards to outstanding entrepreneurs and an increase in commercial information shared with the United States and the Caribbean Basin countries are part of the strategy. Both civil servants and entrepreneurs consider these efforts inadequate. Some improvement is expected in the next few years; however, the ongoing civil war may jeopardize this.

Honduras

Since the beginning of the decade, prices of traditional export products have fallen and around 300 firms have closed. This has led to a recession and social instability. A civilian regime, through the National Development Plan (1982–1986), tried to achieve economic and financial stability. It implemented policies and regulations that encouraged small industrial and handicraft businesses to increase their productivity. In the medium term, this strategy would have set up industrial development centers in priority areas. A financial institution would channel funds to the sector with the support of, and in coordination with, the National Association of Industrialists. The priority areas were: agroindustries, with emphasis on food production; leather goods and textile products; and clothing and household articles. This emphasis characterizes a strategy that provides Honduran S&MSBs with a means for strengthening the sector.

The strategic aims of the National Development Plan did not include deciding on concrete actions to accomplish the plan's goals. Thus, organizations continued to operate without incorporating the changes or inter-institutional arrangements the plan supposed they would. The small industrialists who had pushed for a development law felt frustrated when they realized that the larger firms were being favored. In the first 14 months that the law was in force, only 25 entrepreneurs took advantage of its provisions. The strategy was therefore very unsuccessful.

Costa Rica

Costa Rica's strategy for developing S&MSBs is framed within a government program that recognizes the importance of the industrial sector because of its share in generating value-added,[11] the use of national raw materials, low investment requirements and job creation.

In the midst of the economic and social crisis that has affected all the countries in the area, the absence of labor conflicts in Costa Rica and political stability have made it possible to set up an institutional infrastructure and to carry out a series of programs providing support to the small industry sector.

The fostering of nontraditional exports, the elimination of bureaucratic obstacles, the provision of loans in sufficient amounts, management training for small industrialists and craftspeople, the improvement of technical assistance and the promotion of a joint agreement to facilitate the acquisition of raw materials for the sector are the main proposals of the operational plan for the sector. Partly as a result of this strategy, Costa Rica is the country in the region with the greatest increase in income from nontraditional exports. Credit programs have adjusted to the forecasts and are accompanied by training programs that emphasize the training of workers and, more recently, assistance to and training of managers.

Other aspects of strategy implementation have, however, suffered setbacks. Participation of organizations supporting the sector is still informal and sporadic. The participation of executives of the Interinstitutional Commission on Small Businesses (created to facilitate and coordinate small business ventures) is poor.

In Costa Rica, however, it is likely that the S&MSB sector will develop more rapidly than in the other countries of the region. Concrete export incentives, the widespread recognition by institutions that small- and medium-sized businesses serve as a means of creating jobs and taking advantage of local raw materials, and the fact that practically all private institutions supporting the sector offer technical assistance and training programs accompanied by financing are the key factors for strengthening S&MSBs. The absence of labor conflicts and the democratic system prevailing in Costa Rica have made it possible to create a suitable environment and the infrastructure for institutional support required by the sector.

Nicaragua

Any analysis of Nicaragua must take into consideration the country's economic depression. The fact that nearly 40 percent of the national budget is devoted to defense has made it impossible to fulfill the objectives of reconstructing the production infrastructure. In addition, it has discouraged private investment, destroyed distribution channels and caused the shutting down of businesses and the flight of qualified people.

In this unprecedented framework in the history of S&MSBs, the Ministry of Industry has pointed out that the role of small industry in the national economy should be to help use the labor force and support the integration of the essential sectors for the reconstruction of the production infrastructure. Essentially, the strategy centers on eight key aspects: (1) avoiding the proliferation of small firms; (2) grouping existing firms into cooperatives or collective forms of production; (3) increasing government control by regulating supplies of essential raw materials; (4) encouraging the decentralization of businesses outside the capital; (5) promoting the use of local raw materials; (6) favoring the manufacture of export products; (7) the merging of small firms; and (8) avoiding an increase in unemployment. The strategic aim of discouraging the production of nontraditional goods was achieved by rationing or suspending supplies of raw materials. The net result has been a drastic drop in national production.

The strategy for developing S&MSBs in Nicaragua under the Sandinistas constitutes a special case. In fact, the objectives of favoring collective forms of production, avoiding the quantitative growth of firms and controlling the supply of raw materials are unique in the Central American context. Taken as a whole, these factors do more to restrict than to encourage the development of S&MSBs. These circumstances make Nicaragua the Central American country in which the growth and strengthening of S&MSBs face the greatest obstacles, unless major policy changes are introduced.

Central America

The strategies for developing S&MSBs in Central America can be classified into three categories. The first of these covers only Nicaragua. Nicaragua's strategy is clearly restrictive, because the government does not expect this sector to make any significant contribution to the recovery of the economy (this policy is likely to be different under the new UNO government in Nicaragua). In the second category, we have moderate efforts to encourage S&MSBs. Guatemala is a good example. The third category covers more considerable efforts to provide support for the sector. No country can claim to have a vigorous strategy; however, three of them—El Salvador, Costa Rica and Honduras—exhibit one or two elements that place them in this category. The attention the central authorities pay to the sector, the reasonable institutional structure and the incorporation of management consulting services are indications of a more harmonious development of S&MSBs in these three countries.

V. BARRIERS TO THE DEVELOPMENT OF S&MSBs

The main obstacles to development of the S&MSB sector in Central America can be grouped into three large categories. The first has to do with policymaking and the adoption of national strategies that are congruent with the aim of developing the sector. The second category comprises the set of problems internal to the support institutions, problems that make it impossible for them to provide quality services in a timely manner and in sufficient volume to cover the needs of small- and medium-sized entrepreneurs. The third group of obstacles is at the level of the firms themselves. A strengthening of S&MSBs in the region presupposes deliberate and systematic efforts to remove these barriers.

Strategies and Policies

In the first section of this chapter, I pointed out that governmental and institutional policies were a key element in the development of the sector. However, I stated that these policies had not become an effective tool for support.

In February 1971, Guatemala promulgated a law to develop small businesses; a fund was set up to provide credits up to (US) $1,000 that would allow S&MSBs to secure working capital and to purchase machinery. In 1979, a new law encouraged the decentralization of industry. It forgave up to 100 percent of the import duties on machinery, equipment and raw materials and income tax for ten years. These benefits were of no advantage to the smallest firms, which were able to demonstrate their eligibility only rarely. Larger formal businesses ended up absorbing the benefits.

Under a more aggressive policy in El Salvador, the owner of a business had to join the social security system; the state was to provide training and assistance to small business through several public institutions; and small business organizations were to have consulting and voting rights in the state organizations directly or indirectly linked to the sector. This proposed participation has not been broad enough, and pressure to adopt public policies for strengthening the sector has been insufficient.

In 1978, a law encouraging small industrial and handicraft businesses was promulgated in Honduras. It combined exemption from customs duties and income tax with the provision of technical assistance through specialized organizations. A commission for tax incentives was set up. It was composed of representatives of the sector and public organizations. As in the case of Guatemala, few small businesses have benefited economically from the exemptions. Moreover, the results of the interinstitutional commission are inconsequential, and as a consequence the National Association of Medium-Sized and Small Industries has witnessed a drop in the number of active members.[12]

In Costa Rica, the first attempts to formalize support date to 1976, when small- and medium-sized industry and handicrafts were exempted from import duties. This was complemented in 1978 by the formalization of an interinstitutional coordination committee for small industry and handicrafts. It was to serve in an advisory capacity to the president of the republic.

A year later, a credit program of approximately (US) $5.8 million was set up to buy land or facilities, to purchase machinery or to be used as working capital. It is more likely that in Costa Rica policies on S&MSBs will promote the sector because conditions are similar to those that created a strong and widespread system of cooperatives in the country.

In 1980, the Nicaraguan government announced a policy for the sector. The Provisional Law for the Encouragement, Rehabilitation and Protection of Small Industrial and Handicraft Production recognized that small- and medium-sized industry and handicrafts had remained totally outside the national economy. It was a priority for the new government to foster the organization of small-scale production, because of its capacity to create jobs and its use of local raw materials. Until mid-1989, when credit to the sector was revived, this law was not applied, and Nicaraguan S&MSBs suffered a greater decline than in any of the other countries in the region.

In general, public policy affecting the development of S&MSBs focuses on tax incentives, soft loans and interinstitutional support committees. In Central America, these have not functioned effectively. Small businesses find it hard to benefit from tax incentives and financing has gone mainly to the bigger firms within the sector. In addition, relatively big firms have split legally into smaller entities, so that each part constitutes a small business and has access to the benefits granted to S&MSBs.

The first World Bank projects showed that the success of financing to create viable small enterprises was restricted by the degree to which the policy environment permitted and fostered this improvement. It seems more and more evident that small firms that function in a hostile political environment find it difficult to compete successfully and to cope with government bureaucracy, even if that bureaucracy provides subsidized financing in combination with other forms of assistance.[13]

This seems to be the case for Central America. Although it cannot be asserted that there is an atmosphere hostile to the development of S&MSBs—the laws in all the countries would seem to demonstrate the contrary—the environment for putting those laws into practice is frankly indifferent. Laws that reduce the dependence on financial incentives and encourage the growth of S&MSBs through management training and assistance from a large number of institutions are required. Such training and assistance will raise the sector's share in GDP.

Institutional Barriers

Each Central American country has institutions that directly or indirectly provide support services to the S&MSB sector. The suitable and timely flow of financial, technical and managerial assistance depends on these institutions' capacity and efficiency. Thus, problems at the institutional level become an obstacle to the development of intended beneficiaries. This section presents these problems as they were pinpointed in a diagnostic study carried out by INCAE between 1983 and 1986. In late 1989, the situation still had not changed significantly. Table 6 enumerates the primary institutions supporting S&MSBs in Central America and their main areas of activity.

Guatemala. In October 1984, Guatemala started a process of restructuring the management of CORFINA to try to stop the deterioration in the institution's financial position caused by a default amounting to 20 percent of its portfolio of around (US) $2.4 million. From 1982 to 1985, the training services offered by INTECAP decreased in comparison with 1980 and 1981. In 1986, CORFINA continued its administrative adjustment, but no substantial increase in either its or INTECAP's services in the period from 1986 to 1989 was expected.

In addition to its portfolio problems, CORFINA lacks the operational capacity to successfully carry out the programs entrusted to it. To INTECAP's budget difficulties we must add the fact that its training programs have a theoretical focus, which makes it difficult for trainees to apply the knowledge they acquire.

A gradual increase in the activities of private sector organizations such as FAPE and the Centavo Foundation is foreseen. Their small size (the Centavo Foundation financed only 2,221 small projects between 1962 and 1983), together with the difficulty they have in gaining access to sources of financing are the main weaknesses of these two institutions.

El Salvador. In El Salvador, the institutional jealousy and political polarization make it difficult to carry out any program that requires cooperation. Insufficient information limits the potential user's access to—and understanding of—institutions such as CENAP. Faulty promotion and the lack of coordination between institutions leads, in some cases, to duplication of effort and, in others, such as FIGAPE, to inefficient utilization. In a meeting on 27 January 1989 in San Salvador, 40 representatives of the government sector (policymakers), support institutions and entrepreneurs, pinpointed the following weaknesses in supporting institutions: (1) limited financial resources; (2) lack of coordination between the institutions and the entrepreneurs; (3) concentration of support efforts in suburban areas; (4) absence of integrated services; (5) high costs of financing; (6) poor knowledge about S&MSBs; and (7) financial dependence on foreign aid.

Honduras. The country has a wide range of institutions for supporting S&MSBs; however, these are experiencing difficulties of various kinds. Until 1986, the main weakness of ANMPI, in addition to a drop in the number of active members as a consequence of the frustration brought on by the inattention of policymakers and service institutions, was that studies were not carried out before granting credit. On occasion, this meant difficulties with loan repayment.

Although ANDI has accepted the responsibility for coordinating a system of nationwide technical assistance since 1986, it is still unable to achieve this aim. INFOP consultants are not used to their full capacity; consequently, goals are not met in a number of courses and seminars. In contrast, IDH supervisors are overworked. This suggests a need for internal adjustments in the support institutions before undertaking an am-

TABLE 6

INSTITUTIONS SUPPORTING S&MSBs

Country/Institution	Financing	Technical Assistance	Training	Organizing the Trade	Other
Guatemala Corporación Financiera Nacional (CORFINA) (National Financing Corporation)	For industrial, mining, and tourism sectors for working capital and fixed assets	For setting up, organizing, and operating S&MSBs	—	—	Studies for pinpointing investment opportunities
Instituto Técnico de Capacitación y Productividad (INTECAP) (Technical Institute For Training and Productivity)	—	Varied: from cost systems to feasibility studies	Short courses on managing S&MSBs	—	Drawing up profiles and studies to be evaluated by CORFINA when granting credit
Fundación de Assistencia para la Pequeña Empresa (FAPE) (Foundation For Small Businesses)	Oriented toward people who have no access to other institutions	Monthly visits to supervise progress	Basic training in accounting	—	—
Hogar y Desarrollo (HODE) (Home and Development)	To individual microentrepreneurs; for community-owned enterprises	Administrative techniques to create the habit of planning and control	In drawing up financial statements; in various areas of production	—	Minimal housing; community development; entrepreneurial development for the informal sector
Alianza para el Desarrollo Juvenil	—	Facilitating marketing processes and suitable	—	Forming and strengthening representative	Health and nutrition care; commu-

continued

TABLE 6—*continued*

Country/Institution	Financing	Technical Assistance	Training	Organizing the Trade	Other
(ALIANZA) (Alliance For Juvenile Development)		technology		organizations at the community and municipal levels	nity development; organizing women; rural enterprises
Fundación del Centavo (Centavo Foundation)	For small entrepreneurs	Technical and administrative assistance to small production units in informal sector	For groups of small agricultural enterprises	—	Housing development
El Salvador Fundación Salvadoreña para el Desarrollo Económico y social (FUSADES) (Salvadoran Foundation for Economic and Social Development)	For small and microentrepreneurs	In transfer of technology	—	—	Economic studies
Federación Nacional para la Pequeña Empresa Salvadoreña (FENAPES) (National Federation for Small Salvadoran Businesses)	—	—	Administering international organization scholarships for associates	Representing trade	Studies to regulate industry and commerce
Empresarios Juveniles (Young Entrepreneurs)	—	—	Entrepreneurial and managerial development	—	—
Centro Nacional de Productividad (CENAP) (National Productivity Center)	—	Advice to firms about technological adaptation	Courses for medium-level executives and top-level management	—	Technological research

Federación de Cajas de de Crédito, S.C. de R.L. (FEDECREDITO) (Federation of Loan Banks)	Mainly to small shop-keepers and industrialists	—	—	—	—
Federación de Asociaciones de Ahorro y Crédito de El Salvador de Responsabilidad Limitada (FEDECACES) (Federation of Savings and Loans Associations of El Salvador)	Especially for cooperatives for financing micro- and small enterprises (2nd-tier bank)	In future: assistance in drawing up and evaluating projects, preinvestment financing	—	—	—
Fondo de Financiamiento y Garantía para la Pequeña Empresa (FIGAPE) (Financing and Warranty Fund for Small Businesses)	Firms with assets of less than 120,000 $ C.A.	—	—	—	—
Sociedad de Comerciantes e Industriales Salvadoreños (SCIS) (Salvadoran Businessmen and Industrialists Society)	—	—	—	Setting up cooperatives	Studies for regulating commerce and industry; bill for encouraging S&MSBs
Honduras					
Asociación Nacional de Mediana y Pequeña Industria (ANMPI) (National Association of Medium-Sized and Small Industries)	Handling FOGAPIN loan funds	—	—	Defense of trade	Collaboration in preparing bills for encouraging S&MSBs

continued

TABLE 6—*continued*

Country/Institution	Financing	Technical Assistance	Training	Organizing the Trade	Other
Asociación Nacional de Industriales (ANDI) (National Industrialists Association)	—	In the legal and economic area	—	Representing the trade	Coordination of supporting institutions
Instituto para el Desarrollo Hondureño (IDH) (Institute for Honduran Development)	For small urban and rural entrepreneurs	Drawing up projects, orienting management	Talks on administration and accounting	—	—
Fondo Nacional de Desarrollo Industrial (FONDEI) (National Fund for Industrial Development)	2nd-tier bank	—	—	—	—
Centro de Desarrollo para la Pequeña y Mediana Empresa Industrial y Artesanal (CDI) (Development Center for Small and Medium-sized Industries and Handicrafts)	For firms that do not qualify for bank loans	Accounting, marketing, quality control	—	—	Direct investments in S&MSBs
Instituto Nacional de Formación Professional (INFOP) (National Institute for Professional Training)	—	—	Advice on training; courses and seminars at the managerial level in functional areas	—	—
Consejo Asesor para el Desarrollo de Recursos	—	—	Research on training needs	—	—

Humanos de Honduras (CADERH) (Honduran Consultant Council for the Development of Human Resources)					
Nicaragua					
Cámara de Industrias de Nicaragua (CADIN) (Nicaraguan Chamber of Industry)	—	Basically to cooperatives in the area of food technology	—	Representing trade	Drawing up economic studies
Camara de Comercio de Nicaragua (Nicaraguan Chamber of Commerce)	—	In accounting, tax laws, and labor laws	—	Representing trade	—
Instituto de Promoción Humana (INPRHU) (Institute for Promoting Human Resources)	For small firms, cooperatives, and worker-managed enterprises	Accounting, marketing, and organization	Training agricultural promoters	Encouraging cooperatives	—
Foundación Nicaraguense Desarrollo (FUNDE) (Nicaraguan Development Foundation)	For production cooperatives and savings and loan cooperatives	To agricultural cooperatives	Accounting, finance, and organization of cooperatives	Encouraging cooperatives	Studies on the informal sector
Fondo Nicaragúense de Inversiones (FNI) (Nicaraguan Investment Fund)	2nd-tier bank	—	—	—	—
Banco Nacional de Rollo (BND) (National Development Bank)	Mainly for the agricultural sector	—	—	—	—
Banco de Crédito Popular (BCP) (Popular Credit Bank)	Basically for the informal sector and cooperatives	Marketing, production, and accounting	—	—	—

continued

TABLE 6—*continued*

Country/Institution	Financing	Technical Assistance	Training	Organizing the Trade	Other
Ministry of Industry (MIND)	—	—	—	Encouraging the setting up of production collectives	Sector studies; supply, raw materials
Costa Rica					
Coaliecon Costa Ricense de Iniciativas de Desarrollo (CINDE) (Costa Rican Coalition For Development Initiatives)	Feasibility studies; grants to groups supporting S&MSB	Improving technology	Financing for training in functional areas to medium-sized firms	Strengthening of voluntary organizations	Diagnostic studies; promoting the image of Costa Rica abroad
Cámara Nacional de Artensanía y Pequeña Industria de Costa Rica CANAPI) (Costa Rican National Chamber of Handicrafts and Small Industry)	—	Domestic marketing	Obtaining financial resources for training members	Setting up cooperatives	Organizing handicraft fairs
Cooperativa de Pequeños Industriales, Artesanos y Artistas RL. (COOPEPINARA) Cooperative of Small Industrialists, Craftsmen and Artists)	Savings and loans	Export marketing assistance for large loans	—	Cooperativism	Organizing handicraft fairs; supplying raw materials
Asociación Nacional Pro-Desarrollo de la Artesanía (ANDA) (National Association to Promote Development of Handicrafts)	—	To cooperatives on quality control and prices	Training courses for apprentices	—	Direct sales (outlets)

Asociación de Ayuda al Pequeño Trabajador y Empresario (ADAPTE) (Association for Assisting Workers and Entrepreneurs in Small Enterprises)	For microenterprises	Administrative accounting	Seminars on administration and laws	—	—
Fundación Costarricense de Desarrollo (FUCODES) (Costa Rican Development Foundation)	Small industry, agriculture, and handicrafts	For improvements in production	Management training through INA	Development of membership	—
Dirección General de Asistencia Técnica a la Pequeña Industria y Artesanía (DGATPIA) (Office of the Director General for Technical Assistance to Small Industries and Handicrafts)	—	Technological documentation to obtain financing; coordination of institutions.	—	—	Drawing up feasibility studies for small firms
Instituto Nacional de Aprendizaje (INA) (National Apprenticeship Institute)	—	Advice, according to capacity	Trade training courses; management courses in functional areas	—	Research on suitable technology

Source: Francisco A. Leguizamón, John C. Ickis and Francisco J. Gómez, *El extensionista empresarial: un vínculo para el desarrollo* (Editorial Universitaria Centroamericana, 1987), pp. 48–52.

bitious program for national coordination. Coordination presupposes each organization's capacity to achieve its own goals efficiently. Deficiencies in the promotion of programs and lack of motivation on the part of consultants (mainly in INFOP) are problems that have to be solved.

Costa Rica. In the case of Costa Rica, the lack of financial resources in CANAPI and ADAPTE and the institutional development in CADIN (which enables it to set itself up as an institution that can bring effective influence to bear to assure sufficient support services for the sector) constitute major obstacles to these institutions. The lack of human resources for carrying out promotional activities, training and project analysis in FUCODES and the focus on training workers more than entrepreneurs in INA, together with general and prescriptive teaching material, are additional barriers.

Nicaragua. Support in the form of institutional services supplied to S&MSBs is the most precarious here, in comparison with that in the other countries of the region. By rationing or suspending the supply of raw materials, the Ministry of Industry and Commerce discourages production. This is the first link in the chain of institutional obstacles to the development of S&MSBs in Nicaragua.

The banks—and particularly the BND and the BCP—have been for all intents and purposes unable to facilitate financing for the purchase of imported raw materials in sufficient quantity. Thus, producers not supplied by the ministry must deal with nonofficial sources of supply and must adjust the production and marketing processes for finished articles. In general, public organizations' lack of emphasis on individual firms and the motivation on the part of the officers of these institutions, accompanied by the drop in CADIN and the Chamber of Commerce's operational capacity to defend their members, sum up the institutional barriers in Nicaragua.

Central America. In addition to the internal weakness of the supporting institutions throughout the region, with few exceptions, these institutions have not managed to develop any prestige among the entrepreneurs. The lack of diffusion and coverage, the low level of efficiency, the indifference—when not actual mistrust—of the users, the widespread belief that funds are grants, the high dependence on foreign resources and the antagonism between public and private sector institutions which complicates coordinated efforts, all constitute the main obstacles to the development of S&MSBs from the point of view of the support organizations.

The Businesses

There is a third set of barriers to the strengthening of S&MSBs. We can look at them from two points of view: that of the entrepreneurs themselves in relation to the key factors of their development, and that of the officers of the support institutions, who have difficulty handling the businesses themselves.

Guatemala. To Guatemalan entrepreneurs, there is not yet sufficient long-term political stability. Thus, there is no suitable environment for more intensive investment. The business sector is discouraged by price controls on both imports and exports and by inadequate services, particularly with regard to domestic and foreign credit.

Civil servants point out that the main problems at the business level are: unsuitable production processes, obsolete machinery, lack of capitalization, technically untrained labor and lack of financial control. These factors taken together make the firms highly vulnerable to competition.

El Salvador. In El Salvador, entrepreneurs consider domestic inflation, violence, social insecurity, an excessive tax burden and an unstable supply of electricity to be their main problems. The officers of the support institutions also consider the activity of guerrilla groups a serious problem for the normal development of the economy. Other obstacles mentioned are: stagnation of the Central American Common Market, inflation, inadequate financing, the insufficient use of installed production capacity, deficient management and a lack of managerial and technical training in businesses.

Honduras. In Honduras, the entrepreneurs stressed government corruption and outdated or untimely laws. Institutions are not considered relevant; in fact, most entrepreneurs think that the government consults them only to keep up appearances and not because it has any legitimate interest in the development of the sector.

Civil servants confirmed that there is lack of confidence on the part of the institutions, particularly the banking system, in the sector's capacity to repay loans. They also complain about inefficient technology, irregularities in the supply of inputs and in the marketing of products, insufficient physical infrastructure and a lack of any real entrepreneurial spirit.

Costa Rica. Here, entrepreneurs point out the difficulty of access to raw materials and the lack of a law promoting the development of S&MSBs. The latter is aggravated by the lack of consensus on what should be done. This, in turn, leads to actions by support organizations that are not always in the beneficiaries' best interests. The absence of incentives, financial resources and a broader program of technical assistance are perceived as other barriers to the development of S&MSBs in Costa Rica.

From the institutional point of view, there is a suitable social, economic and political environment; the problems of S&MSBs are at the individual firm level. The goods produced are inferior, owners are more mastercrafts people than entrepreneurs, there is a lack of knowledge about the market and little managerial capacity; therefore, decisions are made on a casual or intuitive basis.

Nicaragua. The state-oriented attitude of the public sector, an increasingly difficult relationship with workers, difficult access to raw materials and financing and few opportunities for investment are the main problems seen by the entrepreneurial sector in Nicaragua under the Sandinistas. All make for a sense of insecurity about the sector's survival.

The institutions diagnose a rather excessive dependence on the agricultural economy and on imported raw materials, technological backwardness, lack of technical assistance and difficulties in financing as the main problems facing S&MSBs in Nicaragua.

Central America. In general, the Central American business sector considers its main problems to derive from a social and economic environment that does not favor its development. There is marked concern about conflicts and political uncertainty. The sector thinks that the government puts obstacles in the way of the private sector; these range from obsolete laws (or the absence of laws) to a variety of bureaucratic stumbling blocks.

Support agencies point out that the main problems are of an administrative nature: lack of managerial skill; inferior products; lack of attention to marketing and financial control; out-of-date technology; and lack of training at all levels. These problems are found in the firms themselves.

Although the evidence is vague, it suggests that the two views are reasonably accurate and that there is a range of barriers for the business sector. Some originate in the handling of the business and others in the environment surrounding it. All aspects form a blockade that the S&MSB sector in Central America now has to face.

VI. CONCLUSIONS AND OUTLOOK

Throughout this paper, I have pinpointed the strategies adopted by the Central American countries to strengthen the S&MSB sector and the problems that have hindered the implementation of support programs. This description leads me to conclude that the economic and social conditions in the region are unsatisfactory for the formation of a sector of small- and medium-sized businesses that could supply the economic drive necessary to satisfy domestic demand and produce an exportable surplus in competitive conditions. Without exception, public policy, financing and technical assistance are—with some differences from country to country—inadequate to meet the requirements of the sector. However, the institutional capacity of the support organizations is one of the most powerful potential resources for carrying out programs to help develop S&MSBs.

The country that requires the most profound adjustment of its policies, readaptation of its system of incentives and reorientation of the institutional programs to eliminate the present restrictions on S&MSBs is Nicaragua. At the other extreme, Costa Rica, with its economic stability, democratic system, governmental attention to the sector, broad institutional structure, focus on multiple credit services, technical assistance and ample freedom to form associations and unions is the country in which S&MSBs could flourish most easily. In the medium term, this would constitute an axis for the national economy.

The majority of the support institutions' aid to the sector is concentrated on financing. People are beginning to acknowledge that isolated credit does not constitute the best tool for strengthening the sector. Institutions are beginning to set up programs covering credit, assistance and training that respond more closely to beneficiaries' needs.

An examination of management assistance programs shows that little importance is given to such programs. Where they are implemented, they are often not very efficient, because of high turnover of staff acting as liaisons between the institution and the beneficiaries, the limited understanding these officers have of the sector's problems, the absence of any strong motivation for working with S&MSB entrepreneurs and lack of skill in communicating with the entrepreneurs and in preparing basic diagnoses of firms.

With the financial support of the InterAmerican Development Bank (IDB), the Central American Institute for Businesses Administration has designed and put into practice a training program oriented toward reducing problems in the relationship of support agencies and small entrepreneurs. Because the program might significantly improve managerial assistance through a group of agents known as "business extensionists," this program is being adopted in all the Central American countries. Table 7 shows how business extensionists change the character of assistance.

One of the most significant changes in the assistance supplied by the extensionists is the highly participative approach to relations between the supporting agent and the entrepreneur. In fact, this participation is accepted as one of the most relevant elements in the consulting process.

Although the first results are promising,[14] replacing traditional managerial assistance routines with more effective ones is no easy task. Both international organizations and local institutions are reluctant to have small entrepreneurs helping identify, analyze and solve their own problems, rather than being forced to adopt solutions suggested exclusively on the basis of the support agent's work.

The strengthening of the agents acting as a link between support institutions and entrepreneurs constitutes merely the first step. The effort should include the strengthening of the small entrepreneurs' trade associations, the readaptation of national strategies so that they adopt the features shown to be the most effective (see Table 5) and, finally, passing laws to encourage S&MSBs after consultation with the sector concerning

TABLE 7

CHANGES IN MANAGERIAL ASSISTANCE CAUSED BY BUSINESS EXTENSIONISTS

Characteristic	Traditional Assistance (47 cases)	Participative Assistance (64 cases)
	(percentages)	
Approach:		
Participative	6.4	90.6
Not very participative	19.1	9.4
Nonparticipative	74.5	0.0
Understanding of S&MSBs problems		
Overall	6.4	54.7
External	4.3	1.6
Internal	89.4	43.7
Disposition toward working with S&MSBs		
High	12.8	92.2
Medium	57.4	7.8
Low	29.8	0.0
Skill in communicating with S&MSBs		
High	4.3	53.1
Medium	36.2	39.1
Low	59.6	7.8
Skill in technical diagnosis		
High	2.1	29.7
Medium	40.4	56.2
Low	57.4	14.1
Skill in participative consultant work		
High	0.0	26.6
Medium	10.6	51.6
Low	89.4	21.9
Basic administrative training		
High	44.7	42.2
Medium	51.1	39.1
Low	4.3	18.7

Source: Analysis of 47 cases of traditional assistance and 64 cases of participative asssitance.

its needs, with the explicit participation of representatives of the sector in policymaking and the implementation of these new laws. Only a concerted effort between policymakers, the support institutions and the entrepreneurs themselves will help entrepreneurs become more dynamic actors in the national economies and stepping stones to a more stable democracy in Central America.

NOTES

1. Many of the statements made in this paper are a result of the research work done in INCAE as part of an agreement with the Bank for Interamerican Development (BID). The main findings are written up in Francisco A. Leguizamón, John C. Ickis and Francisco J. Gómez, *El extensionista empresarial: un vínculo para el desarrollo* (San José: Editorial Universitaria Centroamericana, 1987).

2. There is no regional study that explains to what extent small- and medium-sized businesses create jobs. My estimation has been taken from the more comprehensive notes presented by Philip A. Neck, *Desarrollo de la pequeña empresa: políticas y programas* (Geneva: International Labor Office, 1978), p. 12.

3. World Bank, "New Research: Small Scale Enterprise Development," *Research News* (January 1980).

4. In practically all the meetings, conferences and seminars on the subject of small- and medium-sized businesses, the question of financing is considered a key factor for the development of S&MSBs. See, for example, the Latin American Association of Financial Development Institutions (Asociación Latinoamericana de Instituciones Financieras de Desarrollo—ALIDE), "2nd Central American and Caribbean Seminar on Promotion of Small Businesses," Tegucigalpa, Honduras, October 1985, Group No. 1, pp. 2, ff.
In 1977, the same subject was dealt with in the "Hispano-Andean Seminar on Small and Medium-Sized Businesses," Lima, December 1977, p. 28.

5. The fourth project of the Research Associates Technology and Development Institute, East-West Center, in Honolulu, considers the purpose of technological change to be promoting the spirit of innovation and diffusion of technology through multidisciplinary experiments oriented toward three main objectives: (1) promoting local innovators and launching projects based on a better definition of local needs and on transfer of suitable technology; (2) increasing the local staff and the development of the organizations' capacity to help local entrepreneurs and communities; and (3) speeding up development and the use of information on industrial sectors that help to set up national exchange centers on technology. (Richard Morse, "El empresario y la satisfaccion de las necesidades de la comunidad;" in *Desarrollo*, ed. Neck, pp. 59–60.)

6. "Approach of the Center for Industrial Development (CDI) Program on Rural Technology (PTR), in the "Development of Small and Medium-sized Rural Businesses," paper presented at ALIDE's 2nd Central American Seminar, pp. 4–6.

7. A basic weakness in the development of small business is precisely management. It is generally in the hands of one or two people whose mistakes may affect the very survival of the firm. It is, therefore, logical to pay more attention to selecting, training and perfecting the entrepreneur/manager of such firms. (ILO, "Development of Small Businesses in the Central American Isthmus," Geneva 1981, p. 63.)

8. Joseph E. Stepanek classifies the strategies for speeding up development of S&MSBs in two models: in Model I, the strategy resembles the approaches adopted by the developing countries from 1960 to 1978; in Model II, the strategy

resembles those adopted in developing regions that achieved more accelerated industrialization. (Joseph E. Stepanek, "Estrategias para acelerar el desarrollo de la pequeña industria," in *Desarrollo*, ed. Neck, pp. 45–52.)

9. The research was divided into two stages. In the first, the aim was to pinpoint the strategies and programs of the institutions supporting S&MSBs, we interviewed directors and officers of 37 such institutions, we surveyed 157 entrepreneurs from the five countries and we examined the testimony of 40 of them on the history of their firms. The information we obtained served as a basis for preparing many general diagnoses of the situation of small businesses. (Leguizamón, Ickis and Gómez, *El extensionista empresarial*, p. 98.)

10. Local development corporations were defined by the group as associations of firms in each focal point to achieve scale economies in marketing, financing and purchasing of raw materials. The development focal point is a community of some 12,500 inhabitants who are engaged in productive work and which has a plan for comprehensive development in an atmosphere of freedom, but with microplanning. (Leguizamón, Ickis and Gómez, *El extensionista empresarial*, pp. 126–127.)

11. Luis Alberto Monge, "Programa de gobierno 1982–1986: política industrial," p. 30

12. United Nations Development Organization, "Consultant Report," UNIDO Project SI/MON/79-81, December 1979.

13. J. Levitsky, "Cuestiones de politicas relativas a los programas de asistencia para el fomento de la pequeña y mediana empresa: examen de la experiencia del Banco Mundial con referencia especial a América Latina" (Washington, D.C.: World Bank, April 1985).

14. A detailed explanation of the way this model was applied is to be found in Leguizamón, Ickis and Gómez, "El Extensionista Empresarial (A)." Evolution of the Model and First Results. INCAE, 1986. Ref.: 053.1-7735.

2

Microenterprise and the Informal Sector in the Dominican Republic: Operation and Promotion Policy

Rolando Reyes

I. INTRODUCTION

Microenterprise and the informal sector have acquired a certain prominence among alternatives to deal with the problem of unemployment and poverty in the Dominican Republic. Heightened public debate, a marked increase in the number of organizations that promote the sector and the rising level of national and international resources used in its financing are all signs of this phenomenon. At the same time, academic and research interests in the sector have increased. However, available studies are not yet sufficient to substantiate a recommendation for a long-term strategy or coherent policy aimed at reducing unemployment, underemployment and poverty by promoting microenterprise and the informal sector.

One explanation for the current lack of adequate research is unavailability of reliable data. Most research efforts to date have been restricted to case studies generally limited to point analyses of a given productive activity, geographic area or specific group. Such studies not only fail to yield valid data with general applicability but are also very expensive in relation to the validity of the results obtained.

Given these restrictions, this paper analyzes microenterprise and the informal sector in the broad context of a developing economy experiencing a surplus of urban labor that cannot be absorbed by the modern business sector. More specifically, this paper examines the impact of organizations and programs that seek to promote the informal sector and concludes with an analysis of alternative strategies to improve the levels of employment and income in this sector.

The methodology used consisted basically of a review of prior studies, analysis of available data on the evolution of the labor market and a reordering and analysis of specific data on the sector and organizations promoting it. Section II offers a brief conceptual outline that allows for different interpretations of the performance of the sector in the Dominican case. The building of a conceptual-theoretical framework is necessary to ensure maximum effectiveness of promotional programs.

Section III takes a closer look at the characteristics of small productive units in relation to promotional strategies. The basic objective here is to identify alternative ways of improving the effectiveness of policy in raising employment and income level. This section concludes with a proposal for changing the policy that has so far been followed by both the public and private sectors.

II. MICROENTERPRISE AND THE INFORMAL SECTOR IN THE DOMINICAN REPUBLIC: COMPOSITION AND BASIC CHARACTERISTICS

Any program or strategy intended to promote microenterprise and the informal sector must first study its basic characteristics. Tokman alerts us to the risks involved.[1] These risks become greater when technical and educational advances in the study and understanding of the sector are not taken into account.

Unlike other countries, programs put into effect in the Dominican Republic have not been based on precedent nor have they adopted an interpretive focus. While some were, in fact, based on specific diagnoses, they are no longer current.

Brief Overview of the Informal Sector: Outstanding Aspects in the Case of the Dominican Republic

An explanation of existing economic theories on the sector is beyond the scope of this paper. There is, however, a brief discussion of the theoretical focus upon which the recommendations at the end of this study are based.

Several theories attempt to explain and understand the emergence of informal or underground businesses. Two of the most widely discussed are those which (a) view such activity as the product of excessive government regulation,[2] and (b) attribute the development of the informal sector to the inability of the modern business sector to generate enough jobs to absorb all surplus labor.[3]

Focus on Illegality. The theory of excessive regulation is based on a simple notion—namely, some individuals cannot or will not comply with all conditions imposed by the state to govern production. Thus, they establish productive units at the margin of such conditions. This theory considers any economic activity that is not registered or regulated by law as informal. Therefore, the first policy recommendation stemming from this view would call for less government regulation of economic activity.

Although the importance of this problem and its possible relation to the emergence of some informal activity is recognized, this approach has been refuted by Latin American researchers and academics who have shown its limitations.[4] As Tokman argues, the illegality of informal activities is the result and not the cause of their form of operation.[5]

Focus on the Structural Surplus of Urban Labor.[6] This theory explains the emergence of the informal sector in less industrialized countries as a function of the style of their economic development. It posits two specific types of production: the high-productivity, capital-intensive activities of modern business and small-scale, capital-scarce, low-productivity operations.

It attributes the emergence of noncapital-intensive activities to the inability of the modern capital-intensive sector to absorb all surplus labor. This inability is explained by both the level of technology used in the productive process and the structure of the markets in which modern business activities occur.

Modern capital-intensive activities take place in oligopolistic markets while small productive units tend to exist in small, peripheral markets of low profitability.[7] This lower profitability, in turn, explains their lower capital accumulation and limited possibilities for growth.

Accumulation and Growth: Boundaries between Micro- Small- and Medium Enterprise. Although the relation between levels of profitability and the growth process is still being studied,[8] it is possible to define the heterogeneous informal sector with existing hypotheses. This is particularly important in the case of the Dominican Republic because some institutions do not clearly differentiate between informal activities, microenterprises and small- and medium enterprises. In this sense, academia now accepts that at least three types of productive units can be identified within the informal sector.[9] The first is the individual productive unit as the subsistence level with no prospects for capital accumulation or growth. The high percentage (48.5 percent)[10] of "self-employed" workers in the informal sector suggests that this productive unit is the most prevalent in the informal sector of the Dominican Republic. This figure is even more relevant when we see that informal economic activities accounted for 38.1 percent and 44.1 percent of the 1980 and 1983 Economically Active Population (EAP) for the city of Santo Domingo.[11]

The second type of productive unit is the family business. It too enjoys little capital and labor input, but has more than the individual unit. Its main characteristics are unpaid family labor and all income is used for family consumption. Again, there is limited possibility of capital accumulation and growth. This category of "unpaid relatives" increased its share of informal activities from 2.5 percent in 1980 to 4 percent in 1983.[12]

The third type of productive unit employs paid labor outside of the family. Such units could be considered profit-seeking, although it is not clear if they qualify as "modern" or "informal" enterprises.[13] This is the essence of the debate on the boundaries between micro-, small- and medium enterprises. The volume of capital invested, the number of workers and volume of sales are not appropriate criteria for establishing the difference because they do not take into account technology, production, capital accumulation levels or the skewing effect of inflation on sales and capital. Further discussion of this point is beyond the scope of this study. The importance of these factors in designing any promotional strategy should be recognized, however. Such a strategy—through financing, for example—should address itself primarily to those productive units with slight possibilities of accumulation and growth, but with substantial labor absorptive capacity. There has been no promotional program that intentionally extends credit to small productive units based on relative size. This aspect will be discussed in more detail later. From this point on, references to the sector will include all of the economic players just described.

Despite limitations in delineating the sector, a 1987 study by Miguel Ceara of Santo Domingo found that the greatest relative concentration of small- and medium-sized businesses was in "other manufacturing industries" (sector 39), followed in order of importance by the industries corresponding to lumber (sector 33), metal products, machinery and equipment (sector 38), textiles (sector 32), paper (sector 34), chemical products (sector 35), food, beverage and tobacco products (sector 31) and basic metals (sector 37).[14] Ceara also concludes that small- and medium businesses accounted for 74.1 percent of existing businesses for the 1977–1978 period.[15]

Ceara's study also used various indicators to measure the concentration of small- and medium-sized businesses in each productive area.[16] Some data attest to the heterogeneity of some industries. As noted, the greatest concentration is in sector 39 (other manufacturing). However, the distribution of capital per establishment is heavily concentrated.

According to Regional Employment Program for Latin America and the Caribbean (PREALC) statistics, in 1980, informal labor in the manufacturing industry was 12.7 percent of total informal labor.[17] This percentage rose to 16.6 percent in 1983. However, the share of informal labor in overall labor for the manufacturing industry went from 8.9 percent in 1980 to 12.6 percent in 1983. If we take into account that only those units with less than five employees were considered microenterprises, the earlier figure is a good indicator of the importance of the informal sector in the manufacturing industry.

Size of the Informal Sector. One of the great difficulties in studying employment is the paucity and inadequacy of the few available data. The income and expense surveys conducted in 1976–77 and 1984 did not gather information on how much income was earned by each work category, nor did they record the occupation of members of the houses surveyed. Moreover, the biannual surveys that are being conducted now do not recognize the existence of an informal sector as a separate economic reality. In fact, they assume a unified labor market. Under-employment is defined as less than 35 hours of work in the week prior to the survey, but data on occupation are not offered.

Garcia analyzes the implications of the insufficiency of data for research.[18] He calls attention to the fact that researchers are being forced to become data collectors before they can begin their own work. Garcia suggests mixed surveys as the only solution. These begin by surveying homes and identifying who works in informal units. This permits locating such units and interviewing members on their characteristics and operation.

In 1989, Management Systems International (MSI) set out to do something similar—at least in its initial phase—for the United States Agency for International Development (USAID) and the Dominican Association for Microenterprise (ADOMICRO).[19] Their study found that, as of March 1989, the Dominican Republic had 145,000 microenterprises for a ratio of 5.56 homes per microenterprise. The homes in the survey were selected on the basis of their poor-to-lower-middle income status. MSI's report does not describe the criteria for selection, but, given that it is not possible to form neighborhoods strictly on the basis of income levels, this could allow for significant error. Moreover, this study surveyed only households, so some productive units that do not necessarily operate in the home could not be surveyed. Despite some shortfalls, this study is a valuable contribution to research on the informal sector in the Dominican Republic. Its more important findings include: (a) 54 percent of microenterprise owners are between the ages of 26 and 45, 55 percent are heads of households and 60 percent are men; (b) as expected, commercial businesses make up the largest number of microenterprises (51 percent), services account for 31 percent, microindustry accounts for 18 percent (the latter is composed largely of producers of apparel, 40 percent), wood products (33 percent); and (c) 89 percent of the businesses employ four or fewer people. The average number of employees is 2.75. This figure was extrapolated to estimate the total number of people employed in the informal sector: 398,750.

Relations with the Modern Business Sector. In some modern industries, the installed productive capacity exceeds internal demand, resulting in a utilization index of about 60 percent.[20] In other areas, however, where monopoly over demand does not exist, modern businesses still share the market with informal producers. The latter can divide the market by offering goods at a lower price.[21] However, there is not only competition in the marketplace, but they are integrated in a relationship of dependency in production,[22] marketing and labor.

Subcontracting and machinery and equipment repair services are examples of competition in production. Subcontracting and machinery and equipment repair services are examples of competition in production. Subcontracting part of the productive process by modern sector enterprises can be intended to lower costs in much the same way as coproduction (the *maquila*) is used in international production. Sub-contracting is common in apparel and metal working. Production in the latter is destined essentially for the modern sector, as parts, pieces and equipment.

In relation to manufacturing, one would expect demand for informal goods to be highly dependent on earnings in the modern business sector.

Sixty-five percent of the population is concentrated in the two lowest income levels and consumes 100 percent of its income. This suggests that spending by this segment of the population is oriented largely to informal production.[23]

The relationship between both sectors is even more complex in the labor market. However, its main characteristic is the mobility of labor between the two sectors,[24] with the market as a whole adjusting through the differences between their respective earnings. In a segmented labor market model along the lines of Marquez and Mezera,[25] equilibrium is when average income in the informal sector equals average income in the modern business sector, adjusted by the probability of finding employment in the latter. The high rates of unemployment and the ease of entering the informal sector suggest that the unemployed see a high probability of finding work in the modern sector, this being the only situation in which unemployment is valid. Given that average income is the adjustment variable in the informal sector and that it has fallen more rapidly than average income in the modern sector,[26] the perception of a relatively high probability of finding work in the modern sector appears to be constant over time. If average income in the modern sector is adjusted by the probability of finding work in that sector, the result is less than average income in the informal sector. If this model is valid, one may conclude that urban workers are misreading the labor market by overestimating their chances of finding employment in the modern sector.

The recommendation here is clear: a strategy aimed at reducing open unemployment based on the promotion of informal sector activities must provide the unemployed with information about job opportunities in the sector.

Industrialization and the Labor Market

An analysis of the industrialization process in the Dominican Republic is beyond the scope of this study. However, some of its elements should be taken into account to be able to understand some of the most important relationships between the labor market, the modern sector and the small productive units of the informal sector.

Industrialization began relatively late in the Dominican Republic. Appropriate legislation (Law 299) was not adopted until 1969, and manufacturing did not begin to take hold until the early 1970s; and then it exhibited substantial distortions and limitations.[27] Although the country was able to lower imports of consumer goods between 1970 and 1985, the exact opposite occurred with intermediate inputs. This shows that the model was successful in the former sense, but not in the latter, and intermediate inputs must still be imported. The reasons for this include a narrow national market, an oligopolistic setting which concentrated production among a few producers and a pattern of consumer demand more diverse than production.

On the other hand, this sector brought in new, capital-intensive technology and developed at a faster rate than other, less productive sectors, thereby reducing the market share of the informal sector.

More important, the modern enterprises that developed have not been able to absorb all of the supply of urban labor of the past 20 years. On the other hand, the labor market shows two characteristics peculiar to the Dominican Republic: (1) the rate of unemployment does not fall during periods of economic expansion;[28] at most, there is a drop in underemployment; and (2) the rate of growth of the urban economically active population (EAP) is among the highest in Latin America. This results from heavy rural-to-urban migration, population growth and gross participation rates.[29]

These conditions have resulted in a greater expansion of employment in the informal sector than in the modern sector. Employment in the latter rose by 2 percent between June 1980 and February 1983. However, employment in the informal sector grew 14.8 percent during the same period.[30] The deterioration in the quality of employment that these figures imply can be seen by comparing earned income for both sectors. In 1980, average income in the modern sector was RD$ 308, compared to RD$ 195 in the informal sector. For 1983, these figures were RD$ 300 and RD$ 181, respectively. Another important indicator, the rate of unemployment among male heads of households, rose from 9.5 percent in 1980 to 11.2 percent in 1983.[31]

The Labor Market in Relation to Internal and External Migration

Labor market characteristics analyzed so far suggest the importance of the relationship between internal migration and urban unemployment. In 1960, 60.6 percent of the economically active population worked in the agricultural and livestock sector. By 1983, this figure had dropped to 34.1 percent.[32] This is the best indicator of the strong rural-to-urban migration during this period. The impact of this influx on the high rate of urban unemployment in Santo Domingo and employment in the informal sector have already been discussed.

If heavy internal migration contributes to rising unemployment, would migration abroad not have the opposite effect? If not enough to counteract the effect of internal migration, might it at least reduce its impact? The immediate answer to this question is negative. Despite a large external migration, unemployment has not fallen. This is because of surplus labor's limited ability to migrate.

The most important receiving country is the United States, including Puerto Rico. The gross rate of emigration to the United States for 1970 and

1985 was 3.2 percent and 3.4 percent, respectively. During that period, the Dominican Republic's rate of emigration to the United States was the most stable of any country.[33] However, it is not possible to measure the rate of illegal emigration. Some authors estimate it to be equal to the rate of legal emigration. Other data suggest that the illegal rate is higher in the Dominican Republic than elsewhere in the Caribbean. Among Dominicans applying for legalization under the Immigration Reform and Control Act of 1986, 56 percent could prove they were in the United States before 1 January 1982.[34]

In analyzing the possible effect of an employment strategy on the migratory process, the skill levels and types of jobs held by immigrants in the United States must be taken into account. Professional and technical personnel represented only 7.2 percent of the immigrants admitted in 1987. This was the second lowest percentage in the Caribbean after Cuba, which accounted for 3.3 percent. The Dominican percentage for executives and administrators, sales people and administrative support, was comparable to that of other Caribbean countries. However, the percentage of those in jobs requiring little or no training (artisans, foremen, repairmen, nonagricultural machine operators and labors, agriculture, forestry, fishing, and services) was 77.9 percent.

This suggests that most Dominican emigrants come from a gross labor surplus with little or no skills that could be absorbed by employment strategy based on microenterprise and the informal sector. However, caution is warranted in forecasting the success of any program of this nature in stemming the migratory flow, especially when potential income that might be generated is compared with that earned by immigrants in the United States. The greater the difference, the higher the rate of emigration. Therefore, the problem is not just to create more jobs, but to raise the earning potential of those currently held and those that could be filled under new programs.

The hypothesis that emigrants come from low-skill jobs in urban areas is also confirmed in the case of migration to Puerto Rico. In 1989, 55 percent of all Dominican emigrants to Puerto Rico were in low-skill jobs. Fifty-two percent were from urban areas, and the average level of education was the eighth grade.[35] On the other hand, three of every five emigrants had been employed in the Dominican Republic. This supports the hypothesis that unemployment is not the only motive for emigration; the low earnings of those who are employed are also an important variable. This last is shown by the fact that most of these emigrants were self-employed in the lowest paying occupations of the informal sector, such as vending and personal services.[36]

III. POLICIES TO PROMOTE MICROENTERPRISE AND INFORMAL SECTOR DEVELOPMENT

This section begins with a review of the basic characteristics of the units of production in Santo Domingo which have been financed by the principal existing financing institutions and programs. Existing units of production at the national level will also be considered. This analysis is useful in evaluating the policies of these institutions and will help to estimate the possible effects of a global promotional strategy.

Considering the role the state might play, and parting from a critique of the policies of private institutions, a second section makes some suggestions that might contribute to raising employment levels in the sector and the income of those working in it.

Institutions and Programs that Promote the Sector

Various institutions and programs promote the sector either directly or indirectly. Some institutions have programs which promote productive units together with programs for small business and service unit entities, as well as such activity as street vending.

The three main institutions that promote microenterprise and the informal sector in the city of Santo Domingo are the Association for the Development of Women (*Asociación para el Desarrollo de la Mujer,* ADOPEM) also known as the Women's Bank (*Banco de la Mujer*)[37], the Dominican Development Foundation (*Fundación Dominicana de Desarrollo,* FDD),[38] and the Association for the Development of Microenterprise (*Asociación para el Desarrollo de la Microempresa,* ADEMI). At the regional level, the most important organization is the Program of Assistance to Small Business (*Programa de Asistencia a la Pequeña Empresa,* PROAPE),[39] sponsored by the Association for the Development of the Province of Santiago (*Asociación para el Desarrollo de la Provincia de Santiago*). These organizations sponsor the best programs in terms of definition and structure.[40]

There is another organization, the Economic Development Fund Program (*Programa del Fondo para el Desarrollo Económico,* FIDE),[41] which focuses on larger businesses in the modern sector.

So as not to unnecessarily extend this study, this section considers only the most outstanding results and characteristics of ADEMI, for two reasons. First, ADEMI is the most important of the named institutions because it has been the most successful in terms of funding, number of microenterprises financed and number of jobs created. It has also been the institution most representative of the policy of liberalization, which includes, among other factors, the use of a "market rate of interest and commercial banking criteria in the financing of microenterprise." This policy has been made a condition for funding by important international financial institutions such as the United States Agency for International Development (USAID) and the Inter-American Development Bank (IDB).

Basic Characteristics of the Populations Targeted by Promotional Programs. The most important basic characteristics are distribution of businesses by type of activity, the ratio of capital to employment, size measured by number of employees and volume of sales, and financial and training needs.

These characteristics of enterprises financed by existing institutions in Santo Domingo can be analyzed through a 1988 study conducted by Lora for the Educational Credit Foundation (*Fundación de Crédito Educativo*).[42] The survey included only establishments in Santo Domingo. The sample was taken among establishments financed by the three institutions under reference. Another important survey for the study of microenterprises at the national level is that conducted for the Management Systems International (MSI) study.[43] This was conducted for ADOMICRO[44] and USAID.

As to the type of activities performed by small units of production, the survey directed by Lora found that apparel (19 percent), food preparation and sales (16.5 percent), woodworking and carpentry (12.5 percent) and artisanry (11 percent) predominate. The remaining activities totaled less than 6 percent. The MSI survey confirmed the strong role of apparel and woodworking-carpentry activities (40 percent and 33 percent, respectively) within the microenterprises.

Both surveys confirm the low levels of investment per job and the low levels of sales, although the values differ with the relative sizes of the units of production. Lora's study found that productive units with less than RD $10,000 (US $1,575) of investment had an investment-per-job ratio of RD $1,600 (US $252). Those with between RD $10,000 and RD $50,000 (US $7,874) of investment needed RD $2,500 (US $394) per job, and those with RD $50,000 to RD $100,000 (US $15,748) of investment needed RD $3,000 (US $472) per job. Finally, those with over RD $100,000 of investment created a job with RD $5,000 (US $787).

This same survey found that 19.7 percent of the establishments had an annual sales volume of RD $10,000 or less; 41 percent had sales between RD $10,000 and RD $40,000; 27.1 percent with sales between RD $40,000 and RD $100,000; and only 12.1 percent had sales over RD $100,000.

According to the MSI survey, median monthly sales of the microenterprises were RD $1,083 (US$170), or RD $12,996 (US$2,047) per annum. This figure is consistent with the Lora survey, as the level of sales of the greatest number of enterprises surveyed includes the value of the median sales found in the MSI survey.

If there is any variable that indirectly points to the low income level of those who work in the informal sector, it is the value of sales. If we take into account that the data suggest strong participation in the informal sector by enterprises that employ only unpaid family labor, then the disposable income of all members of the household is the surplus from sales over costs of inputs. Assuming that, on average, this surplus represents 50 percent of sales, then the previous data suggest that in 1988 more than 50 percent of microenterprise households had a monthly income of about RD $500.

Analysis of size as a function of number of employees shows the preponderance of small enterprises. According to the Lora survey in 1988, 50 percent of the establishments had fewer than five workers, and 32 percent had between five and ten workers. The MSI survey is even more revealing; it found that 50 percent of businesses had only one worker, 21 percent had two workers, 9 percent had three workers, 8 percent had four workers, only 8 percent had between five and ten workers, and only 3 percent had more than ten workers. This suggests that, in Santo Domingo, the number of workers per business tends to be greater than the national average when all types of microenterprises are considered (commerce, services and production). However, analysis of only productive units shows more comparable results. Here, 35.5 percent of business has one worker, 19.3 percent has two workers, 16.1 percent has three workers, 9.7 percent has four workers, 12.9 percent has between five and ten workers, and 6.4 percent has more than ten workers.[45]

If, in Lora's survey of Santo Domingo, we take the average value at each level of the number of workers per enterprise and weight it by the average number of employees per business using the average number of workers for each size of business, the average number of workers is 6.43 per business. If we follow a similar procedure with the results of the MSI survey, we obtain a value of 3.22 workers per business in national terms.

Financing is the largest problem for both small- and medium-sized enterprises in the informal sector. It therefore should be the focal point of any promotional strategy aimed at lowering unemployment and poverty in urban areas.

The MSI survey found that 74 percent of existing businesses have no credit. Of the 26 percent of businesses having credit, 6 percent had obtained it through formal channels, and the remaining 20 percent said it has been obtained "more formally." Only 3 percent of the businesses surveyed reported obtaining credit from organizations that finance microenterprises. This last point is a good indicator of the inability of these organizations to reach their targeted populations. The loan average was RD $1,500 over a four-month period. On the other hand, 60 percent of the businesses surveyed were willing to accept a loan if offered.

These figures suggest that the informal sector could be promoted extensively with financing from promotional organizations. However, available financing is exceeded by demand in Santo Domingo alone. The organizations grouped in ADOMICRO had a credit portfolio of over RD $13,000,000 in 1988. Assuming three turnovers per year (average period for loans being four months), these organizations could meet a demand for over RD $39,000,000. On the basis of the MSI survey, Santo Domingo has an estimated 18,100 units of production; given that 60 percent of businesses surveyed are seeking credit, 10,600 establishments in Santo Domingo need to be financed. Assuming that inflation has raised the average need for credit to RD $2500,[46] and, further, assuming demand for three loans per year, total financing required is RD $81,450,000. Therefore, credit available in 1988 was only 47.8 percent of that required under these assumptions. If the small enterprises in the interior of the country are added, the total number seeking credit would rise to 16,260, and total demand would rise to RD $121,195,000. Available credit would then represent only 32.1 percent of total demand. Finally, lack of training and technical assistance also limit growth of the sector. Various studies have shown that areas needing training are sales and marketing, accounting and cost-control and administration of production.[47] Technical assistance is needed in product design, selection of technology and production processes.

Most Important Results and Characteristics of the Association for the Development of Microenterprise (ADEMI). ADEMI was established in May 1983 and began operations with RD $300,000. On December 31, 1988, its loan portfolio amounted to RD $6,006,553, financed by the Technical Secretariat of the Presidency (*Secretariado Técnico de la Presidencia*)—40.8 percent; the *Banco Popular Dominicano*—21.6 percent; the Inter-American Development Bank (IDB)—17.7 percent; and 19.8 percent was self-financed. It has also received donations from international organizations, most notably USAID. ADEMI has 88 employees and offices in 20 provinces.

As of December 1988, ADEMI had financed 5,479 microenterprises through 20,885 loans, indicating that on average each microenterprise received financing 3.8 times. Total loans were valued at RD $32,459,454. The average loan was RD $1,554 (US $245). The average loan to a microenterprise was RD $5,905.

In 1988 alone, the average loan was RD $2,652 (US $418), and the average loan to a microenterprise was RD $11,485 (US $1,808). That year, ADEMI's total costs were RD $1,982,135 or RD $399 (US $63) per loan. This figure is extremely low in comparison to the cost of similar programs in other Latin American countries.[48]

As of December 1988, ADEMI financing had created 6,734 new jobs and had improved 22,705 jobs.[49] In short, ADEMI was able to create one job per RD $4,820 (US $759). This figure for 1988 alone was RD $7,288 (US $1,147) per job created.

More recent figures indicate that, as of June 30, 1989, the loan portfolio has increased to RD $8,814,321; the total number of new jobs rose to 7,680;

and the total number of microenterprises financed increased to 6,650 through 24,267 loans for a total amount of RD $43,413,511. Thus, average loans have been of RD $1,789 and average cost per job created of RD $5,653.

One of ADEMI's most outstanding characteristics is its credit policy. It charges market rates,[50] on the theory that, if ADEMI did not exist, microenterprises would have to borrow at much higher usurious rates. On the other hand, a high interest rate allows ADEMI to capitalize and be self-sufficient.

This interest rate policy and good management has allowed ADEMI to become financially self-sufficient with a loan recovery index of 99 percent. In 1988, income exceeded expenses by 29 percent. From 1987 to mid-1989, the loan recovery index was 99 percent.

Another important feature of ADEMI's financial policy is its maximum repayment period (12 months). This ensures that loans will only be used as working capital. Finally, ADEMI also makes loans to enterprises, in gradually increasing amounts as businesses grow, providing they have been in operation for at least six months; its maximum loan is RD $30,000 (US $ 4,725).

To conclude, in 1989, ADEMI planned to finance 2,000 new microenterprises by increasing its loan portfolio to RD $12,000,000, for a loan total of RD $25,000,000 for the year. Estimates for 1990 indicate that ADEMI will need a loan portfolio of RD$30,000,000 to finance 10,000 microenterprises, which will, in turn, create and improve 60,000 jobs.[51]

Promotional Policy

The above presents an overview of microenterprise and the informal sector, emphasizing its structure and basic characteristics. On the basis of that analysis, it was concluded that the sector's heterogeneity has a differential impact on its ability to generate income and employment.

The first part of this section examined the organizations and programs that promote the sector, stressing the most important aspects of their financial policy. This section will compare the policy to characteristics of the sector and will propose some additional criteria that should be considered. It will also analyze the potential role of the state in a global promotional policy or strategy.

Private Institutions and Programs. The policies of ADEMI and of similar organizations, as well as the conditionality imposed by international lending institutions, are susceptible to four important criticisms that should be considered in the context of constraints on the creation of employment and income in the sector.

First, the very short-term credit policy, which is intended to finance only working capital, seriously limits job creation and growth of income.

This type of financing allows only increases in production that would not be possible without such financing. Such increases can (1) create new jobs only if no limitations are imposed by complementary factors of production (physical capital, training and technical assistance), and (2) increase income only if conditions of supply and demand, competitiveness in the market and costs remain constant. Although these conditions can be met in many cases, it should be added that income for paid workers does not increase since investment and productivity do not increase.

Second, since the same interest rate is applied to all microenterprises, it does not take into account differences in ability to generate surplus income through sales above total costs, including wages. In the final analysis, this implies a transfer of financial resources from less to more profitable businesses. From another perspective, financing at the market rate assumes that the financial market is perfectly competitive, since the same rate applies in the modern sector. Aside from other imperfections, it is well known that "formal" businesses obtain financing at lower interest rates because they represent less risk and greater financial gain to lenders. This situation also results in a transfer of resources from the informal to the modern sector, through the relationship that exists between them in the financial market.[52]

The third important criticism is that existing policy does not provide for selective financing based on ability to create jobs. Elsewhere in this study it is shown that different sectors or activities can generate more jobs per unit of investment than others. In addition, the indirect effect on employment differs from one activity to another,[53] given that the backward and forward linkages of employment are different.[54]

Finally, current policy allows only for financing existing microenterprises and forgoes the possibility of financing and promoting new ones. However, it has been shown that promoting new microenterprises is an effective way to create employment.[55]

From the above, we conclude that a change in policy based on our critique could improve the effectiveness of private institutions devoted to promoting the sector.

The first recommendation is to set aside a loan portfolio for intermediate- and long-term financing of enterprises in the informal sector to allow for growth in productive capacity and productivity. This requires adjustment to new procedures by the institutions, given their lack of experience with this type of lending. As Mezera indicates, "the main obstacle faced by many programs of support for the sector that have tried to step up to meaningful levels of individual lending is that of doing so without even an estimate of the potential profitability of the expansion project prompting the loan application, or incurring an expense to determine that profitability that is not justified by the size of the loan."[56]

The solution to this problem is a simple mechanism that provides for minifeasibility studies at a cost proportionate to the investment. "It is a complete questionnaire—designed for easy use in the field—which would allow a field worker with some training to obtain, in no more than one morning, from the small business, the information necessary to feed and operate an interactive computer program. This program would draw a profile of the investments required by the project and a projection of potential profitability, based on the price of the finished product and the cost of the principal inputs."[57] This method has been used successfully in International Labor Organization (ILO) sponsored projects in Ecuador.

The second recommendation is to explicitly include the employment effect as a criterion of evaluation, for both small loans of working capital and larger loans for development. For working capital loans, a simple criterion for estimating employment effect could be to calculate the ratio of working capital to sales and multiply it by the ratio of sales to number of workers. The result is the number of jobs generated per unit of working capital.

The application of this criterion is more difficult in the cases of development loans, since, in addition to the employment effect, the ability of the project to repay the loan must be considered. This is measured through multiple selection criteria involving simultaneous consideration of the employment effect and profitability. The solution suggested is to maximize a total employment/investment function, subject to the limitation that profitability be greater than or equal to the relevant rate of interest: L is the total number of employees.[58] I is total investment, TIR is the internal rate of return based on market prices, and i is the applicable rate of interest. Given the amount of credit available for development financing, and a number of projects to be financed by that amount, the criterion demands rejection of those projects not in compliance with the above limitation, and ranking the rest on the basis of their employment effect. Projects so chosen would be financed until available resources are exhausted.[59]

The third recommendation involves a modification of the criteria used to set the rate of interest. The previous proposal included a maximization of the employment effect, limited to the financial profitability of the project. This profitability is calculated using market rates, and deducting from sales the value, at market rates, of labor employed in the project, as well as the value of inputs, to reach the flow of funds on which the TIR is calculated. It is possible that profitability so calculated will not equal the interest rate, even when the project has a high employment effect. The proposed solution is to calculate the TIR using prices (*precios de cuenta*), especially in arriving at the cost of labor, accepting the project so long as the TIR so calculated is greater than a parameter that reflects the social opportunity cost of capital,[60] and set a new rate of interest equal to the profitability calculated using prices (*precios de cuenta*).

However, the average interest rate of the loans should be at least equal to the average (*ponderado*) cost of the capital in the loan portfolio. This notwithstanding, projects with high employment effect and with a TIR at costs (*de cuenta*) lower than the institution's average cost of capital can still be accepted so long as the institution makes the necessary adjustments, financing projects at interest rates higher than such costs, so that the average weighted rate of interest in all projects financed equals the average weighted cost of all capital in the loan portfolio. This way, there would be equilibrium between rate of interest and cost of capital, and the institution would avoid deficits and risks of decapitalization, although it would be maximizing the employment effect of available resources. Finally, changing policy to include the promotion of new microenterprises would imply use of the criteria contained in the three previous suggestions.[61]

Role of the State in Promoting the Sector. The state can have significant effect in creating employment and increasing income in this sector through carefully designed promotional policies. In the Dominican Republic, this effect could be achieved through a deliberate strategy that would include three basic elements: (1) facilitating access to financing, training and technical assistance, (2) implementing an economic policy that tends to raise income in the sector and (3) coordinating a global promotional strategy.

An effective way to facilitate access to financing is to establish a National Guaranty Fund, operated by the private organizations already working to promote the sector. The previous section of this paper showed that currently available private financing is exceeded by demand. A Guaranty Fund could raise credit to levels very close to demand, with the advantage that the state would need considerably fewer resources than if a state entity were to make loans directly. Hann (1985) calculated that, if the government were to make 200 loans per month of an average US $2,000, it would need about US $5,000,000 per year. However, if it operated a guaranty fund through which it reimbursed financial institutions for nonrecoverable loans, it would need only 10 percent of that amount, or US $ 500,000.[62] Another advantage of a guaranty fund is that it allows for a lower cost per loan, as loans would be channeled through existing lending institutions.

The latter would forward requests for credit exceeding their resources to commercial banks. Loans would be guaranteed by government funds deposited in these same banks. Assuming that the banks would be willing to accept a guarantee of 20 percent of the value of the loans, the government would need only RD $10,000,000 to raise available financing to RD $50,000,000. However, the disadvantage is that the government cannot dictate the terms of the loans. Above all, the interest rate and the time period, both of which—as seen earlier—should be variables of promotional policy.

The guaranty fund would be devoted essentially to development financing, for two important reasons. First, this type of financing does not exist in the present private lending system. Second, the larger amount of development lending, compared to smaller loans for working capital, would make it more attractive to the banks. Further, the private organizations would do the processing, thereby reducing bank operating costs.

Within the context of a global strategy, training and technical assistance need to be improved. Emphasis has so far been on financing; training and technical assistance have been subordinated[63] to the need for supervision required to ensure repayment of loans.

The state has an infrastructure with which to improve access to training and technical assistance as well as greater resources than the private organizations. Examples of governmental or semi-governmental institutions so equipped are the Institute for Technical-Professional Training (*Instituto de Formación Técnico-Profesional,* INFOTEP) and the Dominican Institute of Industrial Technology (*Instituto Dominicano de Tecnología Industrial,* INDOTEC). INFOTEP programs are oriented mainly toward the modern sector. However, it is capable not only of training existing microentrepreneurs,[64] but also of devising programs that would create new microentrepreneurs by preparing individuals to become self-employed in the sector.

The growth of informal enterprises also requires the development of production techniques and products appropriate to the sector. Attention must be given to modernizing equipment in order to raise the productivity of labor. INDOTEC is the most appropriate organization for this, but it needs to reorder its process and product design activities for the metalworking and food industries.

Although most of the informal sector is not directly affected by government action, this does not mean that it is not influenced by economic policies. This situation can be counteracted with specific measures aimed at the sector. In addition to what has already been discussed, such measures could include legislation[65] targeted at the sector and promoting demand for its goods through government subsidies.[66]

Ideally, the state should design and implement a policy intended to satisfy basic needs by lowering unemployment, underemployment and poverty in a way that takes into account the diversity of the economy. However, explicit promotion of the informal sector will still be necessary because, as previously noted, even if economic policy achieves maximum productivity, thereby absorbing current nonstructural surplus labor, (*componente coyuntural*), one structural surplus will still be unemployed.

NOTES

1. Victor Tokman, *El Sector Informal: Quince Años Después,* Serie Documentos de Trabajo/316 (Santiago: PREALC, 1987).

2. The principal advocate of this thesis is Hernando de Soto. A good presentation can be found in Hernando De Soto, *El Otro Sendero* (Lima: Editorial el Barranco, 1986).

3. This originated with the 1972 report of the International Labor Organization (ILO) mission to Kenya. Known as the Kenya Report, it was developed essentially by PREALC and its researchers. A presentation on the evolution of this theory can be found in Tokman, *El Sector Informal: Quince Años Después.*

4. See Tokman, *Las Relaciones Entre los Sectores Formal e Informal, Una Exploración Sobre su Naturaleza,* En Revista de la CEPAL, Primer Semestre de 1978 (Santiago: CEPAL, 1978); Tokman, *El Sector Informal: Quince Años Después* and *El Sector Informal Hoy: El Imperativo de Actuar,* Serie Documentos de Trabajo/314 (Santiago: PREALC, 1987); Paolo Souza and Tokman, *Sector Informal: Funcionamiento y Políticas.* En Revista Internacional del Trabajo, vol.94, no.3 (OIT: Ginebra, 1976); D. Carbonetto and E.Chavez, *Sector Informal Urbano: Heterogeneidad del Capital y Excedente Bruto del Trabajo,* En Socialismo y Participación (Lima: Socialismo y Participación, 1984); Carbonetto, *Informe Sobre Investigación del Sector Informal Urbano de Lima Metropolitana,* Version Mimeo (Lima: 1985); Carbonetto, *Politicas de Mejoramiento del Empleo en el Sector Informal Urbano (SIU),* En "El Sector Informal Urbano en los Paises Andinos," (Quito: ILDIS-CEPESIU, 1985), among others.

5. Tokman, *El Sector Informal: Quince Años Después,* p. 16.

6. This title has been adopted because it is the main reason for the emergence of the sector. There are, however, elements other than the structural surplus of urban labor that are part of the same. By "structural surplus of urban labor," we mean that part of the EAP that would be unemployed even if the economy were using all of its productive capacity. Another important concept is that of the "excedente conyuntural." This refers to additional unemployment resulting from a decrease in utilization of productive capacity. See Carbonetto, *Informe Sobre Investigación del Sector Informal;* Carbonetto and Chavez, *Sector Informal Urbano: Heterogeneidad del Capital;* Mezera (1987b).

7. Souza and Tokman, *Sector Informal: Funcionamiento y Políticas.*

8. Mizrahi (1987) proposes a model that relates capital accumulation to level of consumption. His basic conclusion is that capital accumulation is possible only at the expense of the consumption levels of workers in the informal sector and their families.

9. Tokman, *El Sector Informal: Quince Años Después.*

10. PREALC statistics, 1983.

11. Informal workers include all those who are self-employed, those employed in microenterprise (less than five workers) with no secondary education and those in

domestic service. See also Noberto Garcia and Mario Valdivia, *Crisis Externa, Ajuste Interno y Mercada de Trabajo: República Dominicana, 1980–1983* (México: El Colegio de México, 1982).

12. Garcia and Valdivia, *Crisis Externa.*

13. The academic community has not studied this problem enough. Some quantitative indicators have been proposed. For example, PREALC defines informal enterprises as those which employ less than five workers. Other possible indicators include the ratio of capital to employment and the ratio of capital to production.

14. Miguel Ceara, *La Concentración Industrial en la República Dominicana,* en Investigación y Ciencia, Año 2, No. 5 (Santo Domingo: Universidad APEC, 1987).

15. This paper has its shortcomings in that it is based on two sources of information and uses two definitions of small- and medium industry. Moreover, the data used are for 1977–78 and 1981 and, thus, do not reflect the changes in the sector that may have resulted from the crisis since 1982. Despite these limitations, this paper is a good indicator of both the volume of small- and medium enterprises by type of activity and the level of concentration by category.

One of the sources (*Secretaría de Estado de Industria y Comercio,* 1977–78) defined small- and medium industry by amount of invested capital: small industries were those which reported an investment of less than RD $150,000; medium ones reported more than RD $150,000, but less than RD $1,000,000. The other source Escuela de Economica del Instituto Tecnologico de Santo Domingo (INTEC, 1982) used total assets and defined small industries as those with assets between RD $10,000 and RD $250,000, and medium ones as those between RD $250,000 and RD $1,000,000; large industries were those with assets in excess of RD $1,000,000.

16. Ceara, *La Concentración Industrial.*

17. PREALC Statistics, 1983.

18. Brigida Garcia, *Desarrollo Económico y Absorción de Fuerza de Trabajo en México, 1950–1980* (México: El Colegio de México, 1982).

19. This is the only existing study based on a household survey. It was based on a sample survey of 612 homes from which inferences on the population were drawn. Despite some mention of its limitations, this study is basic to understanding the importance of the informal sector.

20. Miguel Ceara, *El Ajuste Recesivo en el Sector Industrial,* En Ciencia y Sociedad, vol. XIII, no. 2 (Santo Domingo: INTEC, 1988).

21. Pereira, 1986.

22. There are other theoretical approaches to studying the relationship between the modern and informal sectors. However, current debate and data suggest that in the Dominican case, the relationship is one of complementarity of a dependent nature. For a more detailed analysis, see Tokman, *Las Relaciones Entre los Sectores Formal e Informal.*

23. Banco Central de la Republica Dominicana, *Encuesta Nacional de Ingresos y Gastos de las Familias* (Santo Domingo: Banco Central, 1984).

24. Knowledge of the patterns of labor mobility is basic to promotional policy. At a given time, a worker can be employed in the modern sector, employed in the informal sector, unemployed and seeking employment in the modern sector or unemployed and considering the possibility of entering the informal sector. Since promotional policy affects the differences in income that can be generated in each sector, that policy will affect patterns of mobility. It could also induce an increase in participation of the population in the EAP, as occurred with the Program of Support for Temporary Income (*Programa de Apoyo al Ingreso Temporal*—PAIT), in Peru in 1984. For an explanation of the implications of the mobility of the work force, see Mezera (1987a).

25. Marqueza and Mezera, 1987.

26. PREALC Statistics, 1983.

27. For a detailed analysis of the model of industrialization and its effects, see Miguel Ceara, *Fomento de las Pequeñas y Medianas Empresas: Elementos Macroeconomicos*, Estudios Económicos y Sociales (Santo Domingo: Fundación Friedrich Ebert, 1988).

28. This phenomenon suggests that, in the period of expansion, i.e., when all of the economic productive capacity is being used the rate of absorption of the labor surplus (*componente coyuntural*) is at least equal to the rate of increase of the EAP, on the assumption that the pattern of mobility remains constant.

29. For a more detailed analysis of the labor market characteristics, see Lozano, 1987 and PREALC, 1983.

30. Garcia and Valdivia, *Crisis Externa*.

31. PREALC Statistics, 1983.

32. Isidoro Santana, *Tendencias Recientes y Perspectivas de la Situación Ocupacional en R.D.*, En Población y Desarrollo, Año III, Boletín No. 9 (Santo Domingo: Instituto de Estudios de Población y Desarrollo, 1985).

33. Franc Baez Evertsz, *Migración Internacional en el Caribe: Tendencias y Perspectivas*, Presentado en el Seminario "Migración Internacional en el Caribe: Haitanos en República Dominicana y Dominicanos en Puerto Rico" (Santo Domingo: FLACSO, 4–5 de Septiembre 1989).

34. Michael Laguerre, "American Odyssey: Haitians of New York City," cited by Baez, *Migración Internacional en el Caribe: Tendencias y Perspectivas*. In general, available studies on undocumented migrants are very scarce, and the few available on Dominicans are not very helpful on the question of employment before migration, information needed for studying relationships with the job market.

35. Jorge Duany and Rey Hernandez, *La Fuerza Laboral Dominicana en Santurce: El Impacto de la Inmigración en un Mercado de Trabajo Segmentado*, Presentado en el Sem-

inario "Migración Internacional en el Caribe: Haitanos en República Dominicana y Dominicanos en Puerto Rico" (Santo Domingo: FLACSO, Septembre 1989).

36. Duany and Hernandez, *La Fuerza Laboral Dominicana en Santurce.*

37. The ADOPEM program provides loans for microenterprises managed by women and/or over 50 percent of whose employees are women. Loans range between RD $300 to RD $10,000 and terms are between 12 and 24 months. The monthly interest rate is 2.5 percent, and the commission charge is 3 percent.

ADOPEM operates with funds from the FIDE small-business fund of the Banco Central. As with ADEMI, ADOPEM deposits its funds in a commercial bank, which then issues loans to microenterprises against a letter of credit from the Women's World Bank.

Including its program for group partnerships (supporting groups of women in the establishment of small household businesses, ADOPEM created 2,200 new jobs and improved 1,092 jobs in 1988. Of the latter, 492 were in microenterprises and 600 in partnerships.

38. The FDD operates one program for microenterprises and another for group partnerships. Until recently, it also managed a Center for Technical Assistance as part of the FIDE small-business fund of the Banco Central.

FDD loans range between RD $1,000 to RD $10,000, with a maximum term of one year. FDD charges 1 percent monthly interest and 14 percent in commissions and closing costs. In 1988, FDD's microenterprise program created 184 jobs, while the partnership program created 391 new jobs. So far, it charges a lower rate of interest than the others.

39. In addition to the microenterprise program, PROAPE operates a Center for Technical Assistance (*Centro de Asistencia Técnica*, CAT) and a group partnership program. PROAPE's financial policies are very similar to those of the other organizations mentioned.

40. This observation is based on the fact that these organizations (except ADEMI) also operate programs supportive of other types of informal business activity. However, they employ clear differentiation criteria, defining microenterprises as small productive units.

41. The Center for Small Business Assistance (*Centro de Asistencia a la Pequena Empresa*, CAPE) of the Banco Central's FIDE Fund operates through the centers for technical assistance (CATS), which function at the regional level. There are currently six centers, including PROAPE.

This program was begun in 1982 with a grant from USAID (RD $5,000,000) and matching funds from the Banco Central (RD $2,000,000). This program also called for the establishment of a guaranty fund which, so far, has not had much impact on the flow of financing.

This program classifies small businesses based on sales, fixed capital and working capital. This and other aspects of the results obtained to 1986 (Reyes, 1987) strongly indicate that this program's resources have been going essentially to medium businesses in the modern sector.

42. Although the title of the report refers to small businesses, it is actually a study of informal microenterprises since these businesses were all financed by the orga-

nizations mentioned.

Other surveys have attempted to diagnose the problems of productive units in the sector. The most significant are those by the Santo Domingo Institute of Technology (*Instituto Tecnológico de Santo Domingo*, INTEC) in 1982 and 1983, and by Sonia Lizardo in 1987, among others.

43. Asociación para el Desarrollo de la Microempresa (ADEMI), *Informes Anuales*, Santo Domingo, años 1985–1987.

44. Initially, all of the organizations that had programs to promote microenterprise were grouped under ADOMICRO. According to our information, differences over accepting the conditionality imposed by international financial institutions prompted some organizations willing to accept such conditionality to leave ADOMICRO and form Fund for Micro enterprise (FONDOMICRO). The latter is a mechanism through which to channel resources from these institutions.

45. Fifty-two percent of workers are family members, and 97 percent of all microenterprise owners are employed in their own business. Moreover, 86 percent of microenterprise owners depend on earnings from their businesses; 55 percent are heads of households; 38 percent of the remaining owners are wives of heads of households.

46. This figure is a low estimate for several reasons. First, the average loan from ADOMICRO organizations was RD $2,750 in 1988; second, the average loan suggested by those surveyed in the MSI study was RD $8,000.

47. See Lora (1988); Instituto Tecnológico de Santo Domingo (INTEC), *Diagnóstico del Sector Industrial y de las Pequeñas Empresas no Manufactureras*, Versión mimeo (Santo Domingo, 1982); Rolando Reyes, *La Pequeña y Mediana Empresa en República Dominicana: Un Estudio de su Agremiación y Demanda de Servicios*, Informe de Investigación presentado a la Fundación Friedrich Ebert (Santo Domingo, 1987); Reyes, *Prioridades de Adiestramiento a la Pequeña y Mediana Empresa: Algunas Proposiciones Iniciales*, Conferencia Presentada al Consejo Nacional de Hombres de Empresas (Santo Domingo, 1989).

48. The Department for Small Business of Panama (a government organization) has reported as much as US $4,000 per loan, while a semigovernmental organization in Guatemala has reported costs of US $700 per loan. Hans Hann, *El Sector Informal en Centroamericana*, Investigaciones Sobre Empleo/27 (Santiago: PREALC, 1985).

49. Improved jobs are those existing in the microenterprise before financing, which implies they might disappear if financing does not occur.

50. ADEMI currently charges an interest rate of 38 percent, equivalent to 2.5 percent monthly, as well as overhead of 8 percent.

51. See the President's address to the Annual Assembly, 15 August 1989.

52. The microentrepreneurs deposit part of their capital in commercial banks, a loan requirement.

53. An error made frequently is to multiply the number of direct employees by a fixed coefficient to find the number of indirect employees. That method supposes that in each activity, the number of indirect employees per direct employee is equal.

54. The correct coefficient for measuring indirect employment is the employment multiplier calculated from an input-output matrix. This is a difficult model to apply in the Dominican Republic because of the lack of an adequate and up-to-date input-output table. Nevertheless, it does not mean that an effect cannot be estimated for the different activities and incorporated as a criterion in the evaluation. For a detailed description of the methodology for calculating employment multipliers, see PREALC (1979).

55. For a review of PREALC experiences in support of new microenterprises see Mezera (1987a).

56. Mezera 1987a, p. 18.

57. Mezera 1987a.

58. That is, direct and indirect employment. The difficulty of calculating indirect employment can be dealt with through simple studies of the principal activities where there is the greatest concentration of productive units to determine the total linkages of employment. Another is to work with input-output tables and a third option is to utilize the employment multipliers calculated for countries with a productive structure similar to the Dominican Republic.

59. Other alternative criteria exist to take into account employment effect through a function that also included the effect of other variables; for a description see PREALC (1984).

60. Methodology for a social evaluation of a project using transaction prices can be based on the use of a questionnaire similar to the first one mentioned in note 58. Adequate adjustments must be factored in to move from market prices to transaction prices. These adjustments, as well as the parameters of the social cost of capital, can be found in studies done by the World Bank and the InterAmerican Development Bank. The possibility exists that these studies are not up to date, but local experts can update them.

61. For a detailed description of the methodology of this recommendation, see Reyes, *La Tasa de Interes en el Financiamiento a la Microempresa*, lecture presented at the Seminario Permanente Sobre el Sector Informal (Santo Domingo: Instituto de Estudios Dominicanos, 1989).

62. Hann, *El Sector Informal Centroamericana*.

63. One exception is the Program for Training of Small-Business Owners (Programa de Entrenamiento para Pequeños Empresarios, PEPME), which is implemented by the Educational Credit Foundation (Fundación de Crédito Educativo) with funding from USAID. Through this program, educational institutions design programs targeting the sector, and the Foundation covers tuition costs for small-business owners who participate in the program.

64. Many of the training programs have had little impact. One reason is that they have failed to define specific training needs for businessess with limited access to factors of production other than labor. For a detailed analysis of factors that limit training programs, see Reyes, *Prioridades de Adiestramiento.*

65. Law 22a promotes small business and artisans. Its effect, however, has not been significant. See Ceara, *Fomento de las Pequeñas y Medianas.*

66. The latter could be achieved by having the enterprises and state institutions buy directly from the sector or from industries closely tied to it. Other actions that tend to stimulate demand would include those which limit the competitiveness of the modern sector in the market. See Hann, *El Sector Informal en Centroamericana,* pp. 71–72; Carbonetto, *Informe Sobre Investigación del Sector Informal.*

3

Remittance Inflows and Economic Development in Selected Anglophone Caribbean Countries

Wilbert O. Bascom

I. INTRODUCTION

There is a substantial body of literature on international migration focused mainly on analyzing the microeconomics of labor supply and on measuring the benefits and costs of migration to the host countries. Only some of these studies addressed the impact of economic development, particularly through migrant transfers to the labor-exporting countries.

This paper takes the position that remittances and other private transfers by migrants to their origin countries have been an unexploited source of economic development financing in the Anglophone Caribbean countries. The exploitation of this resource base requires the officials of these countries to recognize more fully that they are in competition with the rest of the world for financial resources, whether in the form of loans, direct investment from multinational companies or remittances and other private transfers from nationals living abroad. This recognition must be demonstrated in the relative competitiveness of the Anglophone Caribbean countries' financial markets as reflected, at least, in their monetary and tax policies, incentive programs, currency convertibility conditions and general financial market efficiency.

It is well known that in recent years international financial markets have experienced substantial product and process innovations and structural change. The forces behind such innovations and change have arisen from the confluence of a series of disparate trends during the 1970s and 1980s. Examples of these are rising inflation rates, volatile interest rates, exchange rates and deregulation.[1] One of the effects of these forces has been the increased efficiency in national and international financial markets. It is argued here that there is a need for a full recognition of these developments by the authorities and policy makers in less developed countries. More specifically, there is a need for the implementation of appropriate measures which would contribute to improving the relative competitiveness of the Anglophone Caribbean countries' financial markets.

In general, this paper attempts to review the literature on the impact of remittances on labor exporting countries. It contends that previous discussion of this impact has underplayed the importance of these transfers in the economic development process. Additionally, it examines available remittance data and attempts to estimate the potential foreign exchange earnings that may be derived from an organized program to attract remittances to the labor-exporting countries.

The paper has four sections. The first reviews the literature and focuses on the need for a broader definition of remittances, as well as on an evaluation of the incentive effects of interest and exchange rate policies. It also specifies the observed costs and benefits of remittances to labor-exporting countries. The second highlights the nature of the interest and exchange rate policies of the Anglophone Caribbean countries to demonstrate the scope for improving the monetary policy environment in these countries. The third examines the available data on the magnitude and growth in remittances in a selection of labor-exporting countries. Information on this section provides a basis for estimating the potential for additional remittance flows to the Anglophone Caribbean countries. The final section suggests facilitating programs which may be instituted in the labor-exporting and labor-receiving countries.

II. REVIEW OF THE LITERATURE

The literature[2] has tended to restrict the definition of remittances to the portion of international migrant workers' earnings transferred to the workers' origin countries. This paper, however, seeks a broader and more appropriate definition. "Remittances" are transfers made from earnings and/or accumulated stock of wealth by individuals who are resident in a foreign country on a temporary or permanent basis. Such individuals remit or could be induced to remit resources to their countries of origin for dependent support, investment or any other purpose.

This broader definition attempts to allow for remittances originating from a portion of the migrants' earnings and from individuals who switch from existing asset portfolios held in the labor-receiving country. Permanent residents and their families in the labor-receiving country, who continue to have an economic interest in their country of origin, are in some cases induced to diversify their asset portfolio.

In addition, this broader definition permits the consideration of some proportion of remittance flows as a source of development finance. It also impresses upon the remittance-receiving countries the need for appropriate financial policies and institutions to facilitate the deployment of some of these flows for economic development purposes. Further, it aims at encouraging policy makers in the remittance-receiving countries to see their countries in the context of a globally integrated financial market place where there can be fierce competition for a given pool of financial resources.

Finally, this broader definition recognizes the limitations imposed by the restricted definition of remittances. For example, the flow of new migrants and the related flow of remittances may dry up because of economic conditions in both the labor-sending and labor-receiving countries. Migrants, with their families, may eventually establish permanent residence in the labor-receiving countries, thus removing one of the basic *raison d'etre* for remittance flows for dependent family support.

The literature, however, argues that permanent residents and their families tend to maintain an economic interest in their origin countries. Rubenstein has observed that:

> Even when migrants do not go back to the West Indies, they may still have a significant impact on conditions in the region. For as long as migrants believe that they will eventually return, they will continue to behave in a manner which will affect their home country . . .[3]

This interest, which has normally been reflected by a continuance of remittances, may be exploited by encouraging the investment of such remittances into competitively priced financial assets. A precondition for competitive pricing in financial markets is the existence of appropriate financial policies and structures which ensure that the potential remitter is not placed at a competitive disadvantage, vis-á-vis a counterpart investor or saver in the labor-receiving country. In other words, remitters interested in acquiring financial assets in the origin country must be given the opportunity to effectively hedge their interest and exchange rate risks. Thus, appropriate exchange and interest rate policies, together with hedging opportunities, would have to be considered as inducements for remittances to flow into financial asset purchases.

Russell[4] has argued that there has been little systematic attention to the influence of exchange rates on remittances. Swamy[5] discovered that neither the exchange rate differentials between official and premium rates, nor those between official and free market rates had any significant effect on total remittances, although they might have contributed to a reallocation of savings among different available accounts. Still, Chandavarkar[6] has maintained that remittances were notably sensitive to any indications of currency overvaluation and were prone to slow down in such cases. Further, currency overvaluation led to the use of unofficial funds transfer channels where more realistic market exchange rates were obtained. This has been the experience of some of the Anglophone Caribbean countries with active unofficial domestic foreign exchange markets.[7] Chandavakar has also claimed that the most important macroeconomic requisite for inducing remittances through official channels was a realistic single rate of exchange for the currency of the labor-exporting country.

Incidentally, the fact that the foreign exchange earnings derived from remittances are captured by the unofficial foreign exchange market could have some developmental impact on the labor-exporting countries' economy. This is likely if the unofficial purchasers of foreign exchange made more efficient allocation choices of these resources than would have been made by the official market players.[8]

The investment incentive value of exchange rate policy may have been underemphasized in some studies. The results presented by Swamy's likely reallocation effect and Chandavarkar's currency overvaluation sensitivity effect, as well as the assumed rational behavior of remitters wanting to add financial assets issued by their origin country to their portfolio, supports such conclusions.

Again, Swamy[9] has found that interest rate differentials between labor-exporting and labor-receiving countries had no effect on total remittances. This finding might reflect the fact that remittances were not for financial asset acquisition. After all, in the case of the Caribbean, remitters are well aware that interest rates in these countries did not normally reflect any risk premium associated with current economic conditions or long-run inflationary expectations. Thus, they might not include relative interest rates in their decision to remit resources for dependent support or to acquire real assets. Chandavarkar,[10] in stating that the confidence felt in the safety and liquidity of financial assets in the labor-exporting countries was a determinant of remittance flows, might have implied that interest rates could reflect a remitter's subjective perceptions about the degree of risk associated with the purchasing of such assets in these countries.

The absence of efficient financial markets in the Anglophone Caribbean countries and the existence of overvalued exchange rates and negative real interest rates (demonstrated by simple models later in this paper) would suggest that financial asset purchases could not have been a primary motivating reason for remittances to the Caribbean. Philpott and Rubenstein,[11] among others, have found that remittances of cash and gifts to dependents in certain Anglophone Caribbean countries were considered important obligations by the migrants. They have indicated that remittances were used primarily to purchase food, clothing, shelter, household furnishings, agricultural land, small businesses, transportation vehicles, livestock, and to finance educational and additional overseas travel.

In emphasizing the costs and de-emphasizing the benefits of remittances to the Caribbean countries, the literature has appeared to indicate that the above expenditures financed by remittances did not have developmental impact, although they might have improved the living standards of the recipients. Still, it may be argued that the use of remittances to purchase newly constructed homes, unproductive real estates made productive after acquisition, or consumer durables produced in the labor-exporting countries could be considered developmentally beneficial to these countries.

In a dynamic sense, a comprehensive program for attracting remittance flows into financial asset purchases in labor-exporting countries may spur structural changes in the Caribbean countries' financial markets and reap economic benefits for these countries. Russell[12] has summarized the benefits and costs associated with migrant remittances as follows:

Benefits:

1) Ease foreign exchange constraints and improve balance of payments;
2) Permit import of capital goods and raw materials for development;
3) Potential sources of savings and investment capital formation for development;
4) Cushion effects of oil price increase;
5) Net addition to reserves;
6) Raise the immediate standard of living of recipients;
7) Improve income distribution (if poor/less skilled migrate).

Costs:

1) Are unpredictable;
2) Are spent on consumer goods, which increases demand and inflation, and pushes up wage levels;
3) Result in little or no investment in capital generating activities;
4) High import content of consumption demand increases dependence on imports and escalates balance of payments problems;
5) Replace other sources of income, thereby increasing dependency, eroding good work habits and heightening potential negative effect of return migration;
6) Are spent on "unproductive" or "personal" investments (e.g. real estate, housing);
7) Create envy and resentment and induce consumption spending among non-migrants.

Notable exclusion from these benefits is the likely catalyst remittances could provide for less developed countries' financial market restructuring and efficiency, as well, as for appropriate monetary and exchange rate policies.

III. MONETARY AND EXCHANGE RATE POLICIES

While the Caribbean countries are mainly commodity exporters (e.g. sugar, rice bauxite, petroleum, etc.), many have been labor exporters, particularly to Europe (United Kingdom) and North America (Canada, United States). Available migration data for Jamaica and Trinidad and Tobago show the United States as the principal destination for their labor exports. Still, economic policy makers in the Caribbean countries have yet to make serious attempts to formalize and promote an economic environment conducive for remittances to flow into financial assets that yield relatively competitive returns to investors.

It is recognized that policy makers have some degree of freedom to direct the proportion of manufactured or commodity export proceeds to be remitted by exporters through the domestic banking system or through other official financial channels and to effectively monitor the implementation of such a policy directive. No doubt there are measures available for exporters to conceal their foreign exchange earnings and influence the amount of export proceeds remitted.[13] However, any directive stipulating the proportion of labor export proceeds that should be remitted by migrants would be of little effectiveness. This is because the amount of remittances from a given income level or from the sale of assets in an existing asset portfolio would, in part, be determined by the economic circumstances of the remitters and their personal perspective of acceptable risks and returns on their financial investments. This perspective would be influenced by the labor-exporting countries' monetary and exchange rate policies.

The role of monetary and exchange rate policies must be evaluated in the context of the other determinants of remittance flows to labor-exporting countries. The principal determinants of remittances are the number of migrants and the level of their earnings and any accumulated savings in the labor receiving countries. Therefore, any administrative measures implemented to control or stop the flow of labor exports, or to restrict the labor-receiving countries' demand for such exports would impair the flow of remittances.

It may be useful to mention that immigration restrictions, unconnected with the economic activity levels or the labor export and absorptive capacity in the sending and receiving countries, could hinder international labor market efficiency. In other words, international labor market efficiency is sacrificed in as much as artificial impediments to the full exploitation of labor complementarity are imposed. Failure to exploit such complementarity could adversely impact the labor receiving country's price level and its relative competitiveness.[14] It could also impact the labor-exporting countries' balance of payments and its developmental potential.

Notwithstanding these observations, the greater the restrictions on labor exports, the greater would be the need for appropriate financial policies in the remittance receiving countries. The maintenance or increase of remittance flows, in spite of expanded immigration restrictions, would depend on the ability of the labor-exporting countries to attract increasing amounts of remittances from current earnings and from the accumulated wealth of both temporary and permanent migrants residing in the labor-receiving countries.

The elimination of an overvalued exchange rate and negative real interest rate environment or the establishment of relatively competitive interest rates may not be sufficient to induce remittances to the labor-exporting countries. But the existence of overvalued exchange rates and negative interest rates can contribute to capital flight from these countries and can discourage the flow of remittances to purchase securities issued by official entities. The observed remitters' preference for real assets may be due to the fact, or to their, perception that the rate of appreciation in the value of these assets has been equal or greater than the labor-exporting countries' inflation rate. Contributing to the high inflation rate are these countries' high import propensity and the practice of acquiring foreign exchange for import financing at the unofficial market rate.

To summarize, the relationship between monetary and exchange rate policy and the size and uses of remittances may be complex. Overvalued exchange rates and negative real interest rates could cause remittances to flow through unofficial channels. This would contribute to increasing the inflation rate, particularly in countries with high import propensities. The high inflation rate, given nominal interest rates which tend to remain fixed for long periods in labor-exporting countries, could cause negative real interest, an avoidance of financial asset acquisition and a preference for real assets, such as land, houses and consumer durables. The implementation of appropriate monetary and exchange rate policy or the deepening of the labor exporting countries' financial markets[15] are considered necessary steps for attracting remittances for economic development financing.

It may be instructive to evaluate the nature of the Anglophone Caribbean countries' monetary policy by examining developments in the countries' real interest rate and exchange rate. This evaluation aims at comparing real interest rates in the Caribbean countries with real interest rates in the United States. It also aims at evaluating the extent of overvaluation of the Caribbean countries' exchange rates. Because the price and interest rate statistics are either suspect or of limited usefulness,[16] the result of this evaluation is merely indicative of the scope for improving the relative competitiveness of the labor-exporting countries' monetary environment or for removing some of the important financial market disincentives for remittances.

Real interest rate (i_r) is defined as the nominal interest rate (i_n) less the expected inflation rate (p^*) or:

$$i_r = i_n - p^*$$

Table 1 compares the annual real interest rate changes in the Anglophone Caribbean labor-exporting countries with those in the United States.

The dominance of negative real interest rates is indicated in the above estimates. At best these are underestimates due to the tendency for official price statistics in the Caribbean to misrepresent the severity of these countries' inflation rate.

For the Caribbean countries, the need for increased remittances as a supplement to their foreign exchange earnings is unquestionable. This may be demonstrated, as in Table 2, by the relationship between the coun-

TABLE 1
REAL INTEREST RATES IN SELECTED COUNTRIES
(percentages)

Year	U.S.	Barbados	Guyana	Jamaica	Trinidad & Tobago
1980	−2.7	−8.9	− 1.5	−17.4	−14.4
1981	5.1	−5.1	−12.2	− 2.9	−11.2
1982	7.1	2.9	− 6.3	2.1	− 8.4
1983	7.4	2.2	0.7	0.8	−12.1
1984	7.6	2.2	−11.2	−14.5	− 9.8
1985	7.0	1.5	− 1.0	− 6.7	− 4.1
1986	8.0	3.1	6.2	5.8	− 3.7
1987	3.7	1.5	−14.7	11.5	− 6.1
1988	4.3	−2.5	− 5.4	9.2	− 3.4
Avg.:	5.3	−0.3	− 5.0	− 1.3	− 8.2

Source: International Financial Statistics, IMF.

Note: Treasury bill rate was used in the real interest rate computation. Changes in the current consumer price level and not a computed expected inflation rate have been considered an adequate for the computation.

tries' stock of unconditional foreign exchange earnings[17] and their current account deficits. The dominance of foreign exchange earnings below current account balances has been represented in Table 2.

The removal of exchange rate overvaluation can have a set of positive effects on the foreign exchange/current account relationship provided the participants in the economic sectors respond as postulated in the literature.[18] For instance, exports are expected to expand, imports and capital flight to contract, and remittances through official channels to increase. It may therefore be useful to obtain some indication of the extent of exchange rate overvaluation in the Caribbean countries. The purchasing power parity theory (PPP) would be used for this purpose.

The PPP is used to compare the price level changes in the labor-exporting and labor-receiving countries and to determine the scope for exchange rate adjustment necessary in the former countries. This theory states that changes in a country's price level, when compared with its major trading partner, should be reflected in proportional changes in its exchange rate. The difficulties in applying the PPP theory are well known[19] and may be demonstrated by the following questions that must be answered before any serious application is done. Which price indices and years should be used to estimate purchasing power parity changes? What is an appropriate base year? Is the base year a year when the balance of payments has been in equilibrium? Should consumer or wholesale prices,

TABLE 2
RATIO OF FOREIGN EXCHANGE TO CURRENT ACCOUNT BALANCE

Year	Barbados	Guyana	Jamaica	Trinidad & Tobago
1980	− 2.7	na	−0.6	6.7
1981	− 0.8	−0.03	−0.2	8.5
1982	− 3.4	−0.05	−0.3	−4.5
1983	− 2.9	−0.04	−0.2	−1.9
1984	6.8	−0.06	−0.3	−2.2
1985	3.4	−0.07	−0.5	−9.7
1986	−27.6	na	−2.4	−0.5
1987	na	na	−1.8	−0.4
Avg.:	− 5.9	−0.05	−0.8	−4.3

Source: International Financial Statistics, IMF.
na: Data not available.
Negative sign (−) indicates deficit balance on current account.

or only prices of traded goods, be used to determine international competitiveness? Apart from these theoretical questions there are practical difficulties in applying the PPP theory, resulting from the unavailability of certain price indices, e.g., the wholesale price indices for some countries and the dubious quality of some of the Caribbean countries' published consumer price indices used in this estimation.

The estimation method is comprised of three steps.[20] First, the ratios of the labor-exporting/labor-receiving countries' prices in any year to a base year is determined. Second, a relationship between the labor-exporting and labor-receiving countries' price ratios is defined. This relationship compares the rate of increase in the price level of the labor-exporting country to that of the labor-receiving country. Finally, the condition required to re-establish purchasing power to the selected base year is determined. This condition is the extent to which the exchange rate in the labor-exporting country needed to be adjusted to bring purchasing power back to the selected base year level.

This simple method has been applied to the 1980s price indices, using 1979 as the base year. The intention was merely to obtain some impression of the overvaluation during the 1980s. No attempt has been made to determine whether 1979, or any other year, was an appropriate base year. Of course, it is recognized that the use of a different base year would certainly provide different rates of overvaluation. However, the overvaluation situation would be caused by the tendency in these countries for exchange rate adjustment to lag behind relative price changes. Price level comparisons were made with the United States, a principal destination for Caribbean labor exports during the 1980s.

The estimates for exchange rate overvaluation are shown in Table 3. Except for Guyana and Jamaica, a tendency for persistent overvaluation has been observed. The apparent undervaluation of the Jamaica dollar from 1984 to 1988 and for the Guyana dollar from 1987 to 1988 might indicate that adjustments in the nominal exchange rates were not adequately reflected in the countries' reported consumer price indices. The significance of these estimates for the remitter is the tendency for the foreign exchange value of financial assets denominated in the labor-exporting countries' currencies to decline. The availability of hedging opportunities therefore becomes a necessary condition for attracting remittances into financial assets.

IV. SIZE AND GROWTH OF REMITTANCES

In spite of inadequate data, Swamy found that in 1978 remittances amounting to about $23 billion were transferred to her sample of labor-exporting to labor-receiving countries.[21] She considered this a substantial flow equivalent to about 10 percent of the value of the countries' merchandise exports. For some countries, the ratio of remittances to merchandise exports was significantly higher. For the 1978–79 period, she showed the percentage of remittances to merchandise was 42.5 percent for Yugoslavia, 76.7 percent for Turkey and 51.3 percent for Morocco. Finally, she found that the growth in the nominal value of remittances differed widely between countries. For example, the labor-exporting countries of Southern and Western Africa have registered annual rates of growth in remittances ranging from 15 percent to 25 percent since 1967. Remittances to Mexico grew at an annual rate of 13 percent and to Colombia and El Salvador at an annual rate of about 20 percent since 1967.[22]

Some idea of the size and importance of remittances for a selection of Caribbean countries has been provided in a number of studies. Rubenstein[23] has stated that the sums sent home by migrants were often substantial. Remittances were the principal sources of hard currency in several small islands. Dirks[24] found that in one small community in Tortola, British Virgin Island, external cash inputs accounted for 45 percent of the income of the average household income. In 1951, the export value of cotton, Montserrat's main cash crop, was nearly nine times the value of remittances; by 1960,[25] the value of remittances was almost four times that of cotton. An almost identical situation was reported by Frucht[26] for Nevis, where revenue for cotton, the islands chief exports, was exceeded by remittances by the early 1960s. Hill also reported that in some years in Carriacou, remittances and other repatriated earnings exceeded local cash in-

TABLE 3

ESTIMATES OF CURRENCY OVERVALUATION/UNDERVALUATION

	Barbados			Guyana			Jamaica			Trinidad & Tobago		
	r	r_a	%	r	r_a	%	r	r_a	%	r	r_a	%
1980	.497	.496	0.2	.355	.393	−9.6	.561	.509	10.2	.417	.405	2.9
1981	.497	.471	5.5	.333	.344	−12.8	.561	.492	14.0	.417	.413	0.9
1982	.497	.443	12.3	.333	.296	12.5	.561	.478	17.4	.417	.359	16.1
1983	.497	.426	16.7	.333	.264	26.1	.517	.434	19.1	.417	.315	32.2
1984	.497	.415	19.8	.261	.215	21.4	.254	.347	−26.8	.417	.284	46.7
1985	.497	.402	23.6	.235	.188	25.0	.180	.277	−35.0	.408	.265	54.0
1986	.497	.387	28.4	.234	.170	37.6	.182	.235	−22.5	.278	.241	15.3
1987	.497	.383	29.8	.102	.135	−24.1	.182	.225	−19.0	.278	.222	25.2
1988	.497	.381	30.4	.100	.112	−10.7	.182	.214	−15.0	.235	.212	10.8
Avg.:	.497	.423	17.5	.254	.235	8.1	.353	.358	−1.4	.365	.302	20.9

Source: International Financial Statistics, IMF.

r = nominal exchange rate US$ per national currencies (r is the market rate in the International Financial Statistics series);

r_a = adjusted exchange rate; and

% = % overvaluation or undervaluation (−) from current nominal values.

come from all sources.[27]

Seasonal migrants also remitted money to their home communities. Foner and Napoli[28] estimated that farm workers in the United States remitted between one-third and one-half of their earnings to their families in Jamaica. For one rural community in Barbados, Sutton and Makiesky[29] reported that 25 percent of adults received remittances from relatives overseas. In the two rural districts of Montserrat, studied by Philpott,[30] over 35 percent of households derived 70 to 100 percent of their income from cash from overseas.

In a sample of 100 households in a rural Vincentian community, Rubenstein found 26 households depended on extra-island cash gifts for at least 25 percent of their support while only 36 households received no external support.

Although only four of the 100 households were almost wholly dependent on non-island residents for support, almost two-thirds of the total received some cash from overseas. Moreover, nearly every village household not currently receiving extra-island support had a history of remittance contributions from present or former members.[31]

Table 4 indicates a tendency for remittances to flow into Barbados and Jamaica at different annual rates and for a slowing in the annual average rate of remittance growth in both countries. In addition, the variability in the growth of remittances would be reflected in the variability in the ratio of remittances to merchandise exports. Table 5 shows that the annual percentage changes in remittances to exports ranged from 15.1 percent to 29 percent for Barbados and from 12.5 percent to 33.7 percent for Jamaica.

Based on the fact that most Caribbean migrants in the labor-receiving countries have a predisposition to maintain their home ties and to eventually return to their native countries, a remittance program may be instituted to facilitate some diversification of their wealth portfolios through the acquisition of financial assets available in these countries. A program which attracts additional remittances solely for financial asset purchases equivalent to about 10 percent of the Anglophone Caribbean countries' merchandise exports could make a substantial contribution to the amount of these countries' available unconditional foreign exchange reserves, as indicated in Table 6.

Available net migration data do not permit an estimation of the per capita remittances that would be required to achieve each country's remittance for investment target. In the case of Jamaica, for which some net migration data are available for the 1980s, it is estimated that the annual per capita remittances required to achieve the 10 percent target would be $1,192.21.[32] This amounts to per capita weekly remittances of about $23.00. If both new and established migrants participate in this program, the per capita remittances would no doubt be lower.

TABLE 4
REMITTANCES TO BARBOS AND JAMAICA
(US$ MILLION)

Year	Barbados	% Change	Jamaica	% Change
1977	27.7	—	50.5	—
1978	29.9	7.9	51.3	1.6
1979	35.3	18.1	94.6	84.4
1980	47.3	34.0	120.7	27.6
1981	56.8	20.0	162.7	34.8
1982	41.9	−26.2	170.7	4.9
1983	41.0	− 2.1	128.5	−24.7
1984	39.2	− 4.4	109.2	−15.0
1985	36.3	− 7.4	191.4	75.2
1986	41.7	14.9	—	—
1987	43.1	3.3	—	—
Avg.:				
1977–85	39.5	5.0	120.0	27.6
1980–85	43.8	2.3	147.2	17.1

Source: Central Bank of Barbados and Bank of Jamaica.

Note: Remittances include private transfers other than from governments and institutions, comprising mainly gifts in cash or kind.

V. FACILITATING PROGRAMS

A well structured remittance for financial asset purchases program would require the setting of realistic remittance targets; the conduct of appropriate monetary and exchange rate policies as well as tax policies; the establishment of facilitating financial structures in the labor-exporting and labor-receiving countries; and the launching of promotional programs to build remitters' confidence in the national economy and the securities issuing institutions. Apart from these necessary preconditions for success, policy makers must be convinced that remittances could make an important contribution to their countries' economic development financing.

An overview of positions on migration, capital movements and trade may provide some general conceptual basis for the promotion of a remittance program. Advocates of barriers to labor exports from less developed countries have argued that trade and capital flows should be substituted

TABLE 5

RATIO OF REMITTANCES TO MERCHANDISE EXPORTS

Year	Barbados	Jamaica
1980	0.208	0.125
1981	0.290	0.167
1982	0.162	0.222
1983	0.127	0.187
1984	0.100	0.155
1985	0.104	0.336
1986	0.151	na
Avg.: 1980–85	0.151	0.189

Source: Table 4; ECLA; IBRD.

na: Data not available.

TABLE 6

NOMINAL VALUE OF TARGETED REMITTANCES

	Barbados	Guyana	Jamaica	Trinidad & Tobago
Exports[1] ($ million)	291.5	268.4	783.9	2,866.6
10% of Exports[2] ($ million)	29.1	26.8	78.4	286.7

Sources: ECLA; IBRD.

[1]Average annual merchandise exports for 1980–85.

[2]Targetted remittance inflows.

for labor movements. However, to the extent that capital flows and trade have occurred, there has been little evidence that labor-receiving countries have actually encouraged trade with labor exporters or that private direct investment preferred labor-exporting countries. Daniels and Radebaugh[33] found that the share of world exports among developed countries increased from 45.9 percent in 1948 to 64.6 percent in 1972. Except for the less developed countries (LDCs) with rapid industrialization and oil exporters, the LDCs' share in world exports for the 1948–72 period has declined.

The United Nations Center on Transnational Corporations[34] shows that the major recipients of direct investment were industrial countries. Of the top 15 recipients only four (South Africa, Brazil, Mexico and Hong Kong) were generally classified as LDCs. About 54 percent of foreign owned affiliates were in Europe and only 31 percent in LDCs. This pattern, as indicated by Daniels and Radebaugh,[35] corresponded to the outward movement of direct investments owned by U.S. enterprises. At the end of 1984, U.S. ownership abroad was $233.4 billion, of which a quarter was located in LDCs. Europe has been experiencing a growing share of U.S. direct investment, while such investment in Canada and Latin America has been declining.

Any attempt by the Caribbean policy makers to increase, if not to divert, remittances into direct or portfolio investment, given the observed patterns of trade and capital flows, should be considered a bold initiative in financial cooperation between these countries' policy makers and the temporary and permanent migrants with return expectations.

With the existence of an appropriate monetary and exchange rate policy environment, programs originating from the labor-exporting countries may include special tax exemption of income received from portfolio and direct investment activities. In addition, programs may also develop to establish remittance facilities and/or arrangements in the home countries as well as in the labor-receiving countries. These would insure that private sector securities issuing entities are operating in a safe and sound manner particularly, with respect to their foreign exchange hedging strategies, and promote an environment of confidence for the remitters.

The labor-exporting country may exempt income derived from securities purchased by remittances from all national government and other local taxes. These may be securities issued by both private and public sector entities. In addition, to ensure that direct investment is not at a competitive disadvantage vis-á-vis portfolio investment, tax exemption should be provided for profits reinvested in direct investment activities and for repatriated dividends from direct investment financed by remittances.

Indigenous banks established in the Anglophone Caribbean countries should establish offices for receiving remittances in the labor-receiving countries. Depending on both the actual and the potential number of remitters, these facilities may include the following: a simple special account arrangement with correspondent banks;[36] a correspondent bank/representative office combination; a branch/agency presence to the more expensive and complicated subsidiary branch arrangement.[37] Programs for facilitating remittances need not be restricted to indigenous banks which in the Caribbean countries are mainly public sector influenced. Such programs may be instituted by private sector firms establishing small money transmitting offices in migrant population centers. But there are particular risks that remitters would face in using the services of these offices. These risks will be alluded to later in this section.

The fact that exchange rate in the Caribbean countries tends to be overvalued and adjustment measures inevitably involve currency devaluation would make remitters hesitate to hold any portion of their financial asset portfolios in the national currency denominated securities of these countries. A program which guarantees a certain exchange rate on the sale of the securities would be workable only if certain management devices are in place. Essentially these would ensure that the security issuing private or public sector entities have neither a net asset nor a net liability position in the remitted currencies.

There are several financial market innovations which offer hedging devices to investors in the developed countries.[38] However, in the case of the less sophisticated financial markets in the Caribbean countries, any foreign exchange rate guarantees may be effective mainly under at least three short-term financing situations. The first would be if a private or public sector firm issues exchange rate guaranteed short-term notes backed by export receivables. The proceeds of these notes would be used to finance working capital directly related to exports. The repayment of the notes would be obtained from the export sales. The second is if a private or public sector entity issues short-term notes to remitters as an interim bridge between the negotiation and the disbursement of external source funding. The third is if banks are allowed to carry special liability and equally matching asset accounts in foreign currencies, free from reserve requirements, and are precluded from lending to any national currency related institution. The liability accounts would be derived from the foreign currency remittances. The benefits of this arrangement would be that the remitters would have no currency risk and the banks would derive for its own use the spread between the interest paid on its liabilities and interest received on its assets.[39]

Providing exchange rate guarantees for long-term securities and for investment in equities is a more complicated issue because of the certainty that the exchange rate would be adjusted on several occasions during the term or for the holding of the assets. The proceeds from the sale of long-term bonds or stocks may be used for the purchase of capital goods or for the reprivatization of certain export oriented industries. The offer of any exchange rate guarantee of such issues would be a bold step by the issuing entities. The only alternative is to ensure that the securities pricing adequately reflects the exchange risk and leaves it to the remitters to purchase whatever quantities reconcile with their own risk-return tolerance. Consider, for example, if a bond issue were offered and the proceeds were to be applied for real estate development that gives the remitter first purchase claim on the units developed at a given price. In such a case, some exchange risk shelter would be provided to the remitter.

It may be easy to offer exchange rate guarantees to remitters. However, it is more difficult to institute a program in a less than sophisticated financial market that would give the remitters confidence that in the long-term the guarantee would be honored. The main short-term hedging strategy is to ensure that remittances are used to finance export activities and that there is a matching of remitted funds with export receivables. This would imply that the limits to remittances for the purchase of short-term paper would be the volume and 'value of the countries' agricultural, manufacturing and other exports. Caribbean Basin Initiative II, which seeks to expand the Caribbean countries' export opportunities to the U.S. market, is therefore integrally linked to the issue of migration, remittances and growth in these countries.[40]

Apart from the uncertainty associated with the time and degree of exchange rate devaluation, remitters' confidence could be influenced by a number of political and social factors. To build their confidence, remitters would want to be assured that public and private security issuing entities are efficiently managed, which would be reflected by their relative profitability and declared returns on assets. Or, as in the case of a government, remitters would want to know that the government has a good track record of honoring its debt obligations on time and that the government's assurances on general economic and taxation issues would be honored. Moreover, remitters would want confirmation that guarantees offered would be legally codified and could not be broken by any single party, and lastly, that dispute settlement would be done in impartially constituted tribunals of law. These are not difficult conditions to be obtained in most of the Anglophone Caribbean countries with a long history of the rule of law in commercial and other transactions.

An effective money transmitting program originating in the labor-receiving countries relates to the supervision of money transmitters. The need for such supervision would be demonstrated by a review of the money transmitting business in Florida, a state which has hosted a substantial proportion of the Caribbean countries' migrants to the United States. But before this is done, a New York case of a money-transmission "rip-off" would help to demonstrate the risk experienced by some migrants.

In 1989, it was reported[41] that an operator of an unlicensed Queens money transmittal service pleaded guilty in a scheme to defraud 300 people who contracted with him to remit a total sum of $400,000 to relatives or associates in several Central and South American countries, principally Colombia. The prosecution was under a state law prohibiting the unlicensed transmittal of money, and was part of a broader investigation conducted by the state's task force on unlicensed money transmitters in New York.

Like other metropolitan areas with large immigrant populations, South Florida has seen the recent development of a small industry serving residents by transmitting money abroad. Literally hundreds of such businesses have been established in Florida, New York, Texas and California.

Customers of these firms often send money weekly or monthly and usually rely on firms that specialize in delivery of funds in one country. These firms, which often advertise in foreign language publications and ethnic radio stations, wire their customers' funds to bank accounts in the foreign country where the funds are disbursed in local currency and delivered to the designated recipients. Sometimes smaller firms contract with larger operations to perform the actual transfer. Sometimes larger firms employ couriers.

It is not uncommon for couriers to deposit the money into their own bank account or place them in the money market for a period of time, however. The couriers therefore benefit from the interest income derived from the float, over which they have complete control, and from their investment activities which are not subject to regulations or prudential supervision in the state. Table 7 provides an overview of the regulation of money transmitters in a selection of states in the United States. The wide differences in regulatory provisions and supervisory practices between these states can be observed.

The money transmission business has clearly arisen in many states to meet a need not fulfilled by the domestic banking industry. Branch banking is scarce in low-income communities, where most of the money transmitters' customers reside. Language difficulties, long delays in international transfers, high fees and poor services are all encountered by migrants seeking this service from state and federal chartered financial institutions. Moreover, many low income migrants do not have two bank accounts—one in the United States and one in their origin country—which are necessary to arrange a transfer. Nor does there appear to be much interest among the larger firms in providing this service to the migrant communities. American Express has been targeting a new MoneyGram service to international tourists and business customers.[42] Deak International Limited, a large money transmitting firm with 75 offices in the United States did most of its business in commercial transfers and Western Union has reported that out of its $2.5 billion in transfers in 1987, only one percent represented international transfers.[43]

Fees charged by the small unregulated money transmitters ranged from 0.5 percent to 5 percent of the funds transmitted. These fees compared favorably with fees charged by regulated transmitters. Western Union, for example, charged a sliding scale, starting at $11, for a transfer of $50 or less, plus a surcharge that varied, depending on the recipient country. Citibank charged $5 for international money order and $22 for an international cable transfer, plus other fees.

Two approaches for improving the remittance system may be considered. The first would be to improve the states' regulation of international money transmitters. Although the potential for abuse has been obvious, the Florida Department of Banking has obtained no evidence of widespread fraud among money transmitting firms. The 1988 failure of Remesas Seguras, a large money transmitting firm, with 19 locations in New York, New Jersey and Florida and which did business with many smaller remitting firms, has cost its clients over $500,000 in lost remittances. In September, 1988, police in Hialeah, Florida, exposed a fraudulent money transmitter claiming to be able to guarantee delivery of funds to relatives in Cuba, a service precluded by federal law. This individual absconded with $40,000.[44]

It has been recognized that full scale regulation of the money transmitting business, with licensing, examination and enforcement powers would be very costly to the migrants remitting funds to their home countries. Bonding and other barriers to competition could hinder what may be honest and legitimate small businesses. In proportion to the large number of firms advertising this service, reported or otherwise known abuses have been few. It is suspected that additional abuses of clients and illegal use of money placed by remitters with these firms may be unreported and thereby undetected. As money transmitters can and have been used as vehicles for capital flight[45] from labor-exporting countries, the importance of official money transmitters from these countries located in the labor-receiving countries cannot be overemphasized.

The second approach is to increase the availability of the international postal money order service to immigrant communities. The U.S. postal service has been establishing new procedures for the issuance of international money orders.[46] These orders can be used for remitting funds to individuals or firms in countries that have entered into agreements with the U.S. postal service for the exchange of money orders. The problem with this facility may not be in the issuance procedures in the United States, but with the postal delivery system in the receiving countries. Migrant dependents in many of the labor-exporting countries have complained of not receiving money orders or other cash remitting instruments mailed to these countries' postal services.

For final consideration and further research by the labor-receiving countries are programs which attempt to exploit the "return expectation" attitude of the Caribbean migrant, as well as the unique climate, language and other cultural elements of these countries, favorable for retirement. Programs which recognize the need of some migrants to retire in their origin countries and which cater for this need would represent the enlightened self-interest of the labor-receiving countries. This self-interest may take the form of implementing measures which would reduce the pressure on the labor-receiving countries' social infrastructure for the aged and release resources for other social purposes, such as education and drug treatment. At the same time, these measures could contribute to the development of the Caribbean countries' social infrastructure. An

TABLE 7

COMPARATIVE REGULATORY ENVIRONMENT FOR MONEY TRANSMITTERS

	Illinois Dept. of Finance	New York Financial Services Div.	Pennsylvania Dept. of Banking	Texas Dept. of Banking	Massachusetts Dept. of Banking—30 Money Remitters	California Dept. of Banking—Money Remitters
License Req.	—over 21 —good moral char.	—sound financial cond. —good moral char. —bus. experience —annual renewal	—min. net worth $500M —5 yrs. bus. experience —good moral char. —no convictions or violations of act	—financially responsible —good moral char. —adequate bus. experience —min. net worth $500M —agents not licensed —audited financial statement	—financial statement —no min. capital req.	—application in writing and under oath —must be a corporation —sound financial cond. —control persons not lacking integrity —applicant competent —reasonable promise of financial success —applicant comply
Fees	$100 initial $25 renew $500	$1000 investig. $500 1st yr. license fee annual renewal	$1000 investigation 1st yr. license fee $300 annual	$500 investigation $500 annual renewal	$50	$1,000 non-refundable filing fee $100 per branch $5 each agency $500 annual fee $4 annual agent
Bond Req.	$250M	$500M discretion of SOB	$1MM bond or security may require additional $1MM	$100M + add'l $50M each location max. $500M securities OK in lieu of bond	$15M Cash/CD	Cash or Securities or Bond sufficient to cover transmitted funds
Exam Req.	No	As deemed nec. at discretion of SOB	Annually	Annually may accept CPA audit by Big 8 firm of another state banking dept.	Annually No standard format	At discretion of SOB

Cost	NA	NA	Borne by licensee or unlicensed entity doing business under this act	Assessed to license	NA	$200 per day
Denial Revocation	—felony conviction —fraud dishonesty —failure to keep proper records	—any grounds for denial original license —violation of law or regs —failure to pay judgement	—bond or security becomes inadequate —violations of act —failure to comply with rules/regs —refusal of examination —any grounds for denial of original application	—any grounds for denial of original license —violation of the act —net worth drops below min.	NA	—C&D for cause unsafe and unsound practices —any grounds for denial of original application —violation of law —refuse to submit books to SOB for inspection —refusal of examination —suspended payment on obligations
Exemp-tions	None	Banks, S&L's Trust Co. Telegraph Co.* with net assets of $750M	Banks, S&L's private banks inc. Telegraph Co., agents of licensee	Banks, S&L's credit unions agents, US or US agency Telegraph Co.'s	NA	Banks, Trust Co's, foreign Bank, Telegraph
Finance of Admin. Cost	General Fund	Assume Gen. Fund	Assume Gen. Fund	Assume Gen. Fund	Assume Gen. Fund	Banking Fund
Other	—	Control change requires SOB approval new investig. fee and insurance fund	—	—	Minimum Staff	—

Source: Conference of State Bankers, 1989.

Note: Michigan—no money remitters. Florida—no jurisdiction over transmitters.

example of these measures is the construction and servicing of health care facilities to be used by migrants returning to their origin countries and even by nationals from the labor-receiving countries seeking competitively equal but less expensive health care services abroad.

VI. CONCLUSION

The Anglophone Caribbean countries have been labor exporters to Canada, the United Kingdom and the United States. They export both skilled and unskilled labor services to these countries. Their labor exports create a tremendous potential source of foreign exchange earnings through remittances, which could be exploited by the government in these countries. Still, it would appear that the countries' governments have not seriously attempted to explore and exploit in an organized manner the economic development potential of this source of foreign exchange earnings.

This paper has recognized that the Caribbean countries are in competition with the rest of the international economy for savings, trade and direct investment flows. They could effectively participate in this competition only if their monetary and fiscal policies are adapted to the rules of the game of international financial competition. This adaptation process might be traumatic under the existing circumstances of some of these countries. The paper has therefore identified a minimum set of steps which might be taken by the labor-exporting and labor-receiving countries to facilitate remittances to the former countries.

Emphasis has been placed on minimizing exchange rate risk to the remitters and the difficulty of implementing foreign exchange rate hedging strategies for long-term securities has been recognized. In addition the importance of the transmission mechanism for migrant transfers to the labor-exporting countries has been recognized. Both the labor-exporting and labor receiving countries have some scope for improving this mechanism.

NOTES

1. B.I.S., *Recent Innovations in International Banking* (April 1986), pp. 1–6.

2. See, for example, Gurushi Swamy, "International Migrant Workers' Remittances: Issues and Prospects," *World Bank Working Papers,* No. 481 (Washington, D.C.: World Bank, 1981); Hymie Rubenstein, "The Impact of Remittances in the Rural English Speaking Caribbean," in *Return Migration and Remittances: Developing a Caribbean Perspective,* RILES Occasional Paper, No. 3, eds. William F. Stinner, Klaus de Albuquerque and Roy S. Bryce-Laporte (Washington. D.C.: Research Institute and Ethnic Studies, 1982); and Sharon Stanton Russell, "Remittances from International Migration," *World Development,* vol. 14, no. 6 (1986).

3. Rubenstein, "Impact of Remittances," 1982, p. 239.

4. Russell, "Remittances from International Migration," 1986, p. 678.

5. Swamy, "International Migrant Worker," 1981, p. 36.

6. A. G. Chandavakar, "Use of Migrants' Remittances in Labor Exporting Countries," *Finance and Development,* July 1980, p. 36.

7. A summary of incentive schemes in some of the labor-exporting countries is given in Chandavaker, "Use of Migrants' Remittances," 1980, as well as in Swamy, "International Migrant Worker," 1981.

8. Guyana provides an outstanding example of an active unofficial foreign exchange market in the Anglophone Caribbean countries. In this country, the official authorities appeared to be in a persistent game of "catch-up" with the devaluation of the Guyana dollar on the unofficial foreign exchange market. The official exchange rate for the Guyana dollar has recently been set at G$30 = US$1. The unofficial market has responded with a rate of G$60 = US$1. It is possible that the non-speculative sector of the unofficial market by reflecting the scarcity value of foreign exchange resources may allocate such resources more efficiently than the official foreign exchange market. It is therefore important to note that different allocative choices between these two markets may not necessary imply less efficient resource utilization by the unofficial market. However, assuming that the government's economic development program has been based on certain priorities and preferences expressed by the people, resource allocation distortions could result if substantial amounts of foreign exchange earnings were in the hands of private speculators in the unofficial market and unavailable for national economic development purposes.

9. Swamy, "International Migrant Worker," 1981, pp. 32–36.

10. Chandavakar, "Use of Migrants' Remittances," 1980, p. 37.

11. Stuart Philpott, "Remittance Obligation, Social Networks and Choice Among Montserratian Migrants in Britain," *MAN,* vol. 3, no. 1 (1968), p. 474; and Rubenstein "Impact of Remittances," 1982, pp. 238–241.

12. Russell, "Remittances from International Migration," 1986, p. 678.

13. By underinvoicing the value of their exports, exporters would remit a smaller amount of their actual export earnings.

14. Some migrants to the United States originating from the Caribbean countries find employment in low wage activities in the agricultural and manufacturing sectors. This has a tendency of holding down domestic price levels lower than it otherwise would have been. Immigration restrictions have caused production problems in some economic activities dependent on cheap imported labor.

15. See Ronald I. McKinnon, *Money and Capital in Economic Development* (Washington, D.C.: Brookings Institute, 1973) and Edward S. Shaw, *Financial Deepening in Economic Development* (London, New York: Oxford University Press, 1973) on the topic of financial repression and financial deepening in economic development.

16. Price statistics are considered suspect when they appear to seriously misrepresent the trend in inflation.

17. These are earnings resulting from normal trading of goods and services, transfers and capital movements not obtained from borrowing from international institutions and world financial markets to replenish depleted foreign exchange reserves.

18. Devaluation is expected to induce an expansion of exports and cause an expansion of domestic activities producing goods and services which substitute for the more expensive imports. These are mainly medium and long-term devaluation related effects influenced by the ability of the economies' real sectors to respond as expected to price stimuli. These effects also depend on the willingness of the labor force to increase production at lower real wages.

19. See, for example, Iani H. Giddy, "An Integrated Theory of Exchange Rate Equilibrium," *Journal of Finance and Quantitative Analysis*, December 1976; R. Z. Aliber, "The Interest Rate Parity Theorem: A Reinterpretation," *Journal of Political Economy*, December 1973; and Alan C. Shapiro, *Multinational Business Finance* (Boston: Allyn and Bacon, Inc., 1982).

20. First, the ratios of the labor-exporting/labor-receiving countries' prices in any year t to a base year was determined as follows:

P_{dt}/P_{db} = the ratio of the labor-exporting country's price level in year t(P_{dt}) to the base year price level (P_{db})

P_{ft}/fb = the ratio of the labor receiving country's price level in year (P_{ft}) to the base year price level $P(_{fb})$

Let:

$P_{dt}/P_{db} = P_d$

and

$P_{ft}/fb = P_f$

Second, the relationship between the labor-exporting/labor-receiving countries' price ratios is.

Finally, the condition to reestablish PPP is as follows:

r = the labor-receiving country's currency per unit of the labor-exporting country's currency.

21. This sample comprised the developing countries of Europe, the Middle East, Asia, Southern and Western Africa and Central and South America.

22. Swamy, "International Migrant Workers," 1981, pp. 7–12.

23. This section on remittances to the smaller Caribbean countries has relied on Rubenstein, "Impact of Remittances," 1982, pp. 239–241.

24. Robert Dirks, "Networks, Groups and Adaptation in an Afro-Caribbean Community," *MAN*, vol. 7, no. 4 (1972), p. 572.

25. Philpott, "Remittance Obligation," 1968, p. 466.

26. Richard Frucht, "Emigration, Remittances and Social Change: Aspects of the Social Field of Nevis, West Indies," *Anthropolica*, vol. 10, no. 2 (1968), p. 208.

27. Donald R. Hill, "The Impact of Migration on Metropolitan and Folk Society of Carriacou, Grenada, 54, Part 2," *Anthropological Papers* (New York: American Museum of Natural History, 1977), pp. 221–223.

28. Nancy Foner and R. Napoli, "Jamaican and Black American Migrant Farm Workers: A Comparative Analysis" *Social Problems*, vol. 25 (1978), p. 483.

29. Constance Sutton and Susan R. Makiesky, "Migration and West Indian Racial and Ethnic Consciousness," in *Migration and Development: Implications for Ethnic Identity and Political Conflict*, eds. Helen Safa and Brian du Toit (The Hague: Mutton, 1975), p. 121.

30. Stuart Philpott, *West Indian Migration: The Montserrat Case*, London School of Economics Monographs on Social Anthropology, (London: Athlone Press, 1973), p. 143.

31. Rubenstein, "Impact of Remittances," 1982, p. 241.

32. The annual per capita remittance estimate has been obtained by dividing the targeted remittance inflow of US $78.4 million by an estimated net migration out of Jamaica of 65,760 for the 1980–85 period.

33. John D. Daniels and Lee H. Radebaugh, *International Business: Environments and Operations* (Reading: Addison-Wesley Publishing Company, 1986), pp. 20–32.

34. United Nations Center on International Corporations (1983), pp. 318–326.

35. Daniels and Radebaugh, "International Business," 1986, pp 20–32.

36. During the time, I held the position of Chief Executive of the indigenous bank in Guyana (1970–1978). I was effective in establishing special account relationships with correspondent banks in the United States and United Kingdom. These relationships allowed for a third party entity to accept remittances and to deposit them into the bank's accounts with its correspondents in these countries. The third party, in turn, provided a detailed listing of the remitters and the amount of

their respective remittances. Within the first two years of this program remittances amounting to over US$2.5 million were received. The foreign exchange derived was held by the bank and used for financing working capital imports into Guyana. The G$ counterpart was credited to the individual remitter's account with the bank and were used mainly as deposits for partial financing of the purchase of homes being constructed in a newly developed subdivision in the greater Georgetown area. In addition, a special Trust Company subsidiary of the bank was established to provide first mortgages to the remitters, receive monthly mortgage payments by way of remittances and service the various needs of the remitters. No doubt, the program had important developmental impact on the economy.

37. I have been informed by the Miami manager of Banco de Bogota that the bank has established New York branch offices used by a substantially large number of permanent and temporary Colombian migrant residents in that city to send remittances to Colombia. This arrangement involved a tie-in with the central bank in Bogota that enjoys the foreign exchange benefits associated with this program. The remittance commission received by the New York operation has been competitive and adequate enough to ensure the profitability of the arrangement.

38. See, for example, B.I.S., "Recent Innovations," 1986, pp. 17–18, 157–168.

39. This arrangement reflects in part the U.S. international banking facilities and international banks' Eurodollar operations. The only difference that can be seen is the arrangement would not permit any lending in national currencies to related financial institutions. This restriction minimizes exchange risk.

40. When the Caribbean Basin Initiative (CBI) legislation came into effect in 1984, the intention was to help create a favorable climate for economic development in the participating countries by facilitating development projects and allowing liberal market entry conditions in the United States. However, the participating countries have been complaining that the CBI arrangement needs liberalizing. The Bush Administration appears particularly keen on such a move in the area of textiles, but spirited opposition from certain interests in the United States has bottled up legislation so that Congress recessed for the year without resolving the matter. An effort will be made to pass CBI II in 1990.

41. See Jill M. Considine, "Florida Man Pleads Guilty in Money Transmission Rip-Off in First Prosecution Under State Banking Law," *New Release* (New York, State Banking Department, 17 May 1989).

42. See *American Banker,* "American Express Expands Moneygram Wire Service," March 1989.

43. See Michael R. Underwood, *Presentation on Money Transmission to the International Banking and Trade Study Commission: A Memorandum* (Tallahassee: Florida Department of Banking and Finance, 10 March 1989).

44. See Underwood, "Presentation on Money Transmission," 1989.

45. The counterpart foreign exchange earnings may never return to the labor exporting countries but may be purchased by nationals of those countries wanting to dispose of their large holdings of national currency balances. These nationals would undertake to deliver the local currency to the recipient in the labor exporting countries at an exchange rate considerably more favorable than that offered in the official foreign exchange market of the countries.

46. *Postal Bulletin*, "International Money Orders," no. 21673 (19 May 1988), pp. 3–5.

4

Tropical Capitalists: U.S.-Bound Immigration and Small-Enterprise Development in the Dominican Republic

Alejandro Portes and Luis E. Guarnizo

I. INTRODUCTION

The purpose of this study is to examine the linkages between Dominican labor migration to the United States and the development of small firms in the Dominican Republic. The motivation for this study is twofold: first, to ascertain the possible effects of labor migration on the economic development of the sending country and, especially, of its small-firm sector; second, to investigate the consequences of successful small enterprise development on both the Dominican migrant outflow to the United States and on return migration.

Although variations abound, three basic positions about the relationship between migration, in particular labor migration, and development of the sending countries can be identified. The most favorable approach comes from neoclassical economic theory that posits that migration flows are a logical consequence of different levels of demand for labor and resulting income advantages of advanced countries over peripheral ones. The neoclassical approach also tends to be uniformly positive regarding the effect of migrant communities on the sending country: remittances can serve as investment capital, support the balance of payments and stimulate demand for goods and services produced in the country of origin. Upon their return, migrants themselves embody new technological knowledge (human capital) which can help inject new dynamism in the domestic economy.[1]

This rosy vision of migration is countered by a series of in-depth field studies conducted in several countries. They make clear, first of all, that becoming a labor migrant is not exclusively a matter of individual decision in a free market because it is subject to a number of political constraints. According to Zolberg, it is precisely these political constraints to migration in the developed world that explain the vast differences in the remuneration to labor between sending and receiving countries.[2] Second, major migratory flows are not coming from the poorest and least developed countries—as would be expected from a theory which emphasizes the "reestablishment of equilibrium"—but from countries at an intermediate level of development. Within these countries, migrants do not generally come from the poorest groups—as again could be anticipated from an emphasis on purely economic gaps—but from middling strata possessing a measure of education, resources and labor experience.[3]

Such negative findings have reinforced a completely opposite vision to that offered by neoclassical theory. This alternative approach, grounded in orthodox Marxism, defines labor migration as another form of exploitation of the resources of poor countries by advanced capitalism, its results being uniformly negative for the sending communities.[4] According to this interpretation, migration simultaneously entails loss of human resources and over-exploitation of immigrant labor, which is placed in a position of great vulnerability *vis-a-vis* employers in the host country. The only beneficiaries of this process are firms in receiving areas which can cut their costs and discipline their domestic work force through the hiring of cheap immigrant labor.[5] Accordingly, immigrant laborers are poorly paid and their remittances barely satisfy their families' subsistence needs; in the exceptional cases where remittances exceed subsistence costs, they tend to generate conspicuous consumption and increase social inequality.

The third position stems from modern economic sociology. This position accepts the findings that throw into question the predictions of neoclassical theory, but resists as an alternative the uniformly negative predictions posited by the critical or orthodox Marxist approach. Instead, economic sociology places its emphasis on the *variability* of outcomes of the migration process and on the existence of socially patterned modes of incorporation into the host society, each having different consequences for immigrant economic behavior. This position begins by noting that both neoclassical and Marxist analyses of labor migration are "undersocialized," that is, that they stem from an excessively individualistic view of economic behavior.[6] Actors are expected to govern their conduct exclusively by prospects for market gain, regardless of its effects and the evaluations of the surrounding social context.

To the contrary, economic sociology assumes that individual profit-seeking is enmeshed in a dense grid of social expectations and reciprocal obligations which constrain its scope. It is not the case that individuals behave altruistically or are guided by value considerations, although such behavior is far more common than given credit by the two previous approaches. Instead, people are restricted from engaging in too blatant a form of profit-seeking when such actions elicit disapproval, pressure and sanctions among those on whom they depend.[7]

This *embeddedness* of individual gain-seeking in webs of social interaction has a liberating as well as a constraining side because social relations can be the source of information and material resources necessary to succeed in market ventures. Just as unconstrained greed is negatively sanctioned, conformity to the expectations of family, group or community endows individuals with resources beyond their own grasp. This *social capital*, generated through stable patterns of interaction, can be added to material capital (money and properties) and human capital (individual skills, experience and aspirations) as resources which individuals can activate in the course of market competition.[8] Economic actors are bound to find very quickly that their "transaction costs" are reduced by the possession of sufficient social capital, while they are significantly increased by its absence.[9]

In the case of migration, the economic sociology approach leads us to pay close attention to the character of the communities of origin as determinants of the type and timing of migration; as well as to the social contexts in which immigrants are incorporated in the host society. Depending on such contexts, immigrants of similar human capital endowments may be channelled toward very different labor market niches, with significant consequences for their mobility prospects.[10] The relation of migration flows to domestic development is, from this perspective, indeterminate because it depends on the contexts greeting migrants in the host country, on their obligations to kin and friends at home and on the binational networks created in the process. Depending on them, labor migration may have the character of a "safety valve" alleviating domestic unemployment and poverty; of a "subsistence strategy" for migrant families which grow reliant on cash remittances; or of a genuine entrepreneurial "engine," stimulated by transfers of capital and know-how from migrants abroad.

II. DOMINICAN IMMIGRATION

Table 1 presents the evolution of recorded Dominican immigration during the last three decades and compares it with those from other Caribbean countries. During the 1980s, the Dominican Republic became the sixth largest source of legal immigrants to the United States, displacing Cuba as the principal source from the Caribbean. Figures in Table 1 do not represent the whole story, however, because they omit a substantial surreptitious inflow. Dominican illegal migration is not so much undocumented as "misdocumented": because the country lacks a land border with the United States, most would-be migrants require some sort of papers to enter. This can take the form of false documentation or of a valid U.S. temporary visa which is then overstayed.[11] Past studies suggest that this is a major channel for unauthorized Dominican migration. The annual flow of nonmigrant Dominicans admitted for temporary residence in the United States has grown between 1975 and 1988, from 78,000 to 135,000 (see Table 2). At present, the Dominican Republic is the third largest source of tourists and other "temporary" arrivals from the region.

How many of these nonimmigrants overstay their visas is in dispute. According to a demographic analysis of Warren,[12] a figure between 350,000 and 400,000 appears to be the most plausible estimate of the total Dominican population residing in the United States. This estimate means that from 5 to 10 percent of the total Dominican population now lives in this country.[13] The impact of this inflow is made more visible by its concentration in a few receiving areas. Unlike other Caribbean immigrants which tend to cluster in South Florida, Dominicans have made New York

TABLE 1
CARIBBEAN LEGAL MIGRATION TO THE UNITED STATES

Country	1951–60	1961–70	1971–80	1981–85	1986–88
Cuba	78,948	208,536	264,863	50,859	74,760
Dominican Repub.	9,897	93,292	148,135	104,797	78,358
Haiti	4,442	34,499	56,335	43,312	61,857
Jamaica	8,869	74,906	137,577	99,089	61,820
Other	20,395	58,980	134,216	63,671	33,296
Total	123,091	470,213	741,126	361,728	310,091

Source: U.S. Immigration and Naturalization Service, *Annual Report, 1988* (Washington D.C.: U.S. Government Printing Office, 1989), Table 2.

their principal point of destination. According to the U.S. Census for 1980, New York accounted for 78 percent of Dominicans living in the continental United States, followed by New Jersey (8 percent) and Florida (4 percent).[14]

Evidence of the network-driven character of Dominican migration is provided by the distribution of visas for legal permanent entry in the United States. Out of a total of 27,189 new arrivals in 1988, 7,562 (27.8 percent) were exempted from national quota limits as parents, spouses and children of U.S. citizens. An additional 19,111 (70.3 percent) came under family reunification preferences of the quota system as spouses, children and siblings of U.S. citizens or permanent legal residents. Only 41 immigrants (0.1 percent) made use of occupational preferences as professionals or skilled workers.[15] Personal ties rather than formal occupational qualifications are obviously the engine governing the process of emigration from the Dominican Republic.

As is the case with other sustained processes of international migration, the growth of monetary transfers from Dominican workers abroad has paralleled the increase of the labor outflow from the country. According to data from the Dominican Central Bank (DCB), family cash transfers and contributions from immigrants represented only 3.2 percent of the Gross Domestic Product in 1977, but increased to 13.2 percent in 1988. It should be kept in mind that the DCB estimates are considered very conservative.

Even then, for every single year for which data are available, the flow of officially estimated remittances exceeded total foreign aid. According to several studies, the average monthly remittance per employed immigrant in 1985 and 1986 was U.S. $170,[16] while the minimum legal wage increased to $85.9 in 1986 from $68.3 in the previous year. The annual family remittance *per capita* of those receiving family transfers reached $408 in 1986,

FIGURE 1
PRINCIPAL SOURCES OF FOREIGN EXCHANGE

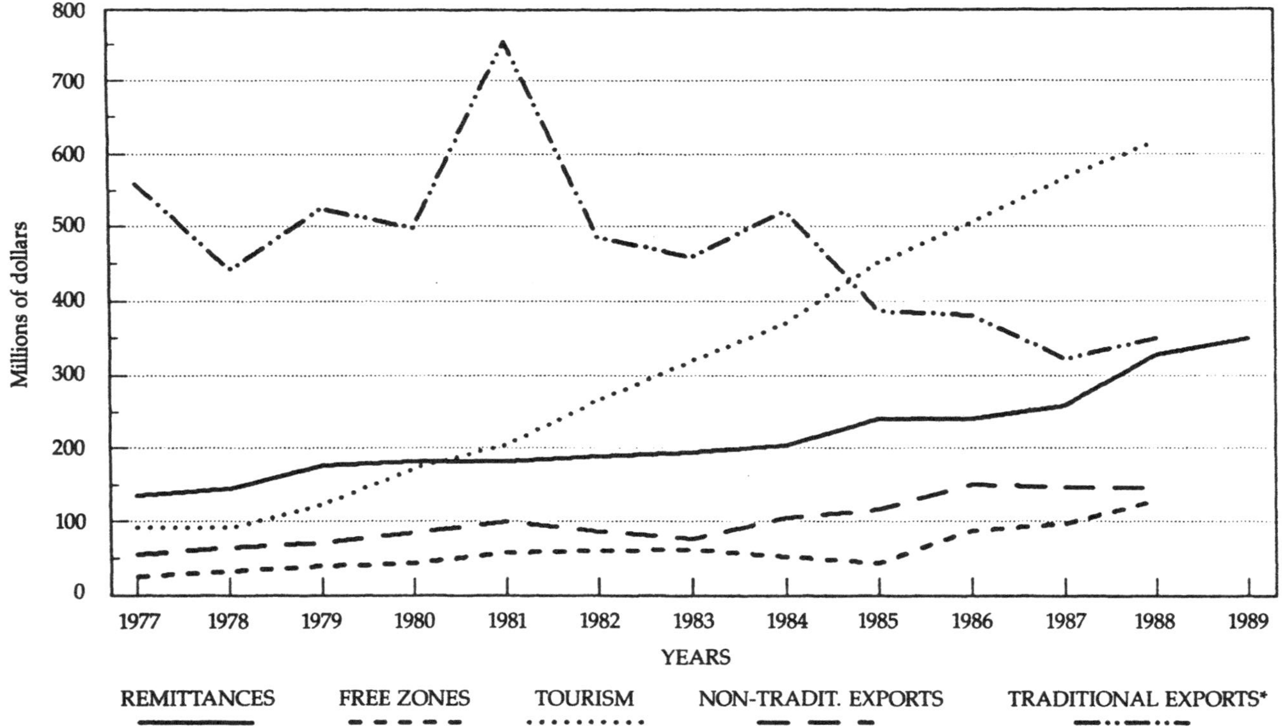

Note: *Sugar, coffee, tobacco

Sources: Banco Central de la República Dominicana, *Boletín Mensual*, vol XII, no. 10, October 1988; Fundación Economía y Desarrollo, *Impacto del Sector Privado en la Economía Dominicana* (Santo Domingo, DR: Acción Empresarial, 1989); and Miguel Ceara, "La Economía Dominicana: Crisis y Reestructuración 1968–1988," Paper presented at Seminar "Economic Crisis and Third World Countries: Impact and Response," University of the West Indies (Santo Domingo DR: CIECA, 3–8 April 1989).

compared to an annual Gross Domestic Product *per capita* of $730 in 1987, and a *per capita* foreign debt of $571.[17] Another illustration of the growing significance of immigrant remittances is presented in Figure 1 which compares the evolution of foreign exchange received by the Dominican Republic under this rubric with those earned by traditional and nontraditional exports, as well as tourism and the new Export Production Zones (EPZs). As the figure shows, receipts from remittances not only experienced a sustained increase between 1977 and 1989 but, by the latter year, matched the *sum* of the country's three traditional exports—sugar, coffee and tobacco. Only receipts from tourism grew faster during this period or surpassed those from remittances in recent years.

III. METHODOLOGY

The limitations of time and resources for this study precluded conducting representative surveys either in the home country or among the expatriate community. Within these limits, we chose to concentrate on the dynamics of immigration and to try to gain a better understanding of the processes linking the New York Dominican community with its home country. To do this, we adopted a three-pronged strategy of data collection based, respectively, on informant interviewing, secondary data collection and a convenience sample of Dominican enterprises linked to migration.

Informants are well-placed individuals who are able to report not only on themselves, but on the character of events and processes in the communities around them. We made extensive use of informant interviewing to gain a preliminary understanding of types of labor market insertion among Dominican immigrants in New York, the destination of their transferred resources, and the economic sectors most affected in the Dominican Republic. A total of 50 informants were interviewed in New York City, Santo Domingo and Santiago. They included migrant entrepreneurs, business leaders, banking managers and government officials.

The final stage of data collection was a survey of small enterprises linked to migration (SELMs) conducted in the cities of Santo Domingo and Santiago de los Caballeros between June and October of 1989. That such firms exist and that they are, in fact, commonplace represent a first substantive finding of the study. Although exhaustive lists do not exist from which to draw representative samples, we experienced no difficulty in locating a sufficient number for a stratified, purposeful sample. The opposite problem actually presented itself, namely how to select from the existing universe and within the time limitations of the study, those units that could yield the greatest and most relevant information.

To avoid having the sample "captured" by a single network of firms, we

TABLE 2

SAMPLED ENTERPRISES: DISTRIBUTION BY CITY AND SECTOR

	Manufacturing	Commerce	Finance	Other Services	Total No.	Total %
Santo Domingo	9	17	13	19	58	51.3
Santiago de Los Caballeros	16	16	11	12	55	48.7
Total No.	25	33	24	31	113.0	
%	22.1	29.2	21.2	27.4	100.0	

adopted two decisions: First, the sample was stratified by sector and location so that interviews were conducted in four different industries and two different cities. Second, identification of eligible firms was based on a strategy of multiple "entry points," through contacts available to individual interviewers, in order to minimize the well-known problems associated with a single snowball-chain. In total, 113 small enterprises were included. Table 2 presents their distribution by city and sector.

The research team composed of Johns Hopkins and FLACSO sociologists also decided to study firms that were somewhat larger than the more abundant, but short-lived microenterprises. This decision was adopted in order to examine the potential effects of migration on a small, but resilient business sector that can make nonnegligible contributions to both national production and employment. As noted in a previous section, this type of enterprise has generally been neglected in past studies of the economic effects of Dominican migration. Eligibility criteria included both capital and labor input limits. To be selected, firms had to have at least five permanent workers but no more than 50; smaller firms were also eligible if they had a minimum capital of U.S. $5,000 (DR $30,000).

To be eligible as SELMs (migration-linked enterprises), firms had to fulfill one or more of the following criteria:

1) be owned by returned migrants or migrants still living abroad;
2) be managed or staffed by returned migrants;
3) receive transfers in cash or kind from migrants abroad;
4) be acquired or started, partially or exclusively, with monies from migrant labor;
5) have major clients among Dominican migrants abroad.

In order to gather comparable data, only the owner or general manager of the firm was interviewed. Table 3 presents the distribution of sampled firms according to their connection to international migration.

Table 4 breaks down this sample by informants' gender and position in the firm. Contrary to stereotypes of an exclusively male entrepreneurial

TABLE 3

SAMPLED ENTERPRISES: CONNECTIONS WITH INTERNATIONAL MIGRATION

	No.	%
Owner is returnee or lives abroad	102	90.3
Firms with returnee workers[a]	81	71.7
Firm receives remittances	48	42.5
Firm started with money earned abroad	101	89.4
Major clients of firm are migrants abroad[b]	11	9.7

Note: [a]Includes owners, administrators and laborers.
[b]Financial firms only.

TABLE 4

DISTRIBUTION OF RESPONDENTS BY GENDER AND SECTOR

Sector	Female Owners	Male Owners	Female Managers %	Male Managers	Total
Manufacturing	31.0	21.0	—	16.7	22.3
Commerce	31.0	27.4	100.0	22.2	29.5
Financial services	3.5	24.2	—	44.4	21.4
Other services	34.5	27.4	—	16.7	26.8
Total %	100.0 (29)	100.0 (62)	100.0 (3)	100.0 (18)	100.0 (112)

class in Latin countries, we find that 32 firms, or 29 percent, of the sample are owned or managed by women. This finding can not be interpreted to mean that one-third of the Dominican small entrepreneurial class is female, but instead that such entrepreneurs exist and that their presence is nonnegligible.

In general, a small incidental sample, no matter how stratified, does not furnish the basis for valid generalizations. Instead, its findings can be used for two purposes: 1) to test null hypotheses about the *existence* of a particular category of individuals or units; and 2) to provide an estimate of the gross order of magnitude between related categories. The sample can answer authoritatively the question "are there zero cases of something?" because their presence in such a small total attests to their existence. Moreover, it can provide a tentative guide as to the possible relative frequency of different such categories in the relevant universe, subject to future empirical validation.

IV. THE DOMINICAN IMMIGRANT COMMUNITY OF NEW YORK: PRELIMINARY FINDINGS

In this section, we present findings based on informant interviews and secondary data collection conducted in New York City. We approached the Dominican immigrant community with well-conceived ideas about its social condition and labor market situation. Both past research on the topic and journalistic coverage had portrayed Dominican immigration as a manual labor outflow providing a source of low-wage workers for the economies of the areas where it concentrates. Indeed, the counterpart of its characterization as a "safety valve" or "subsistence" type of movement in the Dominican Republic is its description as "secondary labor market" immigration in the United States.[18]

This characterization led us to expect other familiar social concomitants of the secondary labor market: concentration of immigrants into ghetto-like surroundings, where ethnic entrepreneurial activity is confined to a few grocery shops and restaurants plus gambling and pervasive street drug selling. We were genuinely surprised to encounter instead a thriving entrepreneurial community. The core of this emerging ethnic economy is located in the Washington Heights area of Manhattan where, according to the 1980 Census, 50 percent of Dominicans living in New York resided.

Employment and participation in ethnic firms offer to migrant newcomers an alternative to the dead-end jobs of the secondary sector. Evidence in support of this characterization comes from reports by various Dominican business associations, themselves proof of prior entrepreneurial development. According to one of them, New York City hosts about 20,000 Dominican-owned businesses. According to the *Federación de Comerciantes e Industriales Dominicanos en Nueva York,* Dominicans own approximately 70 percent of all *bodegas* (corner grocery stores) in New York—with annual estimated sales of $1.8 billion; they also own and operate around 90 percent of the "gypsy cabs" in Upper Manhattan and are owners or major shareholders of three chains of Spanish supermarkets, three newspapers and even two T.V. stations. Allowing for a measure of prideful exaggeration in these figures, they still suggest the diversity of business initiatives in which Dominican immigrants can be found.

For immigrant entrepreneurs, access to a ready pool of labor is only one of the advantages conferred by a concentrated ethnic community. Others include a captive market for culturally defined products and services and access to informal sources of credit. Although formal sources of finance are available to established immigrant businesses, there are significant advantages to the informal route in terms of expeditiousness and absence of paperwork. To be emphasized is that such transactions, often involving large sums of money without a single paper signed, could not take place if they were not securely ensconced in a set of common understandings, common language and mutual obligations enforced by the ethnic community.[19]

These patterns can be illustrated by the experiences of a Dominican businessman interviewed in the course of field work in New York. Nicolás is 38 years old and already owns five commercial shops in New York City and a finance agency (*financiera*) in the Dominican Republic. Nicolás relies exclusively on the informal financial system available in Washington Heights. Sometimes he acts as an investor, sometimes as a borrower. As an investor, he has gained a good reputation that enables him to collect several thousand dollars with no papers signed to be invested in his businesses in New York or Santo Domingo. These investments generally come from older salaried immigrants who do not have enough capital to initiate new ventures themselves. As a borrower, he enjoys ample credit from other well-to-do immigrants. At the time of the interview, Nicolás had two active loans—one for $125,000 and the other for $200,000, only one of which was accompanied by some signed papers. He was paying a monthly interest of around 2.6 percent. Nicolás has 30 employees on his permanent payroll. With the exception of two recently arrived Central Americans, the rest of his staff are relatives, friends or relatives of close friends back in the Dominican Republic.

The case of two of Nicolás' relatives illustrate another facet of the enclave at work. Juan and Carlos both earned graduate degrees in Europe. Upon their return to the Dominican Republic, Carlos married Nicolás' sister. After several years of low earnings in their country, they sought the help of some friends through whom both were hired as temporary instructors by a Manhattan college. Once in New York, the two friends found that their incomes and possibilities for upward mobility were very dim, particularly in comparison with the situation of Dominican entrepreneurs such as Nicolás. As a result, and due to Nicolás' initiative, they both quit their jobs at the college to take over one of Nicolás' *bodegas*.

According to their verbal agreement, Carlos and Juan will become the *bodega*'s owners in five years. Meanwhile, they have to run the store under the loose supervision of Nicolás, who collects a given percentage of the weekly profits and holds the legal property of the business. Under their agreement, the store must be open seven days a week, almost 24 hours a day and secure an agreed minimum weekly payment to Nicolás. Overall, the agreement is entirely informal and based on mutual trust. Not one of the parties involved sees any uncertainty in this kind of arrangement, since the social standing and credibility of each is the collateral securing the deal.

Such experiences, commonplace in the daily life of the immigrant community, can not be captured by a perspective which envisions migration as a question of labor supply and demand among individual market actors. Nor does it fit well the image of a process of relentless exploitation of workers in their country of origin and after migration. Patterns of social interaction within the immigrant community create opportunities that, if not available to everyone or in equal measure, offer to many a means of escaping the drudgery and stagnation of jobs in the secondary sector. By the same token, these relationships pave the way for exchanges of information and eventual investments in the home country, as explained below.

V. THE IMMIGRANT COMMUNITY AND THE DEVELOPMENT OF DOMINICAN SMALL ENTERPRISES

Just as the economic activities of the immigrant community are internally diversified, so are the possible transfers that it can make to its home country. Figure 2 presents a typology of migrant remittances elaborated on the basis of informant reports in New York and in the Dominican Republic. The point highlighted by this typology is that immigrant transfers are not limited to those commonly described in the literature. The predominant mode of transfer for immigrant workers and the few who have gained access to the U.S. public welfare system (retirees, victims of work accidents, single household heads, etc.) are indeed family-oriented small sums of money and consumer goods. The principal domestic effect of such transfers is to subsidize the living standards of the immigrants' kin, a pattern familiar from past studies. Immigrant entrepreneurs and returnees—such as most respondents in our sample—can carry out, however, other types of transfer, including investment capital and producer goods for use in domestic enterprises. These transfers could play a more significant role in the domestic economy than those limited to direct consumption.

Table 5 presents a general description of the small enterprises linked to migration (SELMS) included in our sample. The numbers confirm the small size of these enterprises, which employ only seven workers on the average and highlight the modest wages that they pay. The average worker receives a monthly compensation of U.S. $138 at the official exchange rate. The figure is this high because of the relatively high wages paid by the *financieras,* an average of U.S. $192 at the official rate in both cities. Industrial firms pay the lowest salaries and have the lowest monthly sales per worker.[20]

FIGURE 2
A TYPOLOGY OF MIGRANT TRANSFERS
SOURCE

FORM				
	I. WORKERS IN THE U.S. (WAGES) FAMILY CASH TRANSFERS (F C T)	II. U.S. PUBLIC ASSISTANCE RECIPIENTS (PAYMENTS) FAMILY CASH TRANSFERS (F C T)	III. RETURNEES (SAVINGS) INVESTMENT CAPITAL (I C)	IV. U.S.-BASED ENTREPRENEURS (PROFITS) INVESTMENT CAPITAL (I C)
MONETARY				
NON-MONETARY	CONSUMER GOODS	CONSUMER GOODS	1. SKILLS AND TECHNOLOGY (HUMAN CAPITAL) 2. CONSUMER AND PRODUCER GOODS	PRODUCER GOODS

TABLE 5
SELECTED CHARACTERISTICS OF SAMPLED FIRMS LINKED TO MIGRATION BY CITY AND SECTOR

City and Sector	Average Number of Workers	Average Salary[1] (DR$)	Average Investment per Employee (DR$1000)	Average Monthly Sales per Employee (DR$)	Average Fixed Capital (DR$1000)	Average Firm Age (Yrs)	(No.)
Santo Domingo							
Manufacturing	8	521	43.81	3,183	553.33	8.0	9
Commerce	5	635	54.60	11,095	303.06	6.4	17
Financial services	8	1,227	254.62	41,514	1,945.38	4.0	13
Other services	7	830	83.10	7,448	485.53	5.8	19
Sub-total	7	817	107.09	15,034	769.78	5.9	58
Santiago							
Manufacturing	10	702	21.35	2,224	213.75	11.7	16
Commerce	5	827	70.54	6,667	276.25	4.6	16
Financial services	4	1,200	320.06	128,421	1,431.82	4.3	11
Other services	10	735	50.43	3,348	591.82	8.5	12
Sub-total	8	839	98.59	26,130	557.41	7.5	55
Total	7	828	103.03	20,274	667.38	6.7	113

Note: [1]In 1989, the official monetary equivalence was D.R. $6.25 = U.S. $1.00.

The large amount of capital invested for the creation of a new job in these firms is striking. Again, the smallest amount is in manufacturing and the largest in finance. In Santo Domingo, the average cost of creating a job in an industrial firm is DR $43,810 (US $6,976), while in Santiago the average reported for manufacturing was DR $21,350 (US $3,400). These figures appear quite high compared to those presented by organizations promoting small-scale enterprises. Studies based on 1980 data reported an average capital investment of DR $20,000 in the industrial sector as a whole and DR $3,000 for small scale manufacturing firms. Part of the discrepancy is due to inflation which pushed the real value of the peso in 1989 20 to 30 percent below the official rate. This artifact, which incidentally further reduces the real value of wages paid by these firms, does not explain the entire discrepancy. These SELMs appear better capitalized than the "typical" Dominican small firm, a fact which may reflect their continuing links with outside sources of finance. Such linkages will be explored below.

Table 6 shows that four out of five SELMs were initiated by their present owner and that the remaining 20 percent were purchased or inherited. In seven out of ten cases, the primary source of start-up capital was from savings abroad; only one-fourth of these SELMs were created with savings or loans acquired in the Dominican Republic. Moreover, in the majority of cases where immigrant savings were not the major capital source, they still played a contributing role as secondary investments. In total, nine out of ten SELMs depended, in one form or another, on money savings accumulated abroad for their creation.

The median initial investment was DR $75,000 or around US $12,000. Total investment from migrant savings in our sample thus amount to about 1.2 million dollars. Results in Table 7 show that reliance on immigrant savings as a source of start-up capital has not been decreasing but, if anything, has increased over time. Most firm owners depended on such transfers, but the pattern is still more marked among those returning to the Dominican Republic during the last ten years than among those who came back before 1979.

Forty-two percent of sampled SELMs continued to receive capital from migrants abroad. Partners and co-owners of existing enterprises are the single largest source of working capital. As Table 8 indicates, however, if immigrant relatives are added as a group, they comprise the majority of contributors of new capital inputs. Transfers from siblings are the most common, followed by those from respondents' children.

Investment capital received by SELMs is not always liquid. In our sample, 57 percent of reported transfers came in money form; 37 percent were in kind—producer goods or commodities for sale—and 6 percent were mixed. The mean value of each transfer, as estimated by respondents, was approximately US $5,400, with a median value of US $3,000. The discrepancy between both figures indicates that some firms received transfers significantly higher than the majority.[21]

It is not possible to calculate periodic average values because most capital investments are made at irregular intervals. More than 70 percent of enterprises receiving investments from abroad did so irregularly or occasionally. In many instances, capital was only remitted upon the entrepreneur's explicit request when the need for purchases arose in emergency cases, and so forth.

A related mechanism for capital replenishment consists of owners' periodic trips to stimulate new investments among immigrants. Such promotions may take place directly, through existing kin and friendship networks, or through the mediation of financial and real estate agencies (*financieras*) located in New York, which act as investment brokers. In this manner, migrant investors other than those originally associated with the creation of the firm are incorporated.[22] SELM owners and managers also travel abroad to sell part of their production in hard currency. Proprietors of small garment firms in the Dominican Republic regularly travel to

TABLE 6
FIRM ACQUISITION BY GENDER

Type of Acquisition	Females	Males *(percentages)*	Total
Started by owner	87.5	77.2	80.2
Purchased	9.4	19.0	16.2
Inherited	3.1	3.8	3.6
Total	100.0 (32)	100.0 (79)	100.0 (111)

TABLE 7
IMMIGRANT SAVINGS AS PRIMARY SOURCE OF CAPITAL BY YEAR OF RETURN[1]

	Return Year			
Investment Capital	Before 1979	1980–85 *(percentages)*	1986–89	Total
Savings abroad	76.5	90.0	91.0	87.3
Other	23.5	10.0	9.0	12.7
Total	100.0 (17)	100.0 (30)	100.0 (32)	100.0 (79)

Note: [1]Firm owners only.

TABLE 8
DISTRIBUTION OF CAPITAL TRANSFERS BY TYPE OF SENDER[1]

	No.	%	Cumulative %
Owners and partners	14	29.8	29.8
Parents	4	8.5	38.3
Spouse	4	8.5	46.8
Child(ren)	5	10.6	57.4
Siblings	8	17.0	74.5
Other relative	6	12.8	87.2
Other investors	6	12.8	100.0 (48)

Note: [1]Firms receiving transfers only.

Puerto Rico, New York and other U.S. locations to sell their products. It is common practice to have an informal contract with the buyer abroad and, in some cases, with small clothing stores. On their way back, the informal exporter fills his/her empty suitcases with inputs needed for the business such as fabrics, needles and so forth.

To the uneducated eye, these loaded down international travellers appear as common Dominican migrants visiting their relatives back home. In reality, they are engaged in a growing form of informal international trade, ignored or unnoticed by customs inspectors in both countries. Of all the illustrations that could be offered about linkages between Dominican small firms and the immigrant community in New York, none is more poignant than this dense traffic of entrepreneurially oriented individuals taking advantage of differential demand and prices. The informational requirements of this traffic are invariably channelled through social networks linking places of origin and of destination.

A full 67 percent of SELM owners and managers in our sample travelled abroad during the 12 months prior to the interview. Of these, 72 percent travelled to New York City, 13 percent to other U.S. cities and 11 percent to Puerto Rico. Respondents who travelled for business reasons did so primarily to purchase inputs abroad or to secure new capital through sales, investments or wage work. These categories jointly accounted for 70 percent of business trips; the remainder is composed of individuals who own businesses in the United States. Normally, these businesses are also closely linked to those operating in the Dominican Republic.

As seen above, the skilling potential of labor migration is a hotly debated subject, with free market analysts generally arguing in its favor and critical writers dismissing it. Asked whether they had learned new skills abroad, eight out of ten returnees in the sample responded affirmatively. Table 9 shows that the pattern is the same for males and females. More important, however, is what kinds of skills were transferred and how useful they are in the respondents' current work. Accordingly, respondents were asked: "What skills that you learned abroad are you using now in your business?"

Eighty-five percent of those who acquired new knowledge abroad are putting it to use in their present work. Most of these useful skills are, however, relatively simple ones which do not reflect the "high-tech" transfers sometimes described in the literature. Only 15 percent of respondents who reported learning new skills in the United States did so in production techniques and half of them did so in a notoriously low-tech industry—garment manufacturing. By contrast, one-third learned basic accounting and management techniques necessary to run a business. Typical answers included "aprendí a negociar" (I learned how to do business); "aprendí como administrar una discoteca/bodega" (I learned how to manage a disco or a corner store); or "aprendí a tratar al cliente" (I learned how to deal with customers). The remaining one-third reported mostly low-level service skills such as auto repairing, beautician's training and food preparation.

TABLE 9

DISTRIBUTION OF NEW SKILLS LEARNED ABROAD BY GENDER[1]

Learned New Skills	Females	Males (*percentages*)	Total
Yes	86.4	81.7	82.7
No	13.6	18.3	17.1
Total	100.0 (22)	100.0 (60)	100.0 (82)

Note: [1]Respondents who lived abroad only.

TABLE 10

ACQUISITION OF SKILLS BY OCCUPATION ABROAD[1]

New Skills	Occupation Blue-Collar Worker	Clerical, Sales (*percentages*)	Proprietor, Manager	Total
Yes	78.0	85.7	92.6	84.1
No	22.0	14.3	7.4	15.9
Totals	100.0 (41)	100.0 (14)	100.0 (27)	100.0 (82)

Note: [1]Returnees only.

Table 10 provides some evidence that skill transfers among returnees were more frequent the higher the status of occupations held abroad. Ninety-three percent of those who held managerial positions reported having learned some occupational skill, contrasted with somewhat lower but still majority percentages among blue-collar and clerical workers. A final indication of the usefulness of out-migration for entrepreneurial development came in answers to another question: "Where did you acquire the know-how to run this firm?" Overall, immigration provided the requisite skills for one-third of respondents; formal training and work in the Dominican Republic accounted for the remaining two-thirds. Managers were almost twice more likely to depend on human capital transferred from abroad than owners.

At first glance, these results lend direct support to the neoclassical position. Yet, on closer inspection, the kinds of skills transferred qualify this support and provide evidence for an alternative interpretation. The usual description in the literature concerning the positive effects of human capital transfers assumes that the latter are: a) of a technological nature and

b) acquired while working in mainstream industries of the receiving country. To the contrary, Dominican skill transfers are mostly: a) of a commercial or managerial character and b) acquired through incorporation into an ethnic enclave.

The experiences of our respondents make clear that most of them "learned how to do business" or acquired the rudiments of the garment trade by working in immigrant-owned and managed shops in the United States. Hence, the typical skill transfer does not come from high-tech mainstream companies, but from small and low-tech ethnic firms. Indeed, if our respondents had been confined to manual labor in the New York secondary labor market, the predictions of critical theory would have been, in all likelihood, supported. That they were not is not due to the alternative insertion of large numbers of Dominicans in primary-sector jobs, but rather to the bridgehead role played by their own ethnic community.

VI. CONCLUSIONS

Conclusions Regarding Past Theories of Migration

The findings of this small study can not be used to arrive at definite conclusions concerning the competing theoretical perspectives outlined at the start. However, results point to tendencies worth further examination in the future. If the theoretical scenario were limited to competing neoclassical and critical Marxist views of labor migration, the weight of the evidence would lean in the direction of the former. Migration does have a series of positive consequences for the individuals involved, as well as for the sending and receiving economies.

This conclusion must be immediately qualified, however, by two considerations. First, it is based on a sample deliberately oriented toward the entrepreneurial end of both the immigrant community and the sending country. More negative accounts—which support a critical stance toward the consequences of labor migration—have been based on rural origin or working class samples that have seldom taken into account the diversity of socioeconomic origins of immigrants and their modes of incorporation into the American economy.

The second qualification is that the positive consequences of Dominican migration do not generally accord with the script put forth by neoclassical theory. In the Dominican case, the story is modified by the presence and activities of the immigrant community itself. Immigrants do meet labor demand of New York-area firms, but those who follow to the letter that part of the script are often the least able to accumulate savings or learn skills. Instead, the best opportunities often lie with the networks of entre-

FIGURE 3
PREDICTED AND OBSERVED SEQUENCES OF MIGRATION

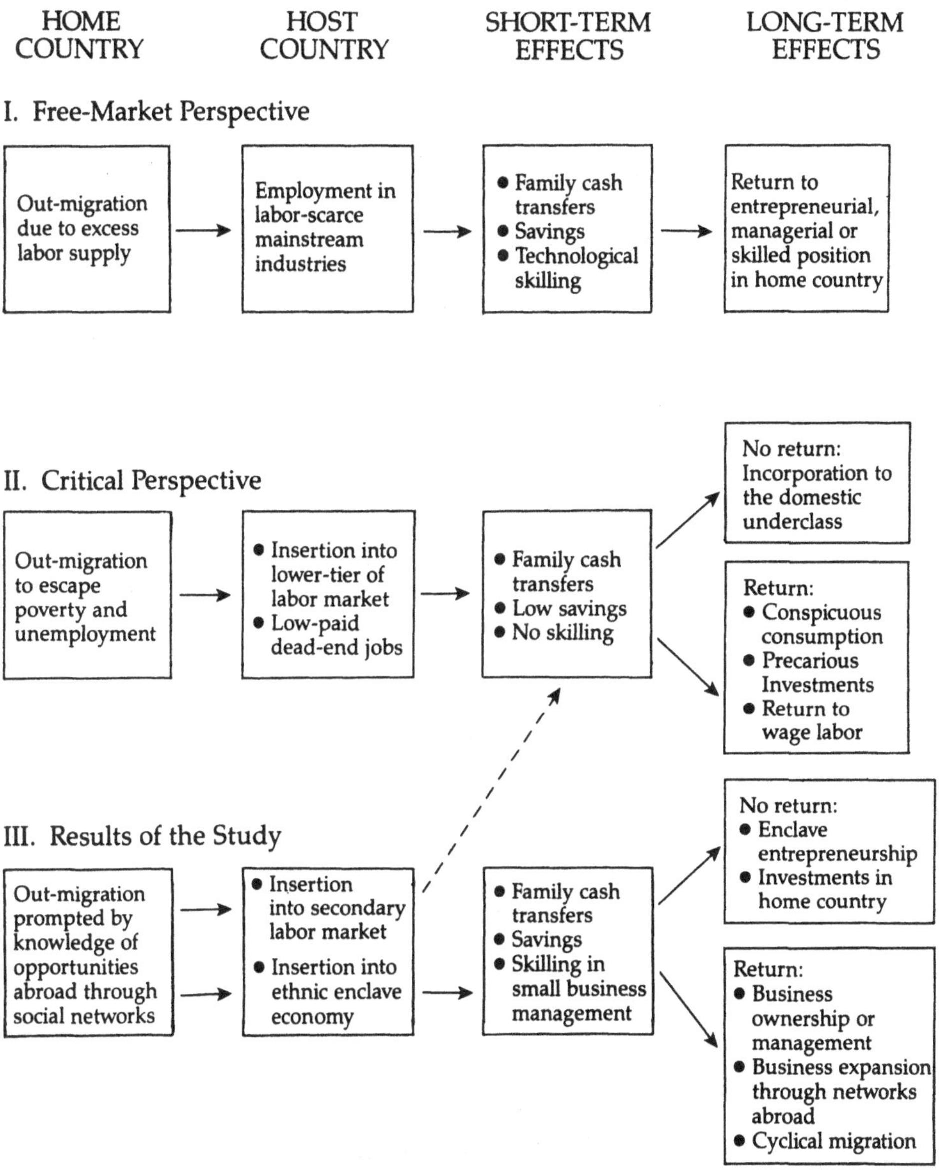

preneurial action created by earlier immigrants. Within this ethnic enclave, barriers of language, culture, legal status or even skin color—so significant in the mainstream labor market—are greatly attenuated.

Nor is the eventual return to the home country the one-way affair envisioned by past writings. Instead, immigrants seem to build a "base" abroad—in terms of property, bank accounts and business contacts—from which to organize their return home. The result is not final departure but the building of a transnational network which facilitates back-and-forth contacts, including cyclical migration. Figure 3 outlines the sequences of labor migration as conceived by the two principal theoretical positions in the field and compares them with those identified in the course of the study.

Social capital gives rise to outcomes that could not be anticipated on the basis of calculations based exclusively on individual profit-seeking. The transformation of university professionals into store owners; the granting of loans for thousands of dollars with a handshake; a class of international informal traders who buy and sell both in New York and in the Dominican Republic are so many examples of these phenomena. The methodological corollary of these results is that researchers would do well in the future to avoid designs focused exclusively on individual traits or on a single class of immigrants. Instead, one must look at *relationships* between immigrants of different class backgrounds and their communities of destination.

Conclusions Regarding Empirical Trends

The discovery of a thriving Dominican economy in New York City; the identification of a plurality of migration-linked enterprises operating in the Dominican Republic; and the tracing of some of the mechanisms through which these enterprises emerge and are sustained over time comprise the principal empirical findings of the study. On these bases, it is possible to anticipate several short- and medium-term trends.

Unless drastic, and so far unforeseen, measures are taken, the small-business enclave in New York is likely to continue to grow, expanding the employment and mobility opportunities for new immigrants as well as the economic weight of the immigrant community in the home country. The strength of binational networks already in place makes it unlikely that the outflow from the Dominican Republic will diminish in the foreseeable future. This is true even if legal avenues for migration are curtailed because an established expatriate community will seek means to bypass new restrictions.

Further, it is not clear why Dominican migration should be repressed since, aside from providing a labor pool for firms in the competitive sector of New York's economy, it reinforces the growth of entrepreneurial activities that have infused new life in formerly decaying areas of the city.[23]

FIGURE 4
MIGRATION-LINKED FLOWS BETWEEN THE UNITED STATES AND THE DOMINICAN REPUBLIC

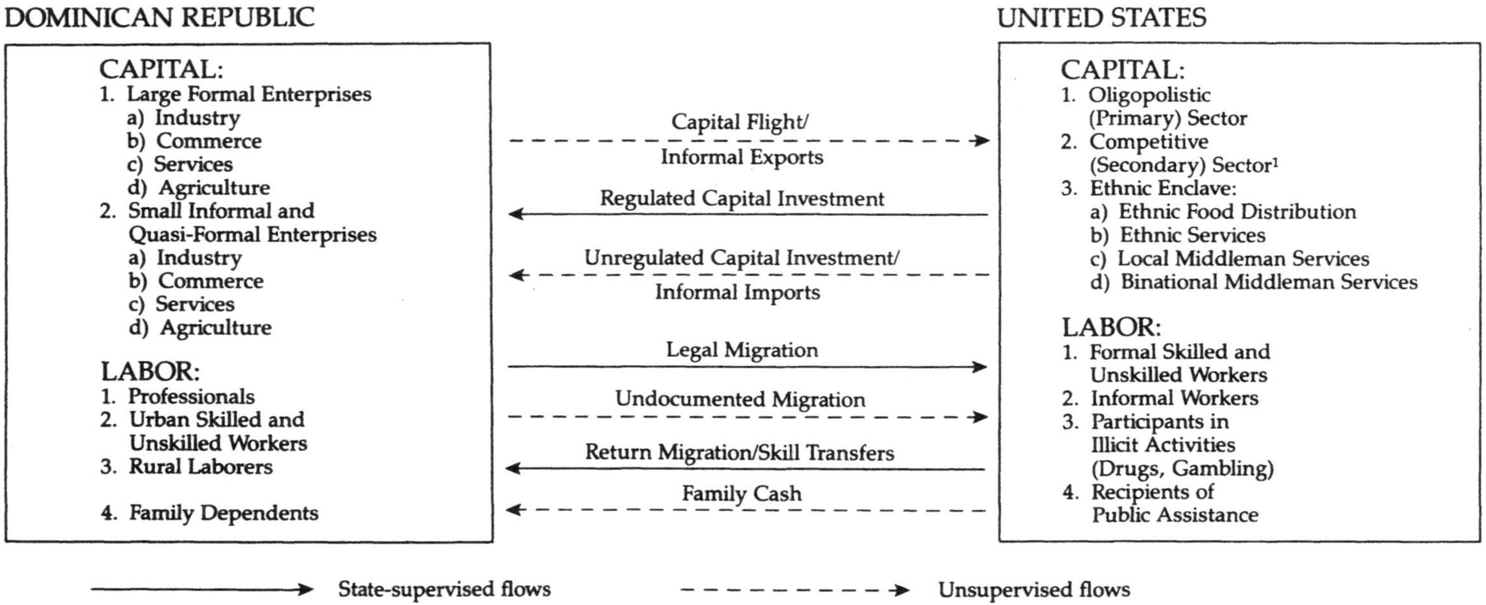

Note: [1]A description of the various types of Dominican Immigrant firms is presented in the full version of this report. See A. Portes and L. Guamizo, "U.S.-Bound Immigration and Small-Enterprise Development in the Dominican Republic," Occasional Papers, Program in Comparative and International Development, Department of Sociology, The Johns Hopkins University, 1990.

This positive aspect of Dominican migration is dependent, however, on its continuing to have an entrepreneurial element, rather than being exclusively a "safety valve" or "subsistence" flow. In other words, the process has few drawbacks to the extent that many immigrants return.

The back-and-forth character of Dominican immigration is illustrated in Figure 4 which portrays the various movements between places of origin and destination. Unfortunately, the continuation of the "return" leg of the process is more difficult to predict with confidence because it depends on the existence of a minimum of economic opportunities and social stability at home. Dominican migrants return and try their hand at business initiatives because they perceive that there are still economic niches and advantages in their country. Their behavior may be fruitfully contrasted with that of Salvadoran or Haitian immigrants, very few of whom seem to return voluntarily even if they succeed economically in the United States.[24] The difference is, of course, that there is very little for these immigrants to "go back to," while there are still enough points of attraction for Dominicans.

Conclusions Regarding Policy

Our policy recommendations are based on the following assumptions, based on the empirical results presented in this report:

1. The emergence of a binational economic community between the United States and the Dominican Republic is essentially benign, provided that the "going" flow does not turn into a flood and that the "returning" ones continue.
   a. Attempts to curtail U.S.-bound Dominican immigration through police measures are not likely to be effective and do not seem desirable given the economic dynamism of the immigrant community.
   b. The best means to control Dominican immigration is through measures in the sending country which stimulate non-migrants to remain and migrants to return.
2. Migrant investments of material and human capital in small enterprises in the Dominican Republic are a fact. The expansion of such investments can play an important role in national economic development.
   a. Other things being equal, migrant entrepreneurs will have a preference for investing in their home country.
   b. Migrant return and entrepreneurial investments are contingent facts, dependent on political stability and economic opportunities at home.
3. The flow of migration-driven resources to the Dominican Republic is not homogeneous, but segmented according to the modes of incorporation of migrants in the U.S.-labor market.

Policies should be fine-tuned according to the diversity of such flows.

U.S. Government Policies

In our view, a program of subsidized credit for small enterprise development will not put a stop to Dominican out-migration because the latter is sustained by a plurality of other forces. In this sense, the hypothesis with which this study started can be safely rejected. However, in combination with other initiatives to facilitate access to profitable opportunities for small investors, a program of subsidized credit would help:

1) control the size of the outflow;
2) maintain its entrepreneurial rather than survival orientation; and
3) stimulate its cyclical character through regular returns to the home country.

The rationale for such a program is based on assumptions 2a and 2b above: given comparable opportunities, would-be entrepreneurs are likely to opt to remain at home or return. Hence, any development which furthers the opportunities for small entrepreneurship in the country of origin is also a means to reduce pressures for out-migration. Programs of credit through private agencies and organizations rather than through government bureaucracies—in the model pioneered by Acción International and the Inter-American Foundation—appear most suitable to support the development of small enterprises.

It should be kept in mind, however, that small firms with the capacity to keep their owners and managers at home generally exceed the size of the typical microenterprise aided by these agencies. Firms of the size included in our sample have the capacity to retain their staff, but they also require injections of capital of considerable magnitude. On the positive side, sampled enterprises were able to negotiate credit with formal sector sources, to meet interest payments and to keep orderly books—characteristics not always found in microenterprises.

Technological aid does not appear to be a high priority for our entrepreneurs but, by the same token, the figures indicate that a large proportion of them learned their skills either by working in other firms or through formal training in the Dominican Republic. These results suggest that technological education in the country of origin can play a major role. Therefore, along with a program of subsidized credit for small firms, aid to financially-strapped public technical and vocational schools is a recommended investment. A deserving example is the Dominican Institute for Technological Promotion (INFOTEP) which operates several good technical schools throughout the country. Reinforcement of technical training and the availability of local credit should go a long way toward expanding the universe of individuals able to pursue entrepreneurial initiatives at home.

Dominican Government Policies

Much of the past literature reduced the effects of Dominican migration on national development to the volume of family cash transfers (FCTs), commonly known as remittances. Attuned to this vision and given the country's need for foreign exchange, official policies have concentrated on maximizing the inflow of monetary FCTs through official channels. Coercive measures and regulation of intermediary firms handling remittances have been recently put in place by the Dominican government.

To gain maximum benefit from migrant monetary and nonmonetary transfers, the Dominican government should work *with*, not against, the immigrant community. To begin with, policies should be attuned to the heterogeneity of such transfers instead of treating them uniformly. At a minimum, FCTs must be distinguished from investments of financial and human capital. A recommended policy for *all* financial transfers is to allow their free convertibility. At present, the Dominican peso is overvalued by a factor of about 30 percent. In this situation, compulsory measures requiring transfers to be converted at the official exchange rate become a heavy tax on immigrants and are doomed to failure.

Another recommended measure is to allow migrants abroad, as well as firms created by returned migrants, to open domestic bank accounts denominated in dollars. Through these accounts, not granted to other nationals, monetary transfers can be made.[25] Foreign exchange deposited in these accounts may be converted into domestic currency at a free rate. This program should be limited to Dominican permanent residents abroad and returnee entrepreneurs able to demonstrate a prolonged stay out of the country in order to discourage its frivolous use. Its major advantage would be to facilitate FCTs and capital investments, providing the government simultaneously with a ready pool of foreign exchange. Its major disadvantage is its potential use for capital flight. The latter, however, is already taking place through numerous channels that escape government control.

The fact that migrants return and invest today, despite bureaucratic barriers and a difficult economic environment, is an encouraging sign that a large potential for future capital investments exists. A number of measures may be taken by the government to activate this potential and channel it toward productive sectors. Copying the laws used to promote foreign investment (Nos. 299 and 861), migrant investors in selected sectors should be exempted from paying taxes on incomes resulting from enterprises in which the initial investment is from savings abroad.

Results from our survey indicate that migrant capital transfers in recent years have been strongly oriented toward the creation of firms in the financial sector. This orientation reflects the new opportunities for profitable investments associated with the shift of governmental policy away from import substitution industrialization. One of the main losers of this shift has been the domestically-oriented manufacturing sector where most small productive enterprises are located. One of the most significant findings of the study in this regard is the survival of many migrant-linked industrial firms by selling part of their production abroad through informal channels. In a sense, these firms have created their own "export promotion" policy.

Such spontaneous initiatives should be brought above board and encouraged. The repatriation of migrant financial and human capital and its reorientation toward productive activities can be significantly accelerated by extending to them the same regime of incentives applied to foreign firms in the EPZs. In addition, the government's council for export promotion should create a specialized agency to inform small industrialists of changing patterns of demand abroad and to help market their products.[26]

In synthesis, the best hopes that the Dominican government has to actualize the potential of past migration for future economic development consists of working *through* the structure and the logic of the immigrant community rather than against them. The surprising achievements of Dominican immigrants, both in the United States and after return, despite the absence of official protection, should inspire policies that build on their ingenuity and resources. Unfortunately, governments have been so far more adept at policing and controlling than at supporting popular economic initiatives. This is, in part, the reason for recommending the private channelling of U.S. credit programs in support of small enterprise development. However, should authorities be willing to adopt a more flexible strategy, firms initiated with migrant capital and know-how can be expected to play a significant role in the success of the new export-oriented model of development.

NOTES

1. George J. Borjas, "Economic Theory and International Migration," *International Migration Review,* vol. 23, no. 3, 1989, pp. 457–485.

2. Aristide Zolberg, "The Next Waves: Migration Theory for a Changing World," *International Migration Review,* vol. 23, no. 3, 1989, pp. 403–430.

3. Douglas S. Massey, Rafael Alarcón, Jorge Durand and Humberto Gonzalez, *Return to Aztlán: The Social Process of International Migration from Western Mexico* (Berkeley and Los Angeles: University of California Press, 1987); Alejandro Portes and Alex Stepick, "Unwelcome Immigrants: The Labor Market Experiences of 1980 Mariel and Haitian Refugees in South Florida," *American Sociological Review,* vol. 50, 1985, pp. 493–514.

4. W. R. Böhning, *Studies in International Labour Migration* (London: Macmillan, 1984); Mario Barrera, *Race and Class in the Southwest: A Theory of Racial Inequality* (Notre Dame, IN: Notre Dame University Press, 1980); Robert L. Bach, "Mexican Immigration and the American State," *International Migration Review,* vol. 12, 1978, pp. 536–558.

5. Manuel Castells, "High Technology, Economic Policies and World Development," BRIE Working Paper (University of California-Berkeley, May 1986); Stephen Castles, "The Guest-Workers in Western Europe: An Obituary," *International Migration Review,* vol. 20, 1986, pp. 761–778; Alejandro Portes, "Toward a Structural Analysis of Illegal (Undocumented) Immigration, *International Migration Review,* vol. 12, 1978, pp. 469–484.

6. Mark Granovetter, "Economic Action and Social Structure: The Problem of Embeddedness," *American Journal of Sociology,* vol. 91, no. 3, 1985, pp. 481–510.

7. Granovetter, "Economic Action"; Robert G. Eccles and Harrison C. White, "Price and Authority in Inter-Profit Center Transactions," *American Journal of Sociology,* vol. 94, Supplement, 1988, pp. 17–51.

8. James S. Coleman, "Social Capital in the Creation of Human Capital," *American Journal of Sociology,* vol. 94, Supplement, 1988, pp. 95–120.

9. Oliver E. Williamson, *The Economic Institutions of Capitalism* (New York: Free Press, 1985).

10. Ina R. Dinnerman, "Patterns of Adaptation among Households of U.S.-Bound Migrants from Michoacan, Mexico," *International Migration Review,* vol. 12, 1979, pp. 485–501; Massey, Alarcón, Durand and Gonzalez, *Return to Aztlán;* Sherri Grasmuck and Patricia Pessar, *Between Two Islands: Dominican International Migration* (Berkeley: University of California Press, 1990); Alejandro Portes and Rúben G. Rumbaut, *Immigrant America: A Portrait* (Berkeley: University of California Press, 1990), Ch. 3; Ivan Light and Edna Bonacich, *Immigrant Entrepreneurs: Koreans in Los Angeles 1965–1982* (Berkeley and Los Angeles: University of California Press, 1988).

11. An exception is the direct illegal flow through a third country. The most com-

mon route is via Puerto Rico. In this case, migrants cross the Mona Passage aboard small boats or "yolas" and disembark surreptitiously on the Puerto Rican coast. Many illegal Dominicans stay on this island, but those with social contacts and greater resources fly to New York. Because Puerto Rico is part of the United States, no immigration formalities need to be observed. See Jorge Duany, "Dominican Immigrants in the Puerto Rican Labor Market," Paper presented at the Seminar on Informal Sector and Social Movements in the Caribbean, FLACSO, Social Science Research Council (Santo Domingo, DR, January 1990).

12. Robert Warren, "Datos sobre la Legalización y Otra Información Estadística Acerca de la Inmigración Dominicana a los Estados Unidos," Fundación Friedrich Ebert (Santo Domingo, DR, 1989).

13. The latest official figure available of total legal and illegal Dominican immigrants in the United States is 169,147 for 1980. See U.S. Bureau of the Census, *1980 Census of the Population*, (Washington, DC: U.S. Bureau of Census, 1984: Table 1). A wide range of "guesstimates," ranging from 300,000 up to one million can be found in the literature.

14. U.S. Bureau of the Census, *1980 Census.*

15. U.S. Immigration and Naturalization Service, *Statistical Yearbook of the Immigration and Naturalization Service, 1989* (Washington, DC: U.S. Government Printing Office, 1989), Tables 5, 7.

16. Franc Moya Pons, "Informe Preliminar de la Encuesta de Migración a los Estados Unidos," *Forum*, vol. 27, 1988, pp. 15–31; Francisco Báez and Francisco D'Oleo, *La Emigración de Dominicanos a Estados Unidos: Determinantes Socio-Económicos y Consecuencias* (Santo Domingo, DR: Editora Taller, 1986).

17. Fundacion Economia y Desarollo, *Impacto del Sector Privado en la Economia Dominicana* (Santo Domingo: Accion Empresarial, 1989); Banco Central de la Republica Dominicana, *Boletin Mensual*, vol. 41, no. 10, October 1988.

18. A number of studies have portrayed the U.S. secondary labor market as composed of small and medium-sized enterprises with labor-intensive systems of production and operations limited to local or regional markets. To survive fierce competition, these firms keep salaries low and labor conditions harsh. Immigrant workers, in particular illegal ones, constitute an ideal labor pool for the secondary market because of the vulnerability built in their tenuous legal status. See Richard Edwards, *Contested Terrain: The Transformation of the Workplace in the Twentieth Century* (New York: Harper Torchbook, 1979); Peter B. Doeringer, "Gender, Skill, and the Dynamics of Women's Employment: Comment," Conference, "Gender in the Work Place" (The Brookings Institution, November 1984); Alejandro Portes and Robert L. Bach, *Latin Journey: Cuban and Mexican Immigrants in the United States* (Berkeley: University of California Press, 1985), Chps. 1 and 7.

19. Alex Stepick, "Miami's Two Informal Sectors," in *The Informal Economy: Studies in Advanced and Less Developed Countries*, (eds.) Alejandro Portes, Manuel Castells and Lauren Benton (Baltimore: The Johns Hopkins University Press, 1989), pp. 111–131; Vittorio Capecchi, "The Informal Economy and the Development of Flexible Specialization in Emilia-Romagna," in *The Informal Economy: Studies in Ad-*

vanced and Less Developed Countries, (eds.) Alejandro Portes, Manuel Castells and Lauren Benton (Baltimore: The Johns Hopkins University Press, 1989), pp. 189–215; Alejandro Portes, "The Social Origins of the Cuban Enclave Economy of Miami," *Sociological Perspectives,* vol. 30, 1987, pp. 340–372; Ivan Light, "Immigrant and Ethnic Enterprise in North America," *Ethnic and Racial Studies,* vol. 7, 1984, pp. 195–216.

20. The average monthly salary in industries sampled in Santo Domingo is DR $521 (US $83), very close to the national minimum wage of DR $500 in 1989; in Santiago, average industrial salaries are significantly higher (US $117). The difference between both cities is a reflection of variations in their respective labor markets created by the presence of export production zones (EPZ). In Santiago, small owners of industrial shops blame the nearby EPZ for the higher salaries that they must pay, as well as for the scarcity of skilled labor. Because of the absence of EPZs and a larger reserve of workers, lower wages can be paid in Santo Domingo where costs of living are actually higher.

21. The arithmetic mean is sensitive to extreme values, while the median is not. The higher mean value, in this case, indicates the "pull" of some disproportionately high transfers.

22. Dominican-based *financieras,* in turn, send their representatives to New York to sell properties or collect dollars to be lent in the Dominican Republic. Such operations generally pass unnoticed by official regulators. In the case of small finance firms, it is the owner or general manager who travels. Normally, transactions are made through family or social connections and are finalized in New York.

23. Saskia Sassen-Koob, "The New Labor Demand in Global Cities," in *Cities in Transformation: Class, Capital, and the State,* (ed.) Michael Peter Smith (Beverly Hills: Sage Publications, 1984), pp. 139–171.

24. Alex Stepick, *Haitian Refugees in the U.S.* (London: Minority Rights Group Ltd., Report No. 56, 1986); Terry A. Repak, "And They Come on Behalf of Their Children: Central American Families in Washington, D.C.," Conference on Migration (The U.S. Department of Labor, September 1988); Edelberto Torres-Rivas, "Report on the Conditions of Central American Refugees and Migrants," Center for Immigration Policy and Refugee Assistance, Georgetown University (Washington, DC, 1985); Segundo Montes-Mozo and Juan José García V., *Salvadoran Migration to the United States: An Exploratory Study* (Washington, DC: Center for Immigration Policy and Refugee Assistance, Georgetown University, 1988).

25. This proposed measure would be different from the "certidolar," which was a certificate of deposit redeemable in dollars, guaranteed by the Dominican Mortgaging Bank.

26. Several highly successful export economies, such as those of Hong Kong and Central Italy, have been created on the basis of cooperative arrangements between government agencies and networks of small entrepreneurs. Government agencies have provided support in the form of training programs, subsidized credit, and marketing facilities. Capecchi, "The Informal Economy"; Manuel Castells, "Small Business in a World Economy: The Hong Kong Model, Myth and Reality," in *The*

Urban Informal Sector: Recent Trends in Research and Theory," Conference proceedings, Department of Sociology, The Johns Hopkins University (Baltimore, MD, 1984), pp. 161–223, Mimeo; U. Sit, S. Wong and T.S. Kiang, "Small Scale Industry in a Laissez-Faire Economy," Working Paper, Centre for Asian Studies, University of Hong Kong (Hong Kong, 1979), Mimeo.

5

Small-Scale Industry and International Migration in Guadalajara, Mexico

Agustín Escobar Latapí
and María de la O Martínez Castellanos

I. INTRODUCTION

In this paper, we summarize the results of our research on small-scale industry and international migration from Guadalajara, Mexico, and offer policy recommendations for diminishing the kind of international labor migration that is linked to small-scale industry.

Mexican industry is changing rapidly. This may be seen as both an internal transformation—in organization, technology and productivity—and an external transformation—in industry's relationships with capital and commodity markets both inside and outside Mexico. Large-scale industry is strengthening its ties with the international economy and has achieved some success in defining more flexible relationships with its markets and labor force. One aspect of this is the growth of *maquiladoras,* which freely import inputs and export partially or completely finished products. Another facet of the same phenomenon is the growing export activity of multinationals located in Mexico that previously sold to the internal market. General Motors, for example, is the second-largest exporter, after PEMEX (Petroleos Mexicanos), the state-owned oil company.

There is considerable doubt about the capacity of small-scale industry to adapt to new economic conditions in Mexico. Alba and Roberts, for example, report that small industrialists were the most skeptical when asked whether the Mexican economy would derive significant benefits from the country's abrupt signing of GATT (General Agreement on Tariffs and Trade) and the corresponding trade liberalization.[1]

Small-scale industry, that is industry that employs 25 or fewer workers, has become the center of growing interest during the last seven years. Its role as employer of a very significant part of the work force has been stressed, and its scanty contribution to GDP has been the reason for many development policies aimed at improving productivity. There are "soft" financing arrangements especially tailored for small scale industry and parts of it are considered the most interesting segment of the informal sector since, unlike street traders and beggars, small-scale industrialists could make a significant contribution to the economy. The sector has, at times, had contradictory ties with the state and has been the focus of considerable debate, since it is viewed as consistently avoiding most taxes and disobeying labor and sanitation laws.

Last, the political, social and personal characteristics of small entrepreneurs must also be considered. They have been studied to see how they compare to traditional capitalist entrepreneurial models. They are feared because of the strong identity they have with their employees. Small-scale entrepreneurs belong to the same social group as their employees, forming a much larger group than large-scale industrialists. Their potential influence on their workers and their communities could be crucial during elections, or when urban communities make specific demands on authorities.

According to the researcher's theoretical bent, this growing interest is naturally biased. Some see small-scale industries and cottage industries as the darkest side of capitalism. Small-scale entrepreneurs pay wages below subsistence levels and extensively exploit labor since capital is often lacking in these units.[2] Other researchers, however, state that this type of organization, or at least segments of it, is a fundamentally cooperative institution created in neighborhoods. It operates on the basis of shared culture and rewards those working in it with incomes higher than those earned by large-scale industrial employees.[3] Research has systematically established that certain types of small-scale industrial workers earn more than their formal counterparts, whether compared by family status,[4] by skill level[5] or by other criteria.

The conception of small-scale industry is not, however, totally determined by the researcher's political leanings. Liberal thinking has praised the entrepreneurial spirit of small-scale industrialists at the same time as it has proposed measures that make it harder for them to exist.[6] The left has also deplored the exploitation of workers, particularly females in home workshops, but it has organized small-scale shops in many parts of Latin America. Some social scientists, such as Friedmann and Salguero, have even stated that the seed of a new social order in the region lies in some of these small economic units.

Whatever the approach, however, there is agreement concerning the importance of employment in small-scale industry in Mexico. The estimate of the number employed depends on the choice of a particular threshold. For example, according to the *Eleventh Industrial Census, 1981*,[7] industries employing fewer than 50 workers accounted for 17.2 percent of the total manufacturing work force in Jalisco, but 43.8 percent of all manufacturing establishments in the state. Other estimates, based on population rather than industrial surveys, estimate the work force in small-scale industry at close to 35 percent.[8] The discrepancy between population and industrial censuses is, therefore, about 2:1; in the case of garment workshops, however, the population census reported five times more workers than the industrial census because most of the work in this industry is carried out in small, unregistered shops or by females in home workshops. This means that policies affecting small-scale industries are crucial for urban employment in general.

Employment and self-employment in small industries have been suggested as primary remedies to stem growing international migration of mostly Mexican workers to U.S. destinations.[9] It is of paramount importance to discern the particular logic of these enterprises and the relationships that exist between them and international migration and remittances. In El Salvador, for example, migrants' remittances are indispensable for creating and keeping alive these small establishments. In other countries, the skills and attitudes learned by migrants lead to the creation of small-scale enterprises based on techniques that may not require large capital outlays but that, nevertheless, are innovative and a significant source of employment in the country of origin.

"Small" industry may mean quite different things in different contexts. Small industry in Guadalajara is made up of two main organizational types: crafts units and microenterprises. In crafts units, the owner works side-by-side with his or her workers, and there is little social difference between them. In microenterprises, the owner does not do manual work and may not be familiar with the skills involved; there is a clear social and hierarchical difference between owner and employee.

Other differences follow from this. First, in crafts units, the number of workers is smaller because supervision has to be combined with the performance of manual work and because craft-type skills do not allow much partitioning. One usually finds the owner, two or three skilled craftworkers and three or four apprentices. Second, per capita investment is usually lower. And, third, the production area can be a part of the owner's house. These differences lead to others that have to do with migration, and that will be dealt with later.

This report is based on surveys of the Guadalajara manual labor market in 1982, 1985, 1987 and 1989, and on case studies of small enterprises first started in 1982. Some persons were repeatedly interviewed until 1989, and 15 case studies were started in this year. The worker surveys carried out in 1982, 1985 and 1987 provided a model of the local and regional operative-level market and served to assess the impact of the crisis on labor and industry. The 1989 survey was carried out specifically to explore the relevance of international migration to small-scale industrial workers. A number of sections in all the surveys remained identical from 1982 to 1987, so that data on wages, work and migration histories and work attitudes are comparable throughout the period. The 1989 survey used the same life history schedule as the others, but approached migration in considerably more detail; however, only a few migrant workers were detected in 1989. The 1982 survey detected 253 international migrants (of whom 223 were labor migrants), and it is, therefore, one that allows finer comparisons between migrant and nonmigrant workers.

Since international migration has been a large-scale phenomenon since well before the economic crisis, we make intensive use of all the surveys and all the case studies. The surveys were not identical in their target populations. The first was aimed at the operative labor market in general, but excluded the private service sector. In the second, we interviewed only workers in informal workshops, that is to say, workshops where the owners did manual work, were not affiliated with a chamber of industry and did not pay taxes. For comparative purposes, the 1987 survey included 302 workers in small-scale workshops and in large factories, and the 1989 survey was applied only to workers in the shops studied that year. This means that the proportion of women is smaller in the first survey than in the others. We will distinguish these differences when appropriate.

The case studies that we have followed since 1982 have allowed us to explore the ways in which these small economic units have responded to the present crisis, what their needs were before and what they are likely to become if economic growth were to resume in the near future.

The first section of this report establishes the importance of small-scale industry in Guadalajara and its responses to the crisis. The second section deals with the shop owners, their migration experiences, the relationship between international migration and the small businesses, and the main characteristics of the small businesses. The third section discusses the work force and migration. In the fourth section, we summarize our findings and make two suggestions.

II. SMALL-SCALE INDUSTRY IN GUADALAJARA

In Mexico City and Monterrey, industrial development may be explained in terms of the leadership exerted by key firms and industries, which led to the establishment of other businesses and a specific type of industrial structure. The large scale of the leading industries and the concentration of capital they entail account for the type of relationship established between local industrialists and government. In both Mexico City and Monterrey, a very small group of large-scale industrialists exerts a determining influence on the rest of industry and on the formulation of economic and industrial policies.

In Guadalajara, on the other hand, industrialists as a group have historically been dispersed, firms tend to be small and they have not been greatly influenced by a single firm or group of enterprises. In his book on elites and economic development, Walton[10] shows the dispersion, lack of consensus and weak links of Tapatío (Guadalajaran) industrialists when compared to those in Medellín, Colombia, and Monterrey. There are some cases of considerable industrial concentration, but even the largest shoe-producing firm in Guadalajara, with 8,000 employees accounts for less than half of local production in that branch of the economy. The branches that show highest average concentration are cement, basic metals and some branches of the food industry. These have not, however, been the basis for Guadalajara's industrialization, which was propelled in the nineteenth century by the textile industry and, in the present, by shoe and clothing manufacture.

Will small-scale industries remain as important in Guadalajara and other cities? What will their needs and problems be? To answer these questions, it is instructive to explain how they have behaved during the present crisis. The U.N. Economic Commission for Latin America and the Caribbean reports that employment in large-scale economic units in Mexico (industrial or otherwise) has shrunk 1 percent in absolute terms since 1980.[11] Informal employment, on the other hand, has increased 80 percent in absolute terms. We have carried out research on the responses of small-scale workshops to the crisis and it shows that during the crisis, small-scale industry has undergone the following macroeconomic changes.[12]

1) Wage levels have dropped in real terms by about 50 percent in the economy as a whole. Wages in small-scale enterprises have dropped even more drastically. (In large-scale industries, men's wages fell 30 to 45 percent, and women's 40 to 55 percent from 1982 to 1987. In our surveys, wages in small-scale industries have dropped 50 percent for men and 60 percent for women. This should give small industrialists an advantage over large-scale industries, since their prices should be lower than those of large enterprises.
2) Investment in productive capital has fallen 50 percent in Mexico.[13] Small-scale enterprises, homeworkers and workshops have invested even less than large industries. This means that the productivity gap between large and small establishments has widened. Alonso[14] found that, in the garment workshops he studied in Ciudad Netzahualcoyotl (a part of Mexico City), real investment per worker dropped significantly after 1982 and especially after 1985, when the earthquake pushed considerable work in this industry away from the central areas of the city. The work force had expanded significantly without new capital investments and this had also pushed piece rates down considerably. In Guadalajara, we also found very little new machinery after 1982.
3) The internal market has shrunk, particularly for goods that used to be within reach of wage-earners. From 1981 to 1987, the construction of dwellings, car production and the production of intermediate consumer goods and household appliances dropped. The market for small-scale industries has, therefore, become smaller and more competitive, and prices have been cut in real terms. While small enterprises used to have some cash reserves, which allowed them to ride out momentary sale problems and to act independently of *acaparadores* (large-scale merchants), in 1986 and 1987 they had expended these reserves and were forced to sell to these *acaparadores* on unfavorable terms. We believe market-related problems and the increasing demand for jobs explain the fall in investment and productivity levels.
4) Large-scale industries had to become more flexible with regard to both labor and market expansion and diminution, as conditions

changed. Rather than investing in expensive equipment, many enterprises have opted to subcontract more. This has led to a search for small, *maquila* shops and an enlargement of the niche they occupy in the local economy.

5) Small industries faced this paradoxical situation in 1987. Their bargaining power had improved *vis à vis* workers, but the crisis and its economic changes have significantly worsened their productivity levels and their position with large-scale merchants or industrialists. They have responded by complying less with tax regulations and other forms of state intervention. In 1982, most of the workshops we studied had some sort of routine, day-to-day relationship with one or more state agencies, even if they were not completely "legal." Since 1982, several of the shops studied have carried out fictional "closures," which served to lower their tax and regulation-related overhead. It was hard for them to remain completely clandestine, but it was evident to us that this was a systematic practice that allowed them to avoid these costs until they were found out and had to register again.
6) There was a tendency toward the peripheralization of shops and small-scale production. Many workshops left Guadalajara and opened in smaller towns and cities in western Mexico. The expansion of outputting networks also was directed mostly away from Guadalajara. By 1989, the ties between *maquileros* (the organizers of domestic outwork) and Guadalajara's hinterland had grown enormously. Thus, small-scale producers had access to a vast labor pool, consisting mostly of women, children and the elderly. These workers were classified as unskilled labor and, therefore, earned lower wages. In these small towns, it was much easier to deal with government agencies since there was little or no supervision of their operations.
7) Workshops were emphasizing their familial characters, that is to say, the importance of trust relationships. We think this has three explanations. First, in a situation of scarce jobs, shop owners can employ their own family or jobless relatives. Second, trust relations diminish the workers' propensity to sue employers and to disclose the existence of the shop. Third, trust relations allow owners to keep all their family's wages or control them. The familial character of the shops has an impact on the distribution of different wage levels. After 1982, if we control for skill, the male children of the owners earned more than non-relatives.

This account sheds light on the internal reorganization of the shops during the crisis. It does not, however, allow an estimate of the relative growth/diminution of small-scale employment. Census data confirm that employment and self-employment in small-scale economic units in general have grown as a proportion of total employment. But a large part of this increase has taken place in the service sector. Concerning manufacturing industry, the *Eleventh Industrial Census 1981*[15] reports that the average number of workers per firm in 1981 was 17.1 in Jalisco; in 1986, the preliminary results of the economic census[16] reported an average of 14.9. The drop indicates that, in general terms, small industries have become more important. This is a rough approximation, since in many smaller *municipios*, a process of concentration has taken place. However, because Guadalajara by far outstrips any other industrial location in Jalisco (73.8 percent of all of Jalisco's industries operate in the city), it is a valid approximation.

As explained before, this does not mean that small industries are experiencing a boom; rather, a combination of factors has pushed large firms to stop expanding, many individuals (especially secondary earners) have entered the labor market and large firms are sub-contracting. This has led to an expansion in the small-scale sector, which is financially weaker than ever. Thus, growth in the importance of this sector has to be qualified.

In conclusion, specific policies aimed at improving the productivity and financial situation of small enterprises may be a very sensible and timely proposition, since the sector seems to be expanding, but under very difficult conditions.

III. SMALL INDUSTRIALISTS, MIGRATION AND THEIR FIRMS

In this section, we seek to establish to what extent and in what ways small-scale industrialists have benefitted from international migration. This relationship can be studied from different perspectives, but, first, it is necessary to establish whether small-scale industrialists actually form part of the migration flow in any significant way. According to the largest survey ever carried out among Jalisco industrialists, 16.6 percent of all small-scale entrepreneurs—those employing up to 25 workers and selling up to 10 million pesos per year in 1981 (under $400,000)—worked in the United States, a proportion far higher than that found among medium- and large-scale industrialists (fewer than ten percent).[17]

We believe this is sufficiently significant to claim that a relationship does exist between small-scale industry and international migration, albeit not on the scale reported for other cities or countries. But little insight is to be gained into the nature of this relationship from a large-scale survey. To explore this in detail, we must understand individual cases and define from their examination what may be significant for the analysis.

The most obvious case of the influence of migration on small-scale industry is when a small industry or workshop is set up, mechanized or reorganized, thanks to money earned in the United States. Most research on migration agrees that most of the money earned in the United States is devoted to non-productive purposes, such as family survival, the construction, purchase or enlargement of a house, education and medical treatment. But there is a relatively important amount devoted to productive purposes as well. Depending on the framework and the type of questions asked, usually under ten percent of respondents state that their savings or remittances are mainly devoted to production. This may include, in small towns, the purchase of land, vehicles, cattle, tractors or financing the season's crops. In larger towns, they are used to buy machinery, raw materials, vehicles and so on. Guadalajara and, to a certain extent, the rest of western Mexico, are particularly suitable, we think, for this sort of relationship, since they are characterized by small-scale industry to a much larger extent than is Monterrey or Mexico City. This relationship can easily be established on the basis of interviews.

Second, migrants may learn specific skills or how to handle special machines, so that when they return they may use these abilities to improve their position in a small firm. This assumption can be explored by determining the occupations of the migrants in the United States and what they have done since they returned and then exploring any apparent coincidences.

There are contradictory points of view on this subject. To some, the skill level of Mexican and Central American migrants' jobs in the United States is very low, since they perform the most strenuous, least-skilled tasks of the host society. However, there is a considerable degree of variety in the jobs these migrants do, and some of these tasks in fact represent new skills. In Morelos and the Valle de Mezquital (in the State of Hidalgo), it is widely acknowledged that tomato cultivation techniques have changed, thanks to the skills brought back by braceros. The same is true of lentil cultivation in Michoacán and chicken raising in Los Altos de Jalisco. This phenomenon has been of extreme importance for Mexico since the Bracero program. Quoting a study on Mexican cotton production, Hancock says: "Another beneficial aspect of the bracero program is seen in the new skills and cultural practices which the Mexicans learn in the United States. United States Department of Agriculture specialists say that the technical skills that braceros brought back to Mexico rank with any single other factor in the increase in cotton production."[18]

This connection should not be over-emphasized, however. The social and technological differences between the two countries may make technological and skill transference difficult. Building techniques, for example, are so distinct that an individual is quite incapable of introducing significant changes. In the construction industry, change has been extremely gradual, and masons' control over the process has militated against rapid increases in productivity, even though this industry employs an above-average percentage of international migrants. A few American-style houses can be spotted in migrant towns and in some sectors of Guadalajara, but they are self-built and have not had an impact on the market.

Technology and skill transfers should not be seen as a manufacturing-only phenomenon. In both countries, the services employ a larger part of the work force than manufacturing. In the United States, the service sector is relatively more labor-intensive than manufacturing, which should make it easier for migrants to bring back the skills and the capital to put the skill to work in the country of origin. Mexican migrants are very significant in hotels, restaurants, domestic service, repair shops and cleaning and maintenance activities. The skills learned in these types of jobs can easily be transferred, given the small scale of the firms and the capital necessary.

But, the very fact that the service sector is labor-intensive also means that most of these skills are not noteworthy innovations in Mexico. What we have found concerning skill transfer in this sector is that it is far more common for Mexican migrants to enter these occupations in the United States if they already possess the basic skills. On the other hand, the best-paid occupations in the service sector in the United States (discounting those involving higher education) usually require a good command of English and are beyond the reach of first-time migrants for at least a few years. Hispanics in these positions usually stay for a long period or are second-generation migrants who are not prone to return to Mexico and bring these skills back. Often, too, the truly innovative skills in this area occur in large-scale organizations and are difficult to copy if the returned migrant cannot exert authority over an organization.

The most significant skills, therefore, remain those in production. They are interesting because they might change the way in which small-scale industries and shops operate. If there is a medium- or long-term productivity improvement, then migration may be making a much more significant contribution to the Mexican economy than remittance estimates might seem to indicate.

Third, migration to the United States can be conceived of as disruption of the norms, attitudes and symbols of a traditional culture. Workers and peasants who migrate could learn new ways to organize their own work and that of others. From this point of view, specific skills are not important. If the cultural "backwardness" of Mexican workers and peasants can be broken by migration, then they can be expected to sow the seeds of change on their return and to participate actively in social, economic and public transformation. This aspect of the influence of migration on Mexican small-scale industry is undoubtedly the most difficult to evaluate. For researchers to do this, entrepreneurs must speak fairly freely about the meaning of migration to them, about their state of mind and their attitudes before and after the experience. Anthropological case studies like the ones we conducted are probably the best way to bring this out.

Initially, we thought we would prove this "culture breaking" concept completely wrong. What happened instead is that we had to give it a small amount of credit. Migration was a very important, watershed experience for several of our interviewees, and two (of our six migrant entrepreneurs) definitely framed the lessons they learned from migrating in these terms. We still believe, however, that this approach is wrong and can be very misleading if it is privileged above others in analyses of migration because it excessively simplifies the cultures and attitudes of the populations living on both sides of the border. The United States possesses diverse cultures (some of them quite traditional) and Mexico is a changing, heterogeneous society (some of it very modern).

This approach, in our opinion, comes from studies that view Mexican and other peasants as "traditional." According to this view, peasant culture contains very significant barriers to modernization and change.[19] As a consequence of the peasants' lack of control over their work and environment, and the prevalence of community over individual interests, peasant culture is fatalistic, superstitious and uninnovative. Individual acquisition of wealth is seen as a threat because wealth is limited. What one gains, another loses.[20] Within this perspective, one could interpret migration as a welcome disrupting force.

There is a growing amount of literature on the fatalistic and superstitious attitudes of workers, particularly female workers in advanced countries. Purcell, for example, studied the interest of British General Electric women workers in astrology and the frequency of their visits to fortune-tellers as a sign of their desire to exert some sort of control over their lives.[21] This new literature explains the attitudes of these groups in the same terms used from 1945 until 1970 to explain the "traditional" values of peasants and other Third World groups. What the newer literature suggests to students of migration and its effects on economic change is that, paradoxically, a Mexican peasant from one of the few remaining isolated, traditional communities might find that his or her deep-seated notions of submission to an authoritarian paternalistic figure and fatalistic approach to life are quite well suited to the role he or she is called on to play in a modern, rational—entrepreneurial—society.

This example is not meant to stereotype the situation of Mexican migrants in the United States, a substantial number of whom have achieved positions of some authority and shown innovative qualities. Rather, we wish to show that reducing the interplay of forces and cultures involved in migration to the clash of "modern" versus "traditional" not only misrepresents the nature of both societies, but also misses most of the substance of the impact of migration on socioeconomic changes and entrepreneurial activities.

Main Characteristics of the Migrant Entrepreneurs

We shall briefly describe the impact of migration on our respondents and their firms. These results do not necessarily reflect the respondents' opinions but, rather, our own conclusions after reading the case studies. Of 19 case studies, we found six in which the owner had worked in the United States, and another two in which relatives' remittances were important in the creation and running of the shop. The roles played by international migration in the lives of our respondents and in the creation and operation of their firms is evident in Table 1. The table is not meant to extract any major statistically sound statement, but to summarize the characteristics of migration for the cases studied.

Case #1 owns a bakery and builds houses on speculation; case #3 owns a small shoe manufacturing factory employing 24 workers; case #4 owns a shop manufacturing "typical" embroidered dresses; case #5 is a successful artistic potter; case #13 barely survives as a self-employed manufacturer of coin purses and derives extra income from helping his brothers sell fresh vegetables at several local itinerant street markets (*tianguis*). Case #15 manufactures eyeglass cases. There were two other cases who profited from relatives' remittances, either as loans or as investments.

The variables used in the table are those discussed in the preceding paragraphs, plus "market," which appeared as significant in two cases (#4 and #5). All variables range rather arbitrarily from 0 to 1. For "Money", the highest value means that the firm was established thanks to substantial resources brought or sent by the migrant from the United States. Zero in this variable means that no savings or remittances were produced, or that they were used for non-productive ends. Case #1 sold a house he owned in Los Angeles and brought substantial savings back to Mexico. Case #5 brought savings and a small electric furnace, but he already had most of what he needed for his shop. Case #13 brought back some savings, which he used to buy indispensable machines, but later he sold his pick-up truck and his house and moved to a smaller one to be able to buy larger quantities of raw materials. Case #15 brought back $20,000, which sufficed to buy what he needed to be self-financing.

"Skills" is similarly used. This kind of influence proved less important than we thought because most of our migrant entrepreneurs already possessed the skills and knew the kind of business they wanted to set up on their return. Case #1, the baker, learned his craft in the United States. Case #5, the potter, learned a few techniques in the United States, but says he does not use them frequently. The rest learned their skills or trades in Mexico, before or after their trip.

"Risk" refers to the impact of migration on changing the migrant's attitude toward innovation and risk. This we evaluated by looking at the mi-

TABLE 1
INFLUENCE OF MIGRATION ON ENTREPRENEURS AND THEIR FIRMS
VARIABLE

Case #	Money	Skills	Risk	Market	Wish to Return to U.S.
1	1.0	1.0	1.0	0.0	0.2
3	0.0	0.0	0.5	0.0	0.0
4	0.0	0.0	0.0	0.2	0.8
5	0.5	0.3	0.0	0.8	0.0
13	0.6	0.0	0.0	0.0	0.2
15	1.0	0.0	0.2	0.0	0.0

Source: Direct investigation.

grants' activities before migrating, comparing them with their activities after their return, and examining what they said about the significance of migration for their general outlook on life and their work. We think this is a fairly subjective variable, both from our point of view and that of the interviewees, since it depends mainly on introspection and on the specific conditions faced by the migrant before and after migration. Case #1 had not attempted anything significant before migrating and he showed an inclination toward risk on his return, when he invested his savings, against general consensus (in real estate), which proved extremely timely and successful. He also toyed with the idea of becoming a Baptist, but abandoned it for fear of social rejection. Case #3 says the basic lesson of his two stays in the United States was, "If you put your mind to it, and work extremely hard, it is possible to succeed, but it is far easier to succeed in Mexico than in the United States, where they discriminate against you." Case #15 says something similar, but he knew exactly what he wanted to do upon his return and did it. He had already tried his luck (and risked his money) at many different things before he left Mexico.

"Market" refers to those cases in which contacts made in the United States have become significant buyers for the small enterprise. As can be seen, only two cases have derived this benefit from migration. In one, the buyers were significant for the firm for a time, then stopped buying. The potter, on the other hand, still sells to U.S. buyers, although they do not represent his main clients (he sells most of his production at tourist spots in Mexico and most of his exports go to Italy). We included this variable because, although it is not important for most cases, most of the interviewees felt that exporting would be one solution to their market problems. Several have tried, but only the potter (a craftsman rather than a small industrialist) was successfully exporting at the time of the interviews. In spite of the reduced importance of the United States as a market for our cases, two of them actually went to the United States, principally to secure contacts and to meet buyers.

All of our migrant entrepreneurs but one behaved as "target" migrants; that is, their trip to work in the United States was dictated by their desire to save a fairly definite amount of money. The one case deviation is case #1, the baker, who went to the United States to "try his luck" (he had a very vague idea of what to migrate for), became a "settled" migrant there, and returned to Mexico only for medical reasons (paradoxically, he is the most successful of all our case studies).[22] Case #3 wanted to save money in the United States to become independent. He later flirted with the idea of staying there when they offered him a job as a journalist in Chicago, but he couldn't stand the weather and returned. On his second attempt (this time in Los Angeles), he also worked as a journalist but was laid off when management changed. He tried to move up the job hierarchy at a large hotel, but failed; finally, he decided to quit and work his way up in Mexico. He returned with no savings and has failed and rebuilt his firm several times since.

Case #4, who manufactures embroidered dresses, went to the United States long after her shop had been established to try to re-establish old contacts and to make new ones. From this point of view, her trip was a failure: her old buyers wanted to buy at lower rates, and new contacts proved extremely demanding. In order to keep looking, she secured a temporary job at a retirement home, where she was cheated, so she had to stay longer to save enough money to return home. She returned penniless. Strangely enough, in spite of her sour experience, she longs to set up a "typical Mexican" garment store somewhere in the U.S. Southwest.

Case #5 already possessed most of the skills of his craft when he went to the United States. He had gone to Italy to study pottery before that. He wanted to learn new skills and save money. He did learn a few skills and saved some money, but living in the United States proved so comfortable that he and his wife decided to stay longer. They returned later than planned, with savings. He does not want to go back because he thinks American potters are neither technically the best nor the most artistic; he prefers to keep in touch with European trends.

Case #13 worked in Guadalajara at a factory manufacturing ladies' purses, where he learned all the skills involved. He went to the United States in order to save enough to be able to set up his own shop. He stayed for almost two years. When he finally was able to save money, he was called back to Mexico because his father was dying. He says he wouldn't go back to the United States because he wants to be close to his family.

Case #15 already possessed the skills necessary to manufacture eyeglass cases when he left and was determined to sell to the clients of the firm where he had learned these skills (he actually copied the list of clients and made time to meet them before going to the United States). In Chicago, he managed a small restaurant, where they housed and fed him. He accumulated substantial savings and his wife saved most of his remittance money. When he came back, he had amassed enough to set up his very successful business.

As has been reported in many other studies, it is impossible to tell, before the migrant dies or returns, exactly what kind of migration is taking place. Decisions are contingent, never definitive. Also, migrants tend to justify and rationalize their experience much as workers rationalize their job satisfaction. Disastrous experiences, such as those of cases #3 and #4, are viewed by the migrants as "valuable lessons." Nevertheless, it is important to note that most of our migrant entrepreneurs went to the United States to save money to be able to return home and set up a business. This incentive to migrate could be replaced by local financing, which has been nearly nonexistent for the last eight years and which has never truly reached the popular sectors in Mexican society. Target migration is very important in Guadalajara, both for setting up small businesses and for making key investments during the life cycle (marriage, purchasing a house).[23] Productive credit, specifically, can counteract this phenomenon and promote local economic growth.

One other thing about our migrant entrepreneurs is that they do not seem to have become migration "addicts." Most stressed that they did not wish to return to the United States. Reasons abounded, but drugs, dangerous neighborhoods and discrimination (sometimes associated with what they feel is an unjust or corrupt police force) were at the top of the list.

Of our six migrant entrepreneurs, half (the baker, the manufacturer of eyeglass cases and the potter) had no trouble crossing the border, finding a job and saving. The others had a rough time for most of their stay. The baker-builder said, during one of the interviews, that he was tempted to return to the United States, but has remained in Guadalajara. It must be noted that he had obtained legal residence in the United States and that his children are American citizens. Also, he is sufficiently affluent to buy a house in a good American neighborhood, away from the *barrio*. Case #13 does not want to return to the United States, but admits it would probably solve his problems. Of the others, only the manufacturer of embroidered dresses wishes to return to the United States to stay a long time—this in spite of her unpleasant experience. Apparently, she thinks running a small store in Texas or Colorado would be a nice way to retire. She has been working hard seven days a week for the past 16 years, since her husband left. During the week, she runs the shop and on Sundays she sets up a booth and sells dresses in Tlaquepaque town square. She does not have a very clear idea of what to do to achieve her dream, however.

Thus, for the people studied, migration is not undertaken because life in the United States is preferable, but because the United States offers certain things that can improve life in Mexico.

The Shops and Their Main Problems

A number of problems are faced by the owners in the day-to-day operation of the firm. Market problems are most often cited. The single most frequent category is "unstable demand," which five workshop owners mentioned. Prices were also mentioned frequently (five times), for several reasons. In one case, there were competing shops close by. In another, the owner pays all his taxes, which he says places him at a disadvantage because other shops do not pay any. In a third, the owner has to sell to wholesalers at one fourth the final price.

The second type of problem mentioned was legal. Thirteen establishments did not comply with all "minimum" tax regulations (federal, local and social security), but only two saw this as a problem. Another had weighed the costs of legality and illegality and decided that it was better to pay taxes. Only two mentioned law suits as a problem. In one suit, a dissatisfied worker wanted higher wages, but the owner proved he had been paying him above the market wage. In another, the Federal Revenue Office (Secretaria de Hacienda) threatened to embargo the shop's machinery to cover overdue taxes.

Labor problems were mentioned only three times, including the lawsuit just mentioned. The other problems mentioned in this connection were worker turnover and scarcity of skilled workers.

Financial problems were mentioned only once, when a small entrepreneur stated he had many times tried unsuccessfully to get a FOGAIN loan. All our other recipients of FOGAIN financial assistance had used the money successfully and had repaid on time. The need for more machinery was mentioned only once.

Additionally, entrepreneurs were asked to talk freely about the Mexican political system, representation, the nature of work and wealth and other topics. Two areas are of interest to our present analysis. One is the opinion of entrepreneurs on the mechanisms of representation at the industry level.[24] Our small industrialists (the microentrepreneurs rather than the craftspeople) complain bitterly about the lack of effective representation in their chambers of industry. Some said chambers of industry worked only for powerful industrialists. Others say chambers of industry were ineffective and mentioned GATT as proof of their uselessness. One entrepreneur mentioned that cheap sandals imported from China had invaded his market. The subject had been brought up at a meeting in his chamber of industry, and its representatives had said there was absolutely nothing they could do. Some view chambers of industry as extensions of the Partido Revolucionario Institucional (PRI) meant to control them and, therefore, questionable and contrived from above. However, many of our case studies—including those who said the government was corrupt—said the PRI was the best party and that it was better for it to remain in power. Some explicitly said they distrusted the Cardenistas (the Partido de la Revolucion Democratica—PDR),[25] and that they would turn the country into a mess if they had the chance. Some viewed voting for the PRI as an unquestioned necessity, something that allowed them to relate to local PRI officers, in order to exert some pressure and to pull some strings when necessary.

The second topic of significance here was the economic crisis and its relation to the creation of wealth and the nature of poverty. Interviewees were asked what made the poor stay poor. Some said it was laziness or lack of education, but an even greater number said some people had it very rough and could not improve their position by themselves. Surprisingly, they did not point at the government, although most of them did think, to varying degrees, that it was corrupt or that it cheated in elections.

The interviewees were divided on the subject of what made the rich stay rich. To some, the rich have worked hard and deserve what they have. To others, the rich are basically lazy (people who inherit money or have contacts) or basically unethical.

In spite of the problems they mention, entrepreneurs don't see their position as too difficult. No one stated that he or she could not go on because of the situation, although they consistently complained about the crisis and the lack of representation.

From our point of view, income is the first area of concern. We believe that owners should earn an income that is higher than that of manual workers in industry and that compensates for the capital invested in the business. The incomes of the owners ranged from .96 times the minimum wage (about $120 per month) to 23.9 times ($3,190). The potter earned most; the sandal manufacturer (case #2), who does not work full time, earns least. On the low side, we also found the manufacturer of coin purses (1.92 times the minimum wage) whose total income is the product of his full-time work and his wife's part-time, unpaid work. The second-highest income was that of the manufacturer of ladies' shoes (case #3) who earns 16.3 times the minimum wage. Very high incomes were also found at the *empanada* factory (case #6) where each partner earns approximately 6.7 times the minimum wage, or 20.1 times the minimum wage for the partnership. In both cases, production workers are paid just above the minimum, except for the most skilled.

Discounting the potter, who earns a very high income because his product is well known, fashionable and respected artistically, the top earners were those we call "microentrepreneurs": the sandal manufacturer (case #2), the factory making *empanadas* (case #6), and the bedspread manufacturer (case #8, see Table 2). Several shops manufacturing sandals and shoes with less capital than these industrialists provided very low incomes for their owners, who act more like self-employed workers than capitalist owners. Their workers are also badly paid. This is a very competitive market and has been depressed since 1983. These manufacturers have stuck with very traditional, labor-intensive lines of sandals, which are increasingly less popular.

The craftspeople, on the other hand, are doing well, especially if we take into account the smaller size of their work force and the smaller amount of capital invested. The ironsmith who manufactures supermarket carts and other things (case #16) earns 12 times the minimum wage, and he also pays his workers very well (one of them is his brother). The cabinetmaker (case #19) earns 8.6 times the minimum and also pays his workers very well (again, one of these is his brother). The pastry shop owners (two sisters, case #7) earn five times the minimum each, and they also pay their employees well (three to four times the minimum wage).

In terms of their ability to produce high incomes for both owners and workers, we must rate the crafts shops higher than the microenterprises. Microenterprises seem to depend on low wages to produce a good income for their owners;[26] the crafts shops do not.

Starting in 1990, all businesses in Mexico now have to register under the same category, which will in effect increase the tax rate paid by small businesses very significantly.[27] In 1989, we found two main categories still in effect and a wide disparity in tax rates.

The sample, in general, showed a marked tendency toward legality. Only two of the 19 cases were completely illegal. Six had workers affiliated with the Mexican Social Security Institute, and 15 were registered with the Internal Revenue Ministry. In some cases, workers were registered only after a surprise inspection; in others, the owners weighed the costs of legality and illegality (secrecy, inability to offer legal sales receipts, bribes) and decided to register. The two completely illegal shops, however, pay very few bribes, which probably explains why they remain outside the law.

The two most common kinds of registration are with the municipal government (an extremely inexpensive *licencia municipal*) and with the Internal Revenue Ministry (as either small or large contributors). Least frequent is registration with the Social Security Institute (Instituto Mexicano de Seguridad Social—IMSS). Apart from those registered as "large taxpayers," this last was the most costly kind of registration and complicated to estimate, since it is based on the firm's risk category and its medical and accident history. We are not surprised at the lack of this type of registration among our crafts shops, since in most the only adult workers are relatives of the owners, and medical expenses arising from accidents and

TABLE 2

THE CASE STUDIES

Case #	Product	Migrant owner	Migration money	Worker total	Paid workers	Relatives	Municipal tax paid	Federal tax paid	Social security	Significant bank credit	Prominent clients	Financed by suppliers	Supplier = buyer	Wish to grow	Wish to grow now
1	Baked goods	Yes	Yes	4	4	1	N.A.	N.A.	N.A.	No	No	No	No	No	No
2	Sandals	No	Yes	4	4	2	No	No	No	No	Yes	No	No	Yes	Yes
3	Shoes	Yes	Yes	14	14	1	Yes	Yes	Yes	Yes	No	No	No	Yes	Yes
4	Embroidered dresses	Yes	No	8	5	3	N.A.	Yes	Yes	Yes	N.A.	Yes	No	Yes	Yes
5	Artistic pottery	Yes	Yes	4	4	0	No	No	No	No	Yes	No	No	No	No
6	Pastries	No	No	4	4	1	N.A.	Yes	No	No	No	No	No	No	No
7	Empanadas	No	No	22	22	2	No	Yes	Yes	Yes	No	Yes	No	Yes	Yes
8	Bedspreads	No	No	6	6	0	Yes	No	Yes	Yes	Yes	Yes	No	Yes	Yes
9	Shoes	No	Yes	24	24	5	N.A.	Yes	Yes	No	No	No	No	N.A.	N.A.
10	Shoes	No	No	2	1	0	No	Yes	No	No	No	No	No	Yes	No
11	Shoes	No	No	2	2	1	Yes	Yes	No	No	No	No	No	Yes	Yes
12	Leather jackets	No	No	2	1	1	Yes	Yes	No	No	No	No	No	Yes	No
13	Coin purses	Yes	Yes	2	1	1	Yes	Yes	No	No	No	No	No	No	No
14	Machinery	No	No	3	3	0	Yes	Yes	No	No	Yes	No	No	Yes	Yes
15	Eyeglass cases	Yes	Yes	2	2	1	Yes	Yes	No	Yes	No	No	No	Yes	Yes
16	Supermarket carts	No	No	4	4	2	Yes	Yes	No	No	No	No	No	Yes	Yes
17	Coin purses	No	No	1	1	0	Yes	Yes	No	No	No	No	No	Yes	Yes
18	Blacksmith	No	No	3	2	0	Yes	Yes	Yes	No	No	No	No	No	No
19	Cabinetry	No	No	2	2	2	Yes	Yes	No	No	No	No	No	No	No

		Need money to grow		Upward social mobility	Profit per unit	Owners average monthly income in minimum wages	Tax to income ratio[a]	Yearly income to capital ratio
		From bank	From other					
1	Baked goods	No	No	Yes	15% owners estimate	N.A.	N.A.	N.A.
2	Sandals	Yes	No	Yes	N.A.	N.A.	N.A.	N.A.
3	Shoes	N.A.	Yes	Yes	1,689	16.28	1:7	1:41
4	Embroidered dresses	Yes	No	Yes	4,232	2.11	1:23	1:78
5	Artistic pottery	No	No	Yes	718,000	23.9	does not pay taxes	1:12*
6	Pastries	No	No	Yes	25,974	each owner 6.7	1:15	1:1.2
7	Empanadas	Yes	No	N.A.	N.A.	5.0	1:75[b]	1:4.8
8	Bedspreads	Yes	No	Yes	5,990	5.99	1:6	1:12
9	Shoes	N.A.	N.A.	Yes	N.A.	N.A.	N.A.	N.A.
10	Shoes	Yes	No	Yes	800	.96	1:6	1:.31*
11	Shoes	No	Yes	Yes	N.A.	2.0	1:36	1:.64*
12	Leather jackets	No	Yes	Yes	N.A.	N.A.	N.A.	N.A.
13	Coin purses	No	No	No	120	1.92	1:35	1:.72*
14	Machinery	Yes	No	Yes	N.A.	4.3	1:4	1:.37
15	Eyeglass cases	Yes	No	Yes	150	3.3	1:3	1:.57*
16	Supermarket carts	Yes	No	Yes	N.A.	12.0	1:56	1:.02
17	Coin purses	Yes	No	No	22% owners estimate	N.A.	N.A.	N.A.
18	Blacksmith	No	No	Yes	45% owners estimate	3.3	1:9	1:.50
19	Cabinetry	No	No	Yes	N.A.	8.6	1:33	1:.12

Source: Direct investigation.

[a]Capital depreciation is not accounted for.

[b]This firm is a partnership. Estimation of this index for the partnership would be 1:2.25.

*Business located in owner's house. House value not estimated as part of the capital.

N.A. not available.

minor illness are paid by the owner directly (not so for prenatal and maternity expenses, which have to be covered in some other way). In one of them, the family of the worker has access to IMSS through his wife's job.

What does surprise us is that the most "formal" entrepreneurs do not pay all of their taxes and fees. But costs explain this reluctance. Among those registered as small taxpayers, payment to IMSS was five times the payment to the Internal Revenue Ministry and ten times the payment to the Mexican Institute for Workers' Housing (INFONAVIT). Among those registered as "large taxpayers" (which are not always the largest in the sample), payments to IMSS and to Internal Revenue were equally large. Among the two largest enterprises, total taxes were equivalent to 5 percent and 2 percent, respectively, of all expenses. The difference derives from the registration of one of them as "small" and the other as "large." This means that between 14 and 20 percent of owners' total income is the amount they pay themselves as directors, plus profit.

But other cases were probably more dramatic. The *empanada* factory (a business employing 22 workers) paid more taxes than each of its partners earned separately, or provided a total income equivalent to only 2.1 times its total tax bill. Of course, a part of this is probably not just "tax," since payments to social security help the owner save money on accidents, illness and maternity leave, but it is, nevertheless, dramatic. Even some of the very small businesses paid significant taxes: a shoemaker (case #10) employing only two workers paid 16.7 percent of his income as taxes and earned less than the minimum wage. The machinist (case #14), employer of three, pays 25 percent; the manufacturer of eyeglass cases (employing two) pays 33 percent. This provides convincing proof of the truth of the ironsmith's (case #18) complaints that other ironsmiths, who avoid taxes altogether, can sell at significantly lower prices than he can. Taxes are high costs associated with extremely small enterprises and certainly do not allow owners to live as comfortably as wealthy industrialists.

The tax reforms enacted in 1990 raise the tax floor and, therefore, will affect our entrepreneurs' cases negatively. This is likely to drive more of them into illegality unless they can secure the advice of skilled accountants who can teach them to avoid these taxes legally (most of our cases did not discount capital depreciation from their profits, for example). Failure to do this might have an inflationary effect on the goods produced by the small-scale sector; increased costs will have to be passed on to clients. It is important for these entrepreneurs to become familiar with the few favorable provisions in the law, especially those related to the tax exemptions arising from investment, since this is likely to make their firms more productive.

In conclusion, we see problems with the firms' relation to their markets, with their access to credit and with the present tax structure. The changes in the tax laws could favor the shops we studied if the owners became familiar with the new provisions and increased their productive investments.

IV. WORKERS AND MIGRATION

There are good reasons to suppose that the labor force working in informal or small-scale enterprises is inclined to migrate to the United States. First, these workers show higher turnover rates than workers in large companies; second, owners provide few incentives for stability and longevity and, since they usually lack formal evaluation and promotion structures, the enterprises themselves are less secure and can cease to exist or can restructure early. Finally, skilled workers have general abilities that are useful in both Mexico and the United States.

This section aims to establish whether these suppositions correspond to the findings obtained from the surveys administered to workers in Guadalajara and southern Jalisco and Atotonilco (Jalisco), and whether the labor force with migratory experience is in a relatively privileged position—that is, proportionately more skilled than the nonmigrant and with higher average incomes—when compared with the labor force that has not migrated to the United States. We assume that, if, indeed, the migrants have advantages, those advantages will generate a "demonstration" effect on other workers and induce repeat migration for those who already have experience.

V. INTERNATIONAL MIGRATION IN THE 1982 GUADALAJARA OPERATIVE LABOR MARKET

In the survey we administered to 1,302 manual workers in Guadalajara and southern Jalisco in 1982, we interviewed workers in 55 enterprises in the following sectors: food, textiles, shoes, paper production, chemicals, rubber and plastic, non-metallic minerals, engineering, electronics, photographic materials, small workshops, construction and local, state and federal government.[28] We do not consider this sample, despite its size, to be a strict random sample of the manual labor force because we did not interview workers in all the industrial branches and because the smaller strata and women are under-represented. It is representative of the people who work in medium and big enterprises, and the small group of informal workshops (N = 32) coincides with the results of other surveys. It is the best sample that exists of the manual labor market of Guadalajara, but our results cannot be extended directly to the total of this labor market.

Of the 1,302 workers, 253 answered that they had migrated to the

United States. Of these, 30 did not provide information on their jobs in the United States; on the contrary, they stated that they had gone there to get to know the country or on holiday. A sizable portion of these were young people belonging to the relatively better off families in the survey. We can thus say that 223 (17.12 percent) went to the United States to work.

The incidence of international migration among these workers can also be analyzed as a percentage of job changes that imply national or international migration. On their first job change, 5.7 percent of the workers migrated; on the second and third, 10 percent; on the fourth, 8.7 percent, and on the fifth, 9.9 percent. As can be seen, the percentage of workers migrating on each job change is almost constant after the first change. Of the job changes involving migration, 0.6 percent (or 10.5 percent of all those migrating) went to the United States on their first job change; 3 percent (or 30 percent of all migrants) on the second and third changes, 2.9 percent (or 33.3 percent of all migrants) on the fourth change; and 3.6 percent (or 36.4 percent) on the fifth change. In other words, almost 3 percent of all the job changes of the workers studied involved international migration; this percentage seems to increase as careers progress. This might be related to advancing life and domestic cycles and also suggests that in Guadalajara, unlike what we found in Los Altos de Jalisco, migration is typically started after an individual has acquired significant work experience.

To explore the relevance of migration to small-scale firms, it is important to establish first whether there is a significant relationship between small industry and migration—that is, whether small-scale industrial workers tend to migrate more (or to show more migration experience) than their large-scale counterparts. Our data show that there is a relationship between size of firm and migration experience since, in the two smaller strata, the mean percentage of migrants is 24.6 and 26.6 percent (if we disregard the self-employed stratum, which is very small). In larger firms, this percentage is down to 17.9 percent.

The relationship between industrial size and percentage of migrants is not by itself an index of a relationship characteristic of the labor market as a whole. It may be that the kind of labor force recruited in different industrial branches differs; therefore, the percentage of migrants varies among them.

There are, in fact, large variations between the branches, even among those where we collected larger sub-samples. The branches showing larger percentages of international migrant workers are also those having a large proportion of workers from rural areas. While, for the sample as a whole, the average of these workers is 27.5 percent, in the case of nonmetallic minerals, 42.3 percent of workers are of rural origin. Construction also is above average in this respect, with 37.5 percent.[29] Both branches also have a higher-than-average proportion of international migrants: 25.6 percent and 20.9 percent, respectively, compared with 19.4 percent labor and nonlabor migrants in the sample. This relationship between the rural origin of workers and international migrants is not always evident. Photography industries employ only 5.4 percent rural-origin workers; nevertheless, they show a high percentage of international migrants (22.5 percent).

The percentage of skilled and non-skilled people is more or less the same between migrants and nonmigrants. The former do not seem to have a clear advantage in terms of skills; however, they do appear to have greater access to supervisory jobs. Our data suggest either that migrants have not had more access to skill-acquiring positions or that they do not systematically use those skills.

Other studies have shown a relationship between life and family cycles and migration. Cohort analysis shows whether this holds in Guadalajara and whether international migration is increasing or decreasing.

Married and widowed workers have, in fact, migrated more frequently than unmarried workers (23.3 percent versus 11.8 percent). But, in large part, this has to do with the age difference between the two groups. The percentage of workers with international migration experience rises from 7.9 percent for those under 21 to 36.1 percent for those over 40. Increases are systematic, except in the 31 to 40 cohort, which is only marginally superior to the immediately younger group. Controlling for marital status partially confirms the preceding, except that the group of young married workers shows a very high percentage of migrants (respective of other groups). It would seem that, in Mexico before 1982, international migration became a more common strategy for newly married workers. Very old unmarried workers (aged 51 and above), a small group, show the highest incidence of international migration, probably explained by their lack of attachment to a family in Mexico.

Men migrate much more than women: 20.3 percent of the men have migrated, against only 8.6 percent of the women. While this holds true in all our samples, our 1982 results were probably biased against female migrants because those women we interviewed were mostly young and relatively educated, which means they had not had much chance to migrate before we interviewed them.

The literature on migration has stressed a positive selectivity of migrants; that is, people migrating in any given community are generally those with higher-than-average socioeconomic status and schooling. These results usually come from studies of small, rural communities. Our sample differs because it has a cluster of unschooled migrant workers, and the incidence of migration does not increase systematically with schooling. The general trend, with important variations, points at the negative selectivity of migration: 31.1 percent of those with no schooling have migrated as opposed to 13.3 percent of those with the highest schooling. This must be related to the better occupational opportunities in large Mexican cities for educated individuals, which means that the "functionality" of migration must be higher for people with fewer skills or less schooling.

In Guadalajara, as in other places, wages depend heavily on skills and on the time necessary for acquiring those skills. The average training period for migrants in our study was 11.3 months, for nonmigrants, 14.54. Thus, the skilled nonmigrants earned the higher wages: 2,810 pesos versus 2,723 pesos for the migrants. Differences are not, however, consistent when the sample is disaggregated by industry.

In conclusion, migration does not produce significant advantages for the migrants in our sample. While it is possible that some of the successful migrants may have become self-employed or moved to non-manual occupations, we believe the conclusion holds for the wage-earning industrial population of Guadalajara.

Before we analyze the results of more recent surveys, we shall describe the most salient traits of the migrants' experience in the United States and their opinions concerning the success of their relatives in that country.

Of the 226 who migrated, 91 could not save at all; 12 saved to get married; 21 to build a house; seven set up a business; 42 gave their savings to their parents; 22 gave them to their wives; and 39 used savings in other ways.

On reasons for returning to Mexico, we got 227 responses. Migration-legal problems were the reason given by 48; the same number said their contracts had ended; 35 "didn't like it"; 50 mentioned family commitments or problems; and 46 gave other reasons. In 1982, only 352 said they would like to go to the United States. The percentage of migrants saying they would like to go back was 33.5, and the percentage of nonmigrants saying they would like to go for the first time was 26.1. Compared with the results of our later surveys, the wish to go to the United States was higher among migrants in 1982, and in the whole sample, the wish to depart was low.

A very high percentage of the workers interviewed in 1982 (89.8 percent or 1,169) said they had relatives living in the United States. Of these, 42.1 percent said their relatives had fared well and had stayed in the United States. In all, 55.4 percent said their relatives had stayed in the United States, and 57.5 percent said they had been successful there. Only 8.7 percent said their relatives had a rough time there. This means that (1) our interviewees do think most of their relatives have settled in the United States, and (2) they think the experience of their relatives is positive.

To sum up our 1982 findings, we can say that migration was not positively selective, skills gained in the United States were not measurably significant and nonmigrants earned more money. Age and marital status did influence migration except in the 31 to 40 cohort. This group deviates because it shows a lower percentage of migrants. The young married sub-sample of this cohort also deviates because it shows a very high percentage of migrants, signaling an increase in migration connected with the basic expenses of setting up a house. There was a large cluster of unschooled, unskilled migrants from rural areas in industries like construction and non-metal minerals.

There is a relationship between size of firm and migration, but it varies from one industry to another. There is a negative relationship between migration and wages but, again, this varies from industry to industry.

VI. INTERNATIONAL MIGRATION AMONG INFORMAL WORKERS IN 1985

In 1985, we carried out a study of small-scale workshops and their workers. We interviewed 100 workers, 90 of whom worked for others and ten of whom were self-employed. We collected information on international migration. A total of 18 percent of the workers interviewed had migrated to the United States and returned, but only 15 percent provided detailed information on their trips. The other three percent probably did not intend to work or could not find work in the North.

In 1985, some changes start to appear in the sample. For the first time, skilled workers show a higher percentage of migrants than the unskilled. This might be related to the changing age structure of the work force in small enterprises since, in 1982, only 26.7 percent of the workers in these shops were under 20, while in 1985, this proportion had grown to 34 percent and to 44 percent in 1987. The percentage of skilled migrants increases because the unskilled are increasingly young and have had less opportunity to migrate.

Again, there are more migrants among the married sub-sample: 23.2 percent as opposed to 14 percent among the unmarried workers.

Another change is evident in our data for the wish to go to the United States. Fifty percent of those with migration experience wanted to go back; 57.3 percent of those lacking this experience also wished to go. The change in respect to our 1982 data is that the wish to go is more prevalent in the sample as a whole in 1985, and more of those lacking migration experience wanted to leave for the United States than those who had already been.

Another change in this sample concerns education. In 1985, migrants had an average schooling of 7.5 years, against a 6.3-year average for the nonmigrants.

Also, in this sample migrants have a wage advantage: 10,388 pesos compared with the nonmigrants' 9,057 pesos. This is explained by the rise in the number of skilled, older migrants in 1985.

Fifteen of the migrant workers we found in 1985 reported the following uses of their savings: eight could not save; one bought a house; two helped their parents; none invested in businesses; and four used their savings for other things. Of the 14 responding to the question on remittances, nine said they had sent money and five said they had not.

Concerning the reasons for their return, we got 14 replies. Two (14.3 percent) blamed migration problems, three said their contracts had ended, two "did not like it," two had family reasons and five gave other reasons.

VII. INTERNATIONAL MIGRATION AMONG INDUSTRIAL WORKERS IN GUADALAJARA AND ATOTONILCO IN 1987

In 1987, we interviewed 302 workers in both small- and large-scale industries in Guadalajara and Atotonilco. These included workers in two large firms we had studied in 1982: a steel mill and the largest shoe factory in Latin America.

Two things stand out in our 1987 results. First, the percentage of migrants drops overall, from 17.13 in 1982 to 3.25 in 1987. Second, the percentage of migrants to the United States is equal among the small and large firms. Third, in 1987, the weight of large-industry employment weakens the relationship between skill and migration which, in 1985, was shown to behave positively. In 1987, as in 1982, migrants were less frequently skilled than nonmigrants and, therefore, earned less than the nonmigrants: 33,570 pesos as opposed to 35,398.

The percentage of international migrants we interviewed is too small to show any systematic relationship between age, marital status and migration.

In the large steel mill, we found 19.1 percent of workers with international migration experience in 1982, but only 2.5 percent in 1987. In the large shoemaking firm, we found 12.5 percent and 2 percent, respectively. Both the sampling techniques and the life-work-migration history schedule remained the same. We believe the drop in the percentage of migrants is not due to changes in the nature of the sample.

VIII. THE WORK FORCE IN SMALL-SCALE ENTERPRISES STUDIED IN 1989

In all, the 19 workshops studied in 1989 employed 125 persons, for an average of 6.6 workers per enterprise. The largest employers were the shoe-manufacturing shops and one pastry shop, but they were also among the worst paying. The shops paying best were the lathe shop (case

#14), the small pastry shop (case #6), the ironsmith (case #18), the manufacturer of eyeglass cases and the cabinetmaker.

There is a small reversal of the trend toward the rejuvenation of the work force. In 1989, 39 percent of the work force was under 20 years of age. This is due, we think, to the greater weight in this sample of workers in crafts shops, who are typically older than the workers in microenterprises. There were, however, very few workers over 30 (9.8 percent).

Schooling shows a disturbing trend: workers under 20 had an average of 5.7 years of schooling; workers between 20 and 29 had an average of 6.2 years of schooling; and older workers, 2.6 years. Young workers showed fewer years of schooling than middle-aged workers, which might reflect the need for early entry into the paid work force during the economic crisis.

Union affiliation is mostly nominal in Guadalajara, but it nevertheless reflects a certain formality and security in the job. Fifty-eight percent of our sample was affiliated.

The size of the town where our interviewees held their first job is an indication of both the sector's ability to absorb rural workers and the age at which they came to Guadalajara. Most of our workers (87.8 percent) held their first jobs in Guadalajara, confirming previous results that indicated that the small-scale sector absorbs mostly urban workers. None came from towns under 5,000 and only one worker (2.4 percent) from towns between 5,000 and 20,000.

We also evaluated the extent to which these workers have stayed in the small-scale sector all their working lives. In 1982, workers moved from small- to large-scale firms easily. Among the workers we interviewed in 1989, 66.8 percent held their first jobs in workshops employing fewer than 20 workers and 29.3 percent in firms employing between 20 and 49 workers. Only one (2.4 percent) held his first job in a firm employing 50 to 99 workers. In other words, the work force we interviewed in 1989 seems to have worked almost exclusively in small enterprises.

There is an increase in the percentage of international migrants in this sample, which is higher than the 1987 average, but lower than the 1982 and 1985 figures. This breaks down to 10 percent for men and 4.7 percent for women. Most of our workers said they had relatives who were willing to help them (or had already helped them) get a job in the United States.

When asked whether they would like to go to the United States soon to work, 51.2 percent replied affirmatively which, again, is higher than in 1982 and just under our 1985 results. When asked why they would like to go, 52.3 percent mentioned that they wanted to see what the country was like, and 28.5 percent said they wanted to work there.

We also asked workers if they would like to settle in the United States if they had a chance to obtain legal residence; 29.2 percent of our respondents said they would.

Almost half the sample knew about the Immigration Reform and Control Act (IRCA). One worker applied for amnesty, and 41.5 percent thought they could have applied but did not. A quarter of the sample knew more than one person who had applied for amnesty. More than half had immediate kin working in the United States (from one to four persons). Almost a quarter (24.3 percent) had relatives who held legal resident status in the United States.

In conclusion:

1) Migration does not by itself produce advantages for workers. When age, skill and marital status are controlled for, migrant workers show shorter periods of training and lower wages.
2) There is a tendency for small-scale industrial workers to migrate more often than large-scale industrial workers, as we anticipated.
3) Concerning the historical behavior of the migration flow and workers' attitudes toward migration, it seems the 1970s were a decade of stagnation in the size of migration flows from the cities. The 31 to 40-year-old cohort in 1982 showed the same percentage of migrants as the younger cohort and a far lower percentage than older cohorts. On the other hand, it seems that, toward the end of the 1970s and in the early 1980s, migration rose again. The rise in the number of migrants among the young married subsample (31 to 40) suggests that conditions were already becoming difficult for workers before the crisis broke in 1982.
4) Concerning the type of worker who is likely to migrate, we found one cluster of workers with migration experience who were typically rural-born, unskilled and unschooled and who earned low wages in Guadalajara. Most of these were older workers who had gone to agricultural jobs in the United States. Among the rest of the sample, migration was far less frequent, but rising.
5) Our data for 1987 and 1989 show that there is a large potential for migration among our samples. Many have contacts, many have immediate kin in the United States and a sizable group has relatives who are legal residents there. The group saying they would prefer to live in the United States if they had access to legal residence is also large.

Table 3 summarizes the characteristics of our four subject groups.

IX. CONCLUSIONS AND RECOMMENDATIONS

Our case studies belong to two main types of enterprise: microenterprises and crafts shops. Microentrepreneurs require larger capital outlays to improve their firms and they usually belong to a different social class than their workers. They do not usually perform manual labor, for example.

TABLE 3

SUMMARY OF SAMPLES

Year	No. of workers interviewed	% Male	% Female	% Migrants	% Male migrants	% Female migrants	Skilled migrants as % of skilled workers	Non-skilled migrants as % of nonskilled workers	Migrant wages (pesos)	Nonmigrant wages (pesos)	Skilled migrant wages (pesos)	Nonskilled migrant wages (pesos)	Migrants average schooling (years)	Nonmigrant average schooling (years)	% of people who want to go to U.S.	% of migrants who want to go to U.S.	% of nonmigrants who want to go to U.S.
1982	1302	91.9	8.0	19.4	20.3	8.6	19.1	18.6	2,409	2,491	2,723	2,120	4.8	5.4	27.0	30.8	26.1
1985	100	69.0	31.0	18.0	23.1	6.4	31.5	9.6	10,388	9,057	10,333	7,666	7.5	6.3	56.0	50.0	57.0
1987	302	53.3	48.7	3.3	5.1	1.3	3.1	4.6	33,570	35,390	34,210	30,970	6.0	6.3	N.A.*	N.A.*	N.A.*
1989	41	46.3	51.2	9.7	15.0	4.7	12.1	0.0	104,250	89,290	104,250	**	6.5	5.2	51.2	50.0	51.3

Notes: 1982: Guadalajara and Southern Jalisco
1985: informal workshops of Guadalajara
1987: Guadalajara and Atotonilco
1989: Guadalajara

*Information not available

**All migrants are skilled

Owners of microenterprises and crafts shops behave differently with respect to migration. We believe that the owners of small, successful crafts shops and the owners of microenterprises that are doing well or that need to grow but require large investments are not candidates for labor migration. The first are too involved in the day-to-day operation of the shop, and the others belong to a different social class than the one involved in labor migration and have larger capital needs than can be furnished by labor migration. These two types are, therefore, retained in Mexico by their firms. In other words, both crafts shops and microenterprises act to retain their owners, albeit for different reasons.

Master craftspeople are retained because they have enough equipment, they are self-employed, production depends a great deal on their presence and supervision, and their standard of living, while not affluent by U.S. standards, is satisfactory to them—they are even proud of it since most come from very poor families. Microentrepreneurs might also be deeply involved in their firms, but we believe they do not migrate because migration is not likely to improve their situation considerably (unless they have gone completely broke and alienated family and friends).

What we mean when we refer to craftspeople is not people who manufacture traditional goods in traditional ways. The potter, the machinist, the manufacturer of eyeglass cases do not produce traditional goods. They are craftspeople because the key to their business is their possession of certain very significant manual skills and because they have reached, in their firms, a scale of operation that is small yet functional. Moreover, they have relatively favorable links with their market; they sell directly to their clients and, if necessary, search for commercial niches. The great difference between the two crafts shops that produce coin purses—one successful, the other not—is that the successful owner sells directly to the public. This allows him to sell his product for three times more on average than the other producer can do.

When we refer to successful microenterprises, we do not want to portray these producers as the incarnation of the capitalist spirit. They are microentrepreneurs because (1) they are not manual workers, which means there is a social division between them and their workers, (2) they attempt to increase their profits, and (3) they are interested in growth, even though they do not always achieve it.

The producers who in our opinion (in some cases, in their own opinion) are inclined to migrate are those who are just starting and need equipment and capital, or the ones who have problems with their small business. We refer not only to the owners themselves, but also to cases like the shoe producer (case #9) for whom savings and remittances from relatives are essential to maintain or expand the shop. Once more, there are thresholds separating different kinds of producers. The clothing or shoe producers (who face a stagnant market) who are workers themselves can migrate if they are still young because there is a "dead" season that requires little work in their shops and because the capital they require is within the reach of international migrants (from $1,500 to $5,000). In spite of her age and bad experience in the United States, case #4 wishes to return to open a new store, since her shop has done badly since 1985. The crafts people who are inclined to migrate are those who cannot maintain the standard of living they wish with the income from their business. In some cases, like that of case #13, the option of migration is strongly rejected, but he admits that the idea is attractive to him.

We must draw attention to the fact that many of the shoe workshops pay bad wages and depend on wholesale business. We believe that a better relationship with the market would allow them to maintain more stock, to be more stable and to pay better wages. This is also true of case #4. The impact of a better relationship with the market was very clear in 1981–1982: the workshops were investing, the workers earned more; the profit margin was greater.

We find that, indeed, there is a certain relationship between the scale of the enterprise and migration (workers in small enterprises migrate more often than do those from the larger ones). At the same time, we deny the idea that the crafts shops are the more insecure or the worst paid. The manufacturer of eyeglass cases, the machinist, the pastry shop owner (case #6) and the cabinetmakers, in general, pay good wages (above the minimum wage and up to 2.5 times more). We also believe this discourages workers from migrating.

On the other hand, workers in clothing and shoe microenterprises (case #4) and the manufacturers of popular shoes (cases #2, #3 and #9) do wish to migrate. Two of them have already done so and others showed great interest in doing it soon. The ones who showed the greatest interest were underemployed skilled workers. One of them is a stitcher who makes barely the minimum wage. The other is officially a stitcher but, in fact, is in charge of repairing and maintaining the machinery of case #3's enterprise. The other two are skilled seamstresses.

The workers who are more inclined to migrate are found either in problematic crafts shops or in the microenterprises that have profited from a buyer's labor market and pay low wages.

We also find that the percentage of workers with international migration experience decreased markedly from 1982 to 1989. This happened even in enterprises in which we found a high number of migrants in 1982. We believe this has two explanations: (1) the rejuvenation of the work force of the workshops, itself a consequence of the general fall in wages—the majority of the workers in these shops in 1989 were too young to have migrated, and (2) many of the migrant workers in 1982 must have returned to the United States or moved to non-manual occupations. It was impossible to estimate this quantity in the studies, but we found several mentions of the phenomenon in different-sized enterprises.

In sum, there is a "type" of worker with migratory experience who normally has rural origins, little schooling and is unskilled. These workers have migration experience, in general, before their arrival in Guadalajara. This type of migration from Guadalajara cannot be stemmed unless this city regains its dynamic role within the region and access to the United States becomes more difficult. It is important to emphasize that greater difficulty in international migration will not by itself restore the role of Guadalajara. Thus, it would be better for Mexico as a whole if migration diminished as a result of the creation of opportunities in the countryside.

Second, the desire to save money to set up a business is common in our case studies and in our interviews with workers. There are a great many target migrants, our second migrant type, who may succeed or not, but who go to the United States with this purpose in mind. We consider this a different type of migrant—of urban origin—who reckons he or she knows a productive process well and who is able to become independent with access to sufficient capital. Unlike the first type, whose experience in the United States is mostly rural, these migrants go or wish to go to urban localities and jobs.

Third, there are also many workers who think they earn less than they should and, given the extreme competitiveness of the labor market in certain areas, they are likely to migrate, not to set up a business, but simply to save money to achieve their basic goals: to marry, to buy a plot of land, to start building a house, to educate their children or to buy a pick-up truck. Unlike the "target migrants," these workers are quite likely to become trapped in the United States: they do not have goals that can be achieved only in Mexico. A job they can live on, the ability to purchase the commodities they cannot afford in Mexico and a better standard of living are likely to convince them to stay in the North. The presence of a large and growing Hispanic population in many American cities also allows them to recreate the way of life they desire. One of the most skilled, hardest-working people we interviewed in 1982 was just such a case. He left for the United States after 1982, got married, and does not want to return. We would say that these workers are typical of microenterprises rather than crafts shops, since the latter tend to pay better wages.

Last, there are some shops that barely make it, that can "go bust" at any moment. This is true of case #13 and many others. We believe these owners are candidates for migration since they have the experience and their needs could be answered by a successful trip to the North.

The migration patterns and migratory types we found in Guadalajara differ from those we found in Jalostotitlàn.[30] In the latter, going "North" is a local cultural imperative. People do not migrate with clear economic purposes—although they do derive economic advantages—but to prove their adulthood or their virility to themselves and their community.

Women push their husbands and older children to migrate.

In Guadalajara, on the other hand, the weight of an individual's reasons to migrate is much greater.[31] In other words, a migration culture does not exist in Guadalajara to the same extent, or with the same intensity, as it does in Jalostotitlàn. For this reason, while the impact of a well designed, anti-migration policy is likely to be felt only in the long term in towns like Jalostotitlàn, we feel that a program offering potential migrants local access to the resources they seek is likely to have much more immediate success in Guadalajara.

Failure to adopt such a development policy would result, on the other hand, in a consolidation of this "migration culture." If it becomes a traditional truth for workers in Guadalajara that they can aspire to marry or to buy a house or to set up their own business only through migration, it will be much harder to stem the flow later. Recent research shows the proportional growth of large-city dwellers in the international flow of migrants,[32] especially among those looking for jobs in casual labor markets. This trend marks the absence of secure migration circuits for these people, the immaturity of their networks. If this trend is allowed to consolidate, the growth in the U.S.-bound population flows could be tremendous: the three largest cities in Mexico house approximately 28 million inhabitants.

As we saw in case studies and in the analysis of worker migration, small-scale industry can, in fact, retain both its owners and its workers, if it meets certain conditions. The economic crisis is the immediate explanation of many of the shops' problems. Wages have been reduced along with demand and job opportunities. We think that the answer to these problems is structural; it will be hard to change these conditions by means of unilateral action.

But small enterprises have been in trouble since well before the crisis. Thus, some problems may be attacked now but will still need attention when economic recovery takes place. Two main areas, if they become the focus of specific policies, could change the way small enterprises behave in the Mexican economy and the extent to which they retain workers and owners.

First is productivity. In the successful cases, increased productivity has a lot to do with the possession and use of machinery. Since 1982, small industries have failed to maintain their capital-to-worker ratio. This is due as much to market difficulties as to the diminishing price of labor. It is important to replace old and expand existing machinery. Machinery purchases depend on (1) capital, (2) availability and information and (3) the owner's evaluation of future market behavior. At present, hopes for an economic recovery are very high, although this is to some extent clouded by the GATT aftershock. Industrialists, at this time, believe the market will expand. Usually, small industrialists buy second-hand machinery. Some have operated successfully with it, but its productive life and its maintenance costs are very uncertain.

What we believe is necessary first, then, is a *plan for the purchase of new machinery on credit*. Mexico's trade liberalization means that it is much easier now to import machinery suitable for small enterprises. However, there is a dearth of information on new machines for this type of industry. Industrialists continue to buy obsolete machines because these are the machines they know. The existence of memory-capable lathes and sewing and cutting machines is unknown to most. The industrialists who have access to this information are those who travel abroad to industrial fairs; they usually do not have the capital problems we associate with small industry (nor are they candidates for labor migration).

For such a plan to be successful, it is necessary to organize *local* (or itinerant) *industrial fairs*, where specially selected machinery can be displayed, demonstrated and sold. These fairs can be attractive, both to the machinery retailers and to the industrialists, and they should be publicized in the popular press and on the radio stations preferred by small industrialists. Publicity should mention the existence of new, preferential finance plans for the purchase of machinery.

In Mexico, credit for the purchase of machinery has been handled mostly through FOGAIN, a central bank agency that channels international and government funds to small industries through commercial banks.[33] Less than 50 percent of the available funding in western Mexico was placed in 1989. Although recovery seems to be high and some of our case studies recognized the importance of these loans, they complained that they take a very long time to be approved and delivered (several months, typically, in two cases over a year). They also stressed the fact that banks "hook" them with promises of FOGAIN loans and then lend to them at commercial rates.

Channeling the loans through the sellers of machinery would be far more efficient because these firms, unlike the banks, would place as many preferential-rate loans as possible. Naturally, credit ratings have to be checked, but if this is done, a repayment is likely if there is sustained growth. In 1989, there was a marked recovery in the sale of many capital goods (both industrial and agricultural), which indicates that this kind of promotional activity would be successful.

Granting loans through a scheme like the one just outlined is more efficient than offering loans to actual or potential return migrants since the loan would be a sort of "prize" for migrants. It is incredibly difficult to ensure that migrants will not return to the United States, so people might be "rewarded" repeatedly for migrating.

Second, we recommend the establishment of a *market information network* in popular industrial areas in the country. It could function like a brokerage house, charging fees to both industrialists and clients. Several of our case studies have problems stemming from the difficulty of locating clients beyond the city limits, often in the city itself. Although these are not the smallest cases studied, they cannot afford to travel solely to find clients. The woman who sells embroidered dresses and the potter traveled to the United States primarily to find clients, but their success was extremely limited. Both stayed in the United States for over a year. Had they known how to gain access to market information, they would not have left Mexico at all.

Timely and precise information on clients and products and the existence of an advisory service to help collect payments and to explain export procedures would make these small enterprises much more profitable than they are at present because they not only would gain market access, they also would be able to sell at better prices. The network could, with existing technologies, handle up-to-date information and interactive systems so that the possibility of responding to obsolete demand would be cancelled. On-line services are now more feasible in Mexico, and the cost of long-distance telephone calls has been cut substantially. This on-line service can also be sold to not-so-small industrialists who could access it from their own terminals. Naturally, some of our case studies depend on local markets and face-to-face interaction with their clients (the bakers, for example), but most would unquestionably benefit from such a network.

While the scheme for the purchase of new machinery does entail costs (i.e., the provision of low-interest credit)—but costs that may be lower than those associated with FOGAIN—the second scheme could turn a profit and still render a very significant service to small entrepreneurs. We don't see all our cases as ideal candidates for the service, but it could significantly transform the way our microentrepreneurs operate and, more important, it would quite likely have an effect on labor relations. When it becomes crucial to respond to quality specifications and deadlines, the reliability of labor becomes as important as its cost, so that owners would be more likely to adopt incentives for punctuality, longevity and quality. Even some of our craft-type entrepreneurs would benefit: the machinist would not depend on the few clients who know him; the coin purse and the eyeglass manufacturers would be able to sell nationally (or even to small buyers internationally); the ironsmith and the cabinetmaker could produce custom-made goods far more cheaply than those available in the United States. Perhaps the hardest-hit of all our cases (those in the shoe industry) would be able to improve their sales considerably since the glut is mostly local and regional, and seasonal fluctuations could be offset by selling away from western Mexico.

Both proposals are subject to some failures, which are likely to be more pronounced at the beginning. But the gradual effects on the small-industry sector would open up a number of opportunities for entrepreneurs who, as one of our respondents put it, "are rowing upstream just to avoid drowning." They would also encourage the permanence in Mexico of many Mexicans who go to the United States, not because they want to, but because it offers them the opportunity to save, to set up a small business and to "quit poverty." Indirectly, workers will also benefit.

These proposals require the Mexican economy to grow and to create better jobs, which it did not accomplish in the 1980s. But, with higher productivity and profits, small enterprises will be capable of providing better jobs.

NOTES

All the work carried out in 1989, including the recovery and re-analysis of the older surveys, was done with funds provided by the Commission for the Study of International Migration and Cooperative Economic Development. The older surveys and case studies were carried out with Ford Foundation and CIESAS (Centro de Investigaciones y Estudios Superiores en Antropologia Social) resources.

1. Carlos Alba Vega and Bryan Roberts, "Crisis, Adjustment and Employment in Mexico: Manufacturing Industry in Jalisco," in *Migration Impacts of Trade and Foreign Investment: Mexico and Caribbean Basin Countries*, ed. Sergio Díaz-Briquets and Sidney Weintraub (Westview Press, 1991), 255–279.

2. José Antonio Alonso, "Crisis, sismos e industria doméstica," in *Mujeres y sociedad: salario, hogar y acción social en el occidente de México* (Guadalajara: Colegio de Jalisco, 1988), pp. 107–124; Lourdes Benería and Martha Roldán, *The Crossroads of Class and Gender: Industrial Homework, Subcontracting and Household Dynamics in Mexico City* (Chicago: University of Chicago Press, 1987); Cristina Padilla, "Marginados o asalariados: el trabajo domiciliar de maquila en una colonia popular," (Licenciatura thesis, Universidad Iberoamericana, 1978).

3. John Friedmann and Mauricio Salguero, "The Barrio Economy and Collective Self-Empowerment in Latin America: A Framework and Agenda for Research," (University of California at Los Angeles, 1988, mimeograph).

4. Mercedes González de la Rocha, *Los recursos de la pobreza: familias de bajos ingresos de Guadalajara* (Guadalajara: Colegio de Jalisco, SPP, 1986).

5. Agustín Escobar Latapí, *Con el sudor de tu frente: mercado de trabajo y clase obrera en Guadalajara* (Guadalajara: Colegio de Jalisco, 1986).

6. Hernando de Soto, et al, *El otro sendero* (Mexico City: Diana, 1987).

7. Instituto Nacional de Estadística, Geografía e Informatica (INEGI), *XI censo industrial, 1981* (Mexico City, 1988).

8. Patricia Arias and Bryan Roberts, "The City in Permanent Transition: The Consequences of a System of Industrial Specialization," in *Capital and Labor in the Urbanized World*, ed. John Walton (London: Sage, 1984).

9. Alejandro Portes, "Unauthorized Immigration and Immigration Reform: Present Trends and Prospects," in *Determinants of Emigration from Mexico, Central America, and the Caribbean*, ed. Sergio Díaz-Briquets and Sidney Weintraub (Westview Press, 1991), pp. 75–97.

10. John Walton, *Elites and Economic Development* (Austin: ILAS/University of Texas Press, 1976).

11. United Nations Economic Commission for Latin America and the Caribbean (ECLAC), "The Dynamics of Social Deterioration in Latin America and the Caribbean in the 1980s," in *Regional Prepatory Meeting for the Eighth United Nations Congress on the Prevention of Crime and Treatment of Offenders* (San Jose, Costa Rica, 1989).

12. Escobar Latapí, "The Rise and Fall of an Urban Labor Market: Economic Crisis and the Fate of Small Workshops in Guadalajara, Mexico," *Bulletin of Latin American Research,* vol. 7, no. 2 (1988), pp., 183–205.

13. Rolando Cordera Campos and Enrique González Tiburcio, "Crisis política y económica: saldos productivos y sociales" (Mexico City: UNAM, 1987, mimeograph).

14. Alonso, "Crisis," 1988.

15. INEGI, 1988.

16. INEGI, *Síntesis de resultados del empadronamiento urbano de Jalisco para los censos económicos de 1986* (Guadalajara, 1986).

17. Departamento de Programación y Desarrollo del Estado de Jalisco (DEPRODE), *La situación industrial de Jalisco* (Guadalajara, 1982).

18. Richard H. Hancock, *The Role of the Bracero in the Cultural and Economic Dynamics of Mexico* (Stanford, CA: Hispanic American Society, 1959), p. 38.

19. E. Rogers and L. Svenning, *La modernización entre los campesinos* (Mexico City: Fondo de Cultura Económica, 1973).

20. George Foster, *Empire's Children: The People of Tzintzuntzan* (Washington, DC: Smithsonian Institution, 1948, monograph series).

21. Kathryn Purcell, "Report on Fieldwork Among Women Workers" (University of Manchester, 1984, mimeograph).

22. This case resembles the ones we compiled in Jalostotitlàn, where migration is a social imperative, a part of the community's way of life, not something that must be explained.

23. In this sense, Guadalajara differs markedly from Jalostotitlàn, a town studied by Gonzalez de la Rocha, et al., in *The Effects of Receiving Country Policies on Migration Flows,* ed. Sergio Díaz-Briquets and Sidney Weintraub (Westview Press, 1991), Chapter 5.

24. Mexican industrial firms have to be registered with a chamber of industry, which represents them before the government.

25. Cuauhtemoc Cardenas was the presidential candidate of an opposition coalition during the 1988 elections. This election front has now become the PRD, a strong electoral party that won many local elections in 1989 and that has occupied many local council buildings.

26. Of all the microentrepreneurs, only the bedspread manufacturer pays wages clearly above the minimum.

27. Discussion of this new *Miscelanea Fiscal* in Congress produced several significant changes in the potential effect of the law. Small-scale industrialists can postpone deciding what fiscal figure they will opt for until September 1990, and will be able to deduct 100 percent of their productive investments from 1990 until

1993. But most of our interviewees did not know this and were unhappy with the changes in the law.

28. Escobar Latapí, *Con el sudor,* 1986.

29. González de la Rocha, et al, "Migratory Patterns and Legislation: The Impact of the Simpson-Rodino Immigration Act on the Village of Altos de Jalisco," Commission for the Study of International Migration and Cooperative Economic Development Working Paper No. 41 (Washington, DC, 1990).

30. Escobar Latapí, *Con el sudor,* 1986, p. 216.

31. Although this means the weight of a "migration culture" is less in Guadalajara, it does not mean that Guadalajara sends fewer migrants, since its sheer size makes for a greater migration flow. Also, there are areas in the city where a migration culture does exist, and the rates of migration are much higher. But it is not as widespread a phenomenon as in Los Altos de Jalisco or Zacatecas.

32. Wayne Cornelius, "Los Migrantes de la Crisis: The Changing Profile of Mexican Labor Migration to California in the 1980s," Paper delivered at conference, Zamora, Michoacán, November 1988.

33. FOGAIN has handled resources from many international agencies, including the World Bank and the InterAmerican Development Bank.

6

Small Business Development in El Salvador: The Impact of Remittances

José Roberto López
and Mitchell A. Seligson

I. INTRODUCTION

Literature on migration is vast, but as Swamy[3] notes in a comprehensive approach to analyzing the impacts of migration, the study of the link to remittances has been very limited. At a minimum, we know that migration and remittances are positively correlated; more migration signifies, at least for a time, more remittances. We also know that despite reforms of migration law undertaken in the United States, continued migration is a near certainty. Cornelius has studied the question from numerous angles[4] as it relates to Mexico. He persuasively[5] argues that the demand for Mexican labor has a structural component to it and therefore, "there is no evidence that any step taken by the U.S. government in the last 100 years to restrict immigration from Mexico has had any appreciable effect on the underlying structural demand for Mexican labor in the U.S. economy." Remittances, from this perspective, may be seen as a permanent component of a structural problem that will not disappear even with further migration reform.

Beyond the question of the linkage of migration to remittances is the issue of estimating the volume of remittances. Several studies, such as those carried out by Shankman[6] and Swamy[7], have attempted to do this. For the purposes of this paper, however, our concern is not directly with the volume of remittances produced by migration of Salvadorans to the United States, but with the impact of those remittances. A study by Connell,[8] concerned with the utilization of remittances, argues that the bulk of them are used for everyday household consumption rather than conspicuous consumption. This view is the prevalent one according to Russell's extensive review of the literature on the subject.[9] In that review she enumerates seven separate potential benefits of remittances, and lists a corresponding cost for each. Russell found that "the predominant view of remittances in the literature of the mid-1970s was negative."[10]

Recent research, however, has indicated a more positive evaluation of the impact of remittances. Macro-economic effects of remittances have been traced by Pastor and Rogers.[11] They argue that although, "they may be large and important as a source of foreign exchange, they remain an unused opportunity for investment." Pastor goes on to speculate that remittances may result in increased inflation and imports, but presents no data to test this hypothesis.

The Salvadoran case gives us an opportunity to study the impacts of remittances. The civil war that has been raging in El Salvador throughout this decade has resulted in the massive migration of Salvadorans to the United States. While estimates vary, no fewer than 700,000 Salvadoran citizens are believed to be residing in the United States, a figure which represents 12 percent of the entire population of the country. One of every five families in El Salvador is believed to have relatives in the United States and as the number of Salvadorans in the United States increases, a growing volume of capital is being repatriated to El Salvador in the form of remittances. These remittances initially were not a significant factor in the Salvadoran economy, but as the war continued and the number of Salvadorans living in the United States grew, they have become an increasingly important, if not vital, factor in the survival of the formal and informal economy of the country.

After enjoying several decades of growth, El Salvador's economy began to experience a protracted decline in 1979. By 1988, Gross Domestic Product (GDP) was less than two-thirds the 1978 level, and real GDP per capita had reverted to 1966 levels. In essence, over 20 years of growth have been lost in the 1980s. The civil war is certainly a major factor in the decline in the economy, one responsible for the destruction of infrastructure and also massive capital flight estimated to have totaled $800 million in the period 1979–1983 alone, but a 50 percent deterioration in the terms of trade between 1977 and 1986 and a reduction in Salvador's primary export, coffee, resulting from war damage and unsuccessful reform programs for agriculture, banking and external trade have also played a role.[12] In addition, inconsistent domestic policies have impeded required economic stabilization.[13]

Under these circumstances, it is not surprising that the hard currency supply in El Salvador is very scarce. Most estimates show that the main source of dollars has been the vast U.S. foreign aid program, currently at a level of more than $1 million a day. Between 1980 and 1987, U.S. foreign assistance totaled some $2 billion, ranking El Salvador as the most important recipient of U.S. economic assistance in Latin America.

By some accounts, however, remittances (i.e., funds earned by El Salvadorans living abroad and sent back by them to family and friends in El Salvador) exceed the foreign aid income. Official estimates place remittances at $350 million in 1986, but Montes[14] calculated a figure almost four times as high, $1.3 billion. Hence, while it is known that remittances are an important, perhaps the most important, source of foreign exchange earnings, there is wide disagreement as to their overall amount.

Our own estimates of net remittances received is more conservative than that provided by Montes. Using what we have termed a "supply approach," we estimated remittances in the range of $286–$630 million for 1986. Using a "demand approach," we estimated $256 million for 1986. The lower estimate we view as minimal because it does not include remittances used to finance smuggling and because it uses a low estimate of capital. We project these figures to 1988, the year immediately prior to the survey, and estimate remittances at a minimum of $381 million and a high of $724 million.

Adding to the problem of obtaining reasonable estimates of the volume of remittances is the difficulty one has in projecting their volume for future years. One major unknown is the impact that the Simpson-Rodino immigration law will have. Under that law, all aliens not qualifying for residence in the United States are to be expelled. Montes[15] estimates that around 48.6 percent of current Salvadoran residents living in the United States who arrived after 1981 do not qualify for admission under the law. He also estimates that if only half of those excluded are repatriated it would cause a $339 million annual loss in the balance of payments. The impact on the economy of El Salvador cannot be underestimated; the loss represents the equivalent of 64 percent of coffee exports for 1986.

Even though future trends in remittances cannot be precisely predicted, remittances clearly represent a major source of income to the economy of El Salvador. This raises the important question of their impact on economic development in El Salvador. To date, unfortunately, we know virtually nothing about their short- and medium-term impacts on the domestic economy. In this study, we examine that question.

II. STUDY DESIGN

Researchers in the Third World normally encounter more obstacles than they would in the developed countries. These problems are multiplied many times in El Salvador as a result of the protracted guerrilla war that has gripped the country. It is impossible to develop a scientific sample design of the country because of the dislocation of population caused by the war coupled with the inability of census takers to carry out their mission in a systematic fashion. As a result, researchers are faced with two options. One option is to give up any thought of carrying out studies because the conditions are so adverse. The other is to conduct the studies as carefully as possible under the circumstances and then to report the results with far wider "confidence intervals" than would be traditional.

Our interest in this study centered on the utilization of remittances by small businesses in El Salvador. Time and resource constraints confined our study to the metropolitan area of San Salvador. We were interested in small businesses in both the formal as well as the informal sectors, and wished to include establishments that had as few as one employee or as many as 19. It was difficult to select a cut-off at the upper end, but we reviewed the eight definitions currently in use in El Salvador and settled on this number as a reasonable standard.[16] Our resources enabled us to design a sample that would produce data from at least 200 respondents. Given that the most systematic work to date had been limited to 35 interviews,[17] we felt that even though 200 was a small number, it was entirely appropriate for the exploratory nature of this study.

The limitation of sample size to approximately 200 imposed certain constraints on our definition of the target population. Estimates are that one out of five residents of metropolitan San Salvador receive remittances. Of those, a smaller percentage operate their own business and invest those remittances in their business. Had we utilized a probability sample of all residents or businesses in metropolitan San Salvador, the number of respondents in our sample of 200 who both receive and invest remittances would have been quite small. Hence, we decided to define the sample as one that would produce data on small businesses in metropolitan San Salvador that receive remittances, some or all of which they invest in their business.

The approach to the sample that we took has one obvious limitation; we cannot say anything about businesses that do not both receive and invest remittances. Determination of why some businesses receive remittances but do not invest them would require another study in which a sample would be drawn targeting that group. Indeed, we can make no overall statement based on our sample about the proportion of businesses that receive remittances, invested or not. On the other hand, our sample does have the virtue of producing data on those who do receive and invest remittances so that we may study what is done with that income.

Based on the considerations outlined above, we constructed a purposive sample rather than a probability sample. In effect, we were developing what is known as a "rare element sample," and in so doing we attempted to construct it in such a way to provide the greatest representation of metropolitan San Salvador even though the sample itself was not of a probability design.

The universe consisted of the small businesses in greater San Salvador, an area comprised of 18 municipalities. Of those, a total of nine were selected for the survey. The selection was made by first eliminating a group of municipalities which, although they are officially within the metropolitan area, are in reality marginal to it (Santo Tomás, Santiago Texacuangos, San Martín, Apopa, Nejapa, Quezaltepeque and Colón). Then, the municipalities of San Salvador and Nueva San Salvador (Santa Tecla) were selected in order to guarantee that these key centers of the urban area would not be excluded owing to random selection criteria. A group of three municipalities (Ayutuxtepeque, Mejicanos and Cuscatancingo) constitute in effect a single urban area and were counted as one unit for sample purposes. The remaining four municipalities (Illopango, San Marcos, Panchimalco and the Auytuxtepeque-Mejicanos-Cuscatancingo group) were selected randomly.

Once the municipalities were selected, the next task was to select the sample areas within each municipality. Normally, one would obtain a list of all communities from the census bureau and proceed to draw the sample from that list, stratified by income. In El Salvador, however, the demarcation of municipality boundaries and communities within those boundaries is poorly specified. Moreover, communities and neighborhoods are extremely heterogenous, with slum areas existing alongside middle and even upper-class neighborhoods. In light of this limitation, it was decided to simply divide each municipality into four segments and to select at random one or more segments within each municipality for creating the sample. In the case of the municipality of San Salvador, which had the largest number of small businesses, all four segments were selected. In Nueva San Salvador, two were selected, and in the remaining municipalities, one each. A single interviewer was assigned to each segment and was told to locate all small businesses and to determine if they were receiving remittances and investing them in their business. The interviewer was to locate and interview the owner of the business or, if the owner had left an individual in charge of the business, to interview that person.

Each interviewer was responsible for obtaining approximately 20 interviews, 9 from small business owners in lower-middle class neighborhoods, 6 from poor neighborhoods and 5 from very poor neighborhoods.[18] This division was determined by Montes' previous work in which he determined that for each lower-middle class family who received remittances, 2.9 did not; for each poor family receiving, 4.8 did not; and for each very poor family, 5.5 did not. In this way, the sample was self-weighing based upon the estimated frequency of families of that social class receiving remittances from the United States.

The sample produced a total of 211 usable interviews, 11 more than specified. The survey was carried out during the month of June 1989. In order to obtain these interviews, a large number of businesses had to be visited. After each business was located, it was necessary to determine if the given establishment received remittances from the United States. Table 1 shows the number of businesses visited in the three types of neighborhoods included in the sample frame (i.e., extremely poor, poor and lower-middle class). As can be seen, approximately five businesses were visited in each type of neighborhood to locate one that admitted to receiving remittances from the United States.

To be included in this study, businesses had to invest their remittances in their own operations. As can be seen in Table 1, an average of two out of five businesses surveyed were not investing remittances in this manner. Once again, there was little difference among the three classes of neighborhoods.

Finally, once we had located business that both received remittances and invested them in the business, we had to obtain the cooperation of the respondent to do the survey. That proved to be less of a problem than we feared, and most respondents cooperated (see Table 1). An average of slightly more than one business rejected the interview for each successful

TABLE 1
SAMPLE CHARACTERISTICS

	Type of neighborhood		
	Low-middle class	Poor	Extreme poverty
Business visited with no remittances			
(Valid N)	(87)	(88)	(36)
Average	5.2	4.7	4.7
Business with remittances but not investing them in business			
(Valid N)	(87)	(88)	(36)
Average	2.1	2.0	2.2
Business with remitt. rejecting the interview			
(Valid N)	(87)	(88)	(36)
Average	1.4	1.2	1.2
Interview duration (in minutes)			
(Valid N)	(87)	(88)	(36)
Average	30.2	28.4	31.6

Source: Survey interviews, June 1989.

interview we carried out.

Once the actual interview began, we found that the average time to complete it was about one-half hour, as is also shown in Table 1. Differences among neighborhoods were insignificant.

III. CHARACTERISTICS OF THE SAMPLE

Types of Small Business Surveyed

We found a great variety of businesses in the sample. We were able to categorize these into four main types plus a catch-all category of "other." This last category includes such establishments as beauty shops, clinics, taxi drivers, food production, funeral homes, etc. Table 2 shows the distribution of businesses in the sample.

The distribution of types of businesses was not completely uniform by neighborhood type. As Table 3 shows, within the extremely poor neighborhoods, stores were less common than in the other two neighborhood types. In contrast, street vendors were far more common in these poorest neighborhoods than in the others. The other observed differences were minor.

The sample was comprised of many informal businesses and a smaller number of better, established enterprises. Several indications of this dis-

TABLE 2
TYPES OF BUSINESSES SURVEYED

Type of business	
Stores (dry goods, grocery, etc.)	
%	39.8%
(N)	(84)
Repair shops	
%	12.3%
(N)	(26)
Street vendors	
%	9.0%
(N)	(19)
Restaurants	
%	10.4%
(N)	(22)
Other	
%	28.4%
(N)	(60)
TOTAL	
%	100.0%
(N)	(211)

Source: Survey interviews, June 1989.

tribution are contained in Tables 4 and 5. Table 4 indicates that only within the restaurant category do more than half of the businesses have a location out of which business is conducted. Table 5 shows that the businesses were relatively young, averaging between two and three years. The initial investment in these businesses was not large. They averaged between 5,000 and 12,000 colones, about $1,000 to $2,000, for the established business and considerably less for the street vendors. The net worth of the businesses at the time of the interview was greater than the initial investment, generally by a factor of two to three times, but sometimes considerably more.

Demographic Characteristics of the Respondents

We were interested in the impact of remittances on small businesses in El Salvador. Our sample consisted of owners (or, in their absence, operators) of small businesses. In order to appreciate the nature of the owners whose businesses are beneficiaries of remittance income, we need first to review their major demographic characteristics and then provide some summary information on their socio-economic characteristics.

Table 6 shows the distribution of the sample by gender. As can be seen, the sample is almost evenly divided between male and female. There are no notable differences among the neighborhood types included in the

TABLE 3

DISTRIBUTION OF BUSINESSES BY NEIGHBORHOOD

	Type of neighborhood					
	Lower-middle class		Poor		Extreme poverty	
Type of business	%	(N)	%	(N)	%	(N)
Store	42.5	(37)	42.0	(37)	27.8	(10)
Repair shop	11.5	(10)	13.6	(12)	11.1	(4)
Street vendor	3.4	(3)	9.1	(8)	22.2	(8)
Restaurant	12.6	(11)	9.1	(8)	8.3	(3)
Other	29.9	(26)	26.1	(23)	30.6	(11)
TOTAL	100.0	(87)	100.0	(88)	100.0	(36)

Source: Survey interviews, June 1989.

sample.

We do note that gender differences emerge in the sample when it is subdivided by type of business. As can be seen in Table 7, females are underrepresented in repair shops and slightly overrepresented in the categories of stores, street vendors and restaurants. No doubt, this is a function of the type of labor required in the repair shops, most of which were auto or truck repair shops. Marital status of the individuals interviewed varied by type of business. Married respondents were far less frequent among the street vendors than among the other types of business. No doubt this is a function of the greater prevalence of street vendors in the very poor stratum, a group in which marital separations are quite common.

Age did not vary much by type of business. As can be seen in Table 8, street vendors and those in the restaurant business were slightly younger

TABLE 4

USE OF PERMANENT LOCALE FOR BUSINESS

	Type of business									
	Store		Repair shop		Street vendor		Rest.		Other	
Use place of business	%	(N)	%	(N)	%	(N)	%	(N)	%	(N)
Yes	31.0	(26)	46.2	(12)	15.8	(3)	59.1	(13)	43.3	(26)
No	69.0	(58)	53.8	(14)	84.2	(16)	40.9	(9)	56.7	(34)
TOTAL	100.0	(84)	100.0	(26)	100.0	(19)	100.0	(22)	100.0	(60)

Source: Survey interviews, June 1989.

TABLE 5

INDICATORS OF VALUE OF BUSINESS

	Type of business				
	Store	Repair shop	Street vendor	Rest.	Other
Years of operation					
(Valid N)	(84)	(26)	(19)	(22)	(60)
Mean	2.7	3.3	2.6	2.5	2.8
Initial investment					
(Valid N)	(58)	(19)	(17)	(20)	(40)
Mean	5,620.9	6,438.9	785.3	5,800.0	12,933.7
Business estimated value					
(Valid N)	(48)	(18)	(12)	(17)	(34)
Mean	13,325.0	13,894.4	1,622.1	20,323.5	42,128.8

Source: Survey interviews, June 1989.

than the others.

Although many of the respondents were not formally married, the overwhelming majority had children. Household size averaged around five people. This number did not vary by type of business (see Table 9).

The level of literacy varied by type of business, with the lowest literacy rates found among those who work as street vendors or in restaurants. The data are contained in Table 10. In contrast, the Inter-American Development Bank lists a national literacy rate of 67 percent in 1984.

Variation was found in the number of years of schooling among occupational categories, as shown in Table 11. As expected, street vendors had the lowest level of education, but surprisingly, restaurant owners were somewhat better educated than repair shop and store owners.

Monthly income for the head of the household was measured and reported in Salvadoran colones (see Table 12). The exchange rate at the time

TABLE 6

GENDER OF RESPONDENTS BY NEIGHBORHOOD TYPE

	Type of neighborhood					
	Lower middle class		Poor		Extreme poverty	
Gender	%	(N)	%	(N)	%	(N)
Male	54.0	(47)	48.9	(43)	52.8	(19)
Female	46.0	(40)	51.1	(45)	47.2	(17)
TOTAL	100.0	(87)	100.0	(88)	100.0	(36)

Source: Survey interviews, June 1989.

TABLE 7

GENDER AND MARITAL STATUS OF RESPONDENTS BY BUSINESS TYPE

	Type of business									
	Store		Repair shop		Street vendor		Restaurant		Other	
	%	(N)	%	(N)	%	(N)	%	(N)	%	(N)
Sex										
Male	40.5	(34)	73.1	(19)	42.1	(8)	40.9	(9)	65.0	(39)
Female	59.5	(50)	26.9	(7)	57.9	(11)	59.1	(13)	35.0	(21)
TOTAL	100.0	(84)	100.0	(26)	100.0	(19)	100.0	(22)	100.0	(60)
Marital status										
Single	10.7	(9)	15.4	(4)	10.5	(2)	9.1	(2)	6.7	(4)
Married	44.0	(37)	50.0	(13)	26.3	(5)	50.0	(11)	56.7	(34)
Widow(er)	11.9	(10)	7.7	(2)	.0	(0)	4.5	(1)	5.0	(3)
Divorced	6.0	(5)	.0	(0)	5.3	(1)	4.5	(1)	1.7	(1)
Common law union	17.9	(15)	15.4	(4)	26.3	(5)	22.7	(5)	20.0	(12)
Separated	9.5	(8)	11.5	(3)	31.6	(6)	9.1	(2)	10.0	(6)
TOTAL	100.0	(84)	100.0	(26)	100.0	(19)	100.0	(22)	100.0	(60)

Source: Survey interviews, June 1989.

TABLE 8

AGE BY TYPE OF BUSINESS

	Type of business				
Age	Store	Repair shop	Street vendor	Restaurant	Other
(Valid N)	(84)	(26)	(19)	(22)	(60)
Mean	46.3	48.2	43.5	43.1	46.4

Source: Survey interviews, June 1989.

TABLE 9

HOUSEHOLD SIZE AND TYPE OF BUSINESS

	Type of business				
Persons living in the house	Store	Repair shop	Street vendor	Restaurant	Other
(Valid N)	(84)	(26)	(19)	(22)	(60)
Mean	5.1	5.1	4.7	5.5	5.0

Source: Survey interviews, June 1989.

TABLE 10

LITERACY BY TYPE OF BUSINESS

	Type of business									
	Store		Repair shop		Street vendor		Restaurant		Other	
Literacy	%	(N)	%	(N)	%	(N)	%	(N)	%	(N)
Yes	90.5	(76)	92.3	(24)	63.2	(12)	77.3	(17)	90.0	(54)
No	9.5	(8)	7.7	(2)	36.8	(7)	22.7	(5)	10.0	(6)
TOTAL	100.0	(84)	100.0	(26)	100.0	(19)	100.0	(22)	100.0	(60)

Source: Survey interviews, June 1989.

TABLE 11

YEARS OF EDUCATION BY TYPE OF BUSINESS

	Type of business				
Education	Store	Repair shop	Street vendor	Restaurant	Other
(Valid N)	(83)	(26)	(19)	(22)	(60)
Mean	7.6	7.0	4.2	8.1	8.1

Source: Survey interviews, June 1989.

TABLE 12

MONTHLY INCOME BY NEIGHBORHOOD

	Type of neighborhood		
Monthly income, head of household	Low-middle class	Poor	Extreme poverty
(Valid N)	(80)	(80)	(28)
Mean	1,822.4	956.7	556.2

Source: Survey interviews, June 1989.

TABLE 13

HEAD OF HOUSEHOLD MONTHLY INCOME BY TYPE OF BUSINESS

	Type of business				
Monthly income	Store	Repair Shop	Street vendor	Restaurant	Other
Head of household					
(Valid N)	(74)	(25)	(18)	(20)	(51)
Mean	1,122.6	1,012.0	784.2	1,410.0	1,710.1

Source: Survey interviews, June 1989.

TABLE 14

INDICATORS OF LEVELS OF LIVING BY TYPE OF BUSINESS

	Type of business									
	Store		Repair shop		Street vendor		Restaurant		Other	
	%	(N)	%	(N)	%	(N)	%	(N)	%	(N)
Radio owner										
Yes	94.0	(79)	96.2	(25)	78.9	(15)	95.5	(21)	96.7	(58)
No	6.0	(5)	3.8	(1)	21.1	(4)	4.5	(1)	3.3	(2)
Telephone owner										
Yes	28.6	(24)	26.9	(7)	5.3	(1)	40.9	(9)	31.7	(19)
No	71.4	(60)	73.1	(19)	94.7	(18)	59.1	(13)	68.3	(41)
Refrigerator owner										
Yes	91.7	(77)	65.4	(17)	36.8	(7)	86.4	(19)	85.0	(51)
No	8.3	(7)	34.6	(9)	63.2	(12)	13.6	(3)	15.0	(9)
Indoor toilet										
Yes	88.1	(74)	96.2	(25)	73.7	(14)	81.8	(18)	90.0	(54)
No	11.9	(10)	3.8	(1)	26.3	(5)	18.2	(4)	10.0	(6)
Potable water										
In home	90.5	(76)	88.5	(23)	57.9	(11)	95.5	(21)	86.7	(52)
Public source	6.0	(5)	7.7	(2)	42.1	(8)	.0	(0)	8.3	(5)
Other	3.6	(3)	3.8	(1)	.0	(0)	4.5	(1)	5.0	(3)
Car owner										
Yes	27.4	(23)	19.2	(5)	15.8	(3)	27.3	(6)	41.7	(25)
No	71.4	(60)	80.8	(21)	84.2	(16)	72.7	(16)	58.3	(35)
DK	1.2	(1)	.0	(0)	.0	(0)	.0	(0)	.0	(0)
Cooking instrument										
Wood	6.0	(5)	7.7	(2)	26.3	(5)	18.2	(4)	10.0	(6)
Kerosene	1.2	(1)	3.8	(1)	15.8	(3)	.0	(0)	1.7	(1)
Gas	81.0	(68)	69.2	(18)	57.9	(11)	54.5	(12)	75.0	(45)
Electricity	11.9	(10)	15.4	(4)	.0	(0)	27.3	(6)	11.7	(7)
DK	.0	(0)	3.8	(1)	.0	(0)	.0	(0)	1.7	(1)
TOTAL	100.0	(84)	100.0	(26)	100.0	(19)	100.0	(22)	100.0	(60)

Source: Survey interviews, June 1989.

of the interviews was 5.6 colones to the U.S. dollar. The data show that the incomes varied by neighborhood type, with the poorest heads of household earning less than one-third of those in the more affluent group. As shown in Table 13, those in the "other" category earned the greatest income. Surprisingly, restaurant owners earned more than store owners, although the difference was not very large.

One final table portrays the respondents' living standard. Once again street vendors came out at the bottom of the list. (see Table 14).

IV. VOLUME AND IMPORTANCE OF REMITTANCES FOR SMALL BUSINESSES

Table 15 compares the volume of remittances received by small businesses to the overall income stream of the respondents. The most important calculation is shown on line five. As we can see, for each type of business, remittances represent about half of total income and are the main source of household income. This is a large figure, but not surprisingly large. In the detailed Massey study of migration from western Mexico, income from U.S. migrant labor to the households ranged from a low of 66 percent to a high of 87 percent.[19] The results of the El Salvador study differ from those of Mexico in that the remittances flowing to small businesses in El Salvador are much more likely to be invested than they are in Mexico. In Mexico, productive investment ranges from none to a high of 25 percent, depending upon the location (urban vs. rural) and age of the respondents.[20]

We know, then, that remittances play a very important role in the overall economy of these small business families. But what of the use of remittances in the businesses themselves? We also attempted to determine how much of the remittances received was invested in the businesses and how much was spent in other ways. The direct impact of remittances on small business development is shown in Table 16, which depicts the percentage of total remittance income invested in the various businesses. In each of the business types, 44 percent to 48 percent of the total was invested directly in the business. Thus, the investment would have a subsidiary role which, in most cases, probably substitutes or reduces the demand for bank credit.

Further impacts of remittances are indirect. For example, note the impact of employment generation by the small businesses included in the sample. The economic impact of employment generation can be measured by examining employee salaries. The data in Table 17 indicates that significant sums are paid to employees of the business studied. We cannot trace here how much of those salaries can be directly or indirectly attributed to remittances, but we can see that salaries for family workers are

TABLE 15

MONTHLY INCOME (IN COLONES) FROM VARIOUS SOURCES

	Type of business				
	Store	Repair shop	Street sale	Restaurant	Other
Income, head of family					
(Valid N)	(74)	(25)	(18)	(20)	(51)
Mean	1,122.64	1,012.00	784.17	1,410.00	1,710.08
Net business income					
(Valid N)	(49)	(19)	(12)	(18)	(34)
Mean	817.65	1,511.40	598.61	801.39	1,388.55
Remittance income					
(Valid N)	(84)	(26)	(19)	(22)	(60)
Mean	1,122.20	1,229.85	756.00	948.18	1,478.03
Total gross income of family head (Remittance income plus other income, i.e., 1 + 3)*					
(Valid N)	(74)	(25)	(18)	(20)	(51)
Mean	2,312.48	2,279.84	1,563.50	2,380.20	3,223.84
Remittances as percentage of gross income (3/4).					
(Valid N)	(74)	(25)	(18)	(20)	(51)
Mean	.51	.57	.52	.45	.47
Net business income as percentage of gross income (2/4)					
(Valid N)	(49)	(19)	(12)	(17)	(31)
Mean	.40	.41	.37	.42	.40

Note: *Net business income cannot be added since it is not known if family head always considers this income in his/her estimate of gross income. Our assumption is that such income is included.

Source: Survey interviews, June 1989.

lower than salaries for non-family workers in all categories. The salaries of nonfamily workers are, except for the "other" category, close to the minimum wage range of 330–450 colones per month. We are able to see that the absence of greater remittance flows is viewed as a barrier to greater investment.

We noted that nearly half of all of the respondents invested remittances in their businesses. As shown in Table 18, other uses of remittances covered many areas, the most important of which was food consumption. Expenditures for housing, often reported as the largest use of remittance income, was quite limited in the El Salvador sample. For example, one survey in Turkey showed that 49 percent of remittance income was used

TABLE 16

PERCENTAGE OF REMITTANCES INVESTED IN BUSINESS BY TYPE OF BUSINESS

	Type of business				
	Store	Repair shop	Street vendor	Restaurant	Other
Percent of remittances invested in business					
(Valid N)	(84)	(26)	(19)	(22)	(60)
Mean %	44	44	46	45	48

Source: Survey interviews, June 1989.

TABLE 17

AVERAGE MONTHLY SALARIES (IN COLONES) PAID TO EMPLOYEES BY TYPE OF BUSINESS

	Type of business				
	Store	Repair shop	Street vendor	Rest.	Other
Salary of family workers					
(Valid N)	(32)	(10)	(4)	(13)	(24)
Mean	156.3	430.0	375.0	261.5	323.3
Salary of non-family workers					
(Valid N)	(8)	(13)	(0)	(11)	(16)
Mean	243.8	508.1	—	356.8	1,261.8

Source: Survey interviews, June 1989.

for housing, while another study in Portugal found that housing absorbed 38 percent of the total income.[21]

V. THE IMPORTANCE OF REMITTANCES IN SMALL BUSINESS DEVELOPMENT

The picture that emerges from the data is that for those small businesses receiving remittances in El Salvador, the income plays a very large role in economic development. Although our sample is small and does not represent all small businesses in El Salvador, the results nevertheless show how important remittances can be.

This important finding relates directly to the controversy surrounding the economic impact of remittances. Several studies on remittances, according to the extensive review conducted by Russell,[22] demonstrate neutral or negative consequences on the domestic economy of countries re-

TABLE 18

USE OF REMITTANCES
(Monthly means, in dollars)

	Type of business				
	Store	Repair shop	Street vendor	Restaurant	Other
Food					
Mean	37.0	55.0	34.8	23.9	50.8
(%)	(18.4)	(25.3)	(25.7)	(14.1)	(19.2)
House payment					
Mean	12.8	8.1	13.2	11.8	13.0
(%)	(6.4)	(3.7)	(9.8)	(7.0)	(4.9)
Clothes and shoes					
Mean	8.1	11.9	5.5	5.7	9.9
(%)	(4.0)	(5.5)	(4.1)	(3.4)	(3.7)
Health					
Mean	9.5	12.6	6.0	8.3	15.0
(%)	(4.7)	(5.8)	(4.4)	(4.9)	(5.7)
Education					
Mean	11.2	14.6	8.9	28.4	9.4
(%)	(5.6)	(6.7)	(6.6)	(16.8)	(3.6)
Car payments					
Mean	1.8	0.0	0.0	2.3	5.8
(%)	(0.9)	(0.0)	(0.0)	(1.4)	(2.2)
Business expenses					
Mean	88.4	95.2	62.1	75.7	127.0
(%)	(44.0)	(43.7)	(46.0)	(44.7)	(48.1)
Savings					
Mean	16.8	17.4	4.5	9.2	20.6
(%)	(8.4)	(8.0)	(3.3)	(5.4)	(7.8)
Miscellaneous					
Mean	15.0	2.9	0.0	4.0	12.4
(%)	(7.5)	(1.3)	(0.0)	(2.4)	(4.7)
Total					
Mean	200.7	217.7	135.0	169.3	264.0
(%)	(100.0)	(100.0)	(100.0)	(100.0)	(100.0)

Source: Survey interviews, June 1989.

ceiving remittances. Many of those studies have focused on issues such as the potential inflationary impact of remittances, or more specifically, on the stimulation of conspicuous consumption. For example, in a study conducted in Pakistan, 62 percent of remittances were found to be used for current consumption.[23] Russell concludes:

> In assessing the value of the use of remittances, most observers acknowledge that the benefits accrue largely to the individual migrant's family. The benefits to the economy and the society at large

> are viewed as being much more questionable, given the effects of remittances on increasing consumer demands, fueling inflation and increasing imports.[24]

Little attention has been placed upon the impact of remittances on economic development.[25] The limited research that has been conducted has focused on the multiplier effects of investments in housing, for example. One study conducted in Mexico, however, reports some important impacts on small business development.[26] In that study it was found that 9 percent of the businesses in one community and 16 percent of businesses in another community were established with money Mexican migrants earned in the United States.

Given the large percentage of remittance income spent on small businesses in our sample and the significant amount of remittance income as a proportion of total income, serious questions need to be raised about the economic viability of the businesses supported by remittance income. Without the remittances the enterprises might not survive, and the remittances are therefore merely subsidizing nonviable enterprises. We used our survey to provide at least a partial answer to this question, as shown in Table 19.

The first variable displayed in Table 19 shows that from one-quarter to more than one-third of the businesses in San Salvador sample were established as a result of the availability of remittances. This figure is substantially higher than that found in the Mexico survey, lending credence to the view that a significant percentage of the businesses would not have existed if the remittances had not been available. The second item in the table reinforces and magnifies the remittance-dependence thesis. From one-third to more than two-thirds of the respondents reported that their future economic situation depended upon the continuous flow of remittance income.

What is most disturbing about the results of the first two questions in the table is that even though a large percentage of the respondents believe that their economic future rests on remittance income, only a limited percentage (ranging from 9 percent to 39 percent) of the respondents believe that the remittance flow is likely to be permanent. However, approximately half of all of the respondents did not guess as to how long the remittance flow would continue.

The findings presented in Table 19 provide at least a partial indication of the nonviability of a significant proportion of the small businesses receiving remittances in El Salvador. Using strict economic criteria, one could easily argue that this evidence further supports the negative view of the role of remittances in development. However, such an interpretation has to be conditioned by five factors.

TABLE 19

IMPORTANCE OF REMITTANCES TO SMALL BUSINESSES

	Type of business									
	Store		Repair shop		Street vendor		Rest.		Other	
	%	(N)	%	(N)	%	(N)	%	(N)	%	(N)
Business was open due to remitt.										
Yes	32.1	(27)	38.5	(10)	26.3	(5)	27.3	(6)	35.0	(21)
No	67.9	(57)	61.5	(16)	73.7	(14)	72.7	(16)	65.0	(39)
TOTAL	100.0	(84)	100.0	(26)	100.0	(19)	100.0	(22)	100.0	(60)
Future dependence on remittances										
Yes	53.6	(45)	69.2	(18)	52.6	(10)	45.5	(10)	38.3	(23)
No	46.4	(39)	30.8	(8)	47.4	(9)	54.5	(12)	60.0	(36)
DK	.0	(0)	.0	(0)	.0	(0)	.0	(0)	1.7	(1)
TOTAL	100.0	(84)	100.0	(26)	100.0	(19)	100.0	(22)	100.0	(60)
Expectation of remittances in future										
A few more months	3.6	(3)	3.8	(1)	5.3	(1)	9.1	(2)	10.0	(6)
1–2 years more	8.3	(7)	7.7	(2)	.0	(0)	9.1	(2)	.0	(0)
More than 2 years	16.7	(14)	7.7	(2)	15.8	(3)	22.7	(5)	11.7	(7)
Forever	26.2	(22)	38.5	(10)	15.8	(3)	9.1	(2)	25.0	(15)
DK	45.2	(38)	42.3	(11)	63.2	(12)	50.0	(11)	53.3	(32)
TOTAL	100.0	(84)	100.0	(26)	100.0	(19)	100.0	(22)	100.0	(60)

Source: Survey interviews, June 1989.

TABLE 20
RELATIONSHIP BETWEEN INITIAL AND FUTURE DEPENDENCE ON REMITTANCES

	Business was opened due to remittances			
	Yes		No	
	%	(N)	%	(N)
Economic future depends on remittances				
Yes	75.4	(52)	38.0	(54)
No	23.2	(16)	62.0	(88)
DK	1.4	(1)	.0	(0)
TOTAL	100.0	(69)	100.0	(142)

Note: Chi-square < .001; Tau b = .36
Source: Survey interviews, June 1989.

1. Even though many businesses seem dependent upon remittances, many clearly are not.
2. While as many as one-third of the businesses were started because of remittances, two-thirds and more were not.
3. As shown in Table 20, the businesses that are viewed by their owners as most likely to fail as a result of the termination of remittances are the ones that were started with remittances in the first place. Of the 32 percent of the businesses started with remittances, 77 percent would fail without them. On the other hand, nearly two-thirds of the business not established with remittances are viewed by the respondents as being able to survive such a withdrawal.
4. Even among the businesses established with remittances, and acknowledging that most of those would fail as a result of remittance withdrawal, one-quarter are viewed by their owners as surviving.
5. These points must be viewed in the context of the Salvadoran Civil War. Survival of small businesses in prosperous industrialized countries is the exception rather than the rule. Survival rates for developing countries are likely to be even lower. In the extremely uncertain environment of war-torn El Salvador, the finding that many businesses would fail without remittances should come as no surprise, but is not necessarily a reason for minimizing the developmental role of those remittances.

VI. STIMULATING THE PRODUCTIVE USE OF REMITTANCES

The question now becomes how to help channel these remittances to stimulate small business development. In the final section of this paper, we attempt to provide some answers to that question.

TABLE 21

PRINCIPAL REASONS FOR NON-INVESTMENT OF REMITTANCES

	Type of business									
	Store		Repair shop		Street vendor		Rest.		Other	
	%	(N)	%	(N)	%	(N)	%	(N)	%	(N)
Small amount of remittances										
Yes	52.4	(44)	50.0	(13)	68.4	(13)	59.1	(13)	41.7	(25)
No	45.2	(38)	42.3	(11)	31.6	(6)	36.4	(8)	56.7	(34)
DK	2.4	(2)	7.7	(2)	.0	(0)	4.5	(1)	1.7	(1)
TOTAL	100.0	(84)	100.0	(26)	100.0	(19)	100.0	(22)	100.0	(60)
Does not know where to invest										
Yes	16.7	(14)	11.5	(3)	5.3	(1)	4.5	(1)	13.3	(8)
No	79.8	(67)	80.8	(21)	89.5	(17)	86.4	(19)	85.0	(51)
DK	3.6	(3)	7.7	(2)	5.3	(1)	9.1	(2)	1.7	(1)
TOTAL	100.0	(84)	100.0	(26)	100.0	(19)	100.0	(22)	100.0	(60)
Irregularity of remittances										
Yes	38.1	(32)	15.4	(4)	26.3	(5)	18.2	(4)	21.7	(13)
No	59.5	(50)	76.9	(20)	68.4	(13)	72.7	(16)	76.7	(46)
DK	2.4	(2)	7.7	(2)	5.3	(1)	9.1	(2)	1.7	(1)
TOTAL	100.0	(84)	100.0	(26)	100.0	(19)	100.0	(22)	100.0	(60)
Bad climate for investment										
Yes	28.6	(24)	23.1	(6)	21.1	(4)	27.3	(6)	18.3	(11)
No	69.0	(58)	73.1	(19)	73.7	(14)	63.6	(14)	80.0	(48)
DK	2.4	(2)	3.8	(1)	5.3	(1)	9.1	(2)	1.7	(1)
TOTAL	100.0	(84)	100.0	(26)	100.0	(19)	100.0	(22)	100.0	(60)
Does not need to invest										
Yes	22.6	(19)	19.2	(5)	15.8	(3)	18.2	(4)	18.3	(11)
No	75.0	(63)	73.1	(19)	78.9	(15)	72.7	(16)	80.0	(48)
DK	2.4	(2)	7.7	(2)	5.3	(1)	9.1	(2)	1.7	(1)
TOTAL	100.0	(84)	100.0	(26)	100.0	(19)	100.0	(22)	100.0	(60)

Source: Survey interviews, June 1989.

We asked the respondents to identify their concerns about not investing more remittances in their businesses. Table 21 shows their replies. Approximately half of all of the respondents stated that the small volume of remittances was a principal problem. In contrast, a much smaller percentage of the respondents stated that they did not know where to invest the money, that remittances were irregularly received, that they did not think the business climate was favorable for investment or that they did not need to invest. One can deduce from these findings that the business owners interviewed believe that greater volumes of remittances would translate into greater investment. Stimulation of the volume of remittances may result, therefore, in an interactive effect that would increase investment beyond the increased volume of remittances. In effect, there may be a threshold level beyond which remittance investment in the small businesses would increase, but beneath which significant portions of the money would be spent in consumption or on other nonbusiness expenditures.

Table 21 demonstrates that from the point of view of the small business people interviewed for this study, the small irregular remittance flows are the primary constraints to increased business investments. This suggests that to increase investment, one must increase the volume and regularity of the remittance flow. Consequently, two policy issues arise: how to increase the flow of remittances, and how to provide for a greater regularity in that flow.

Policies to increase or keep constant the flow of total remittances must be linked to the determinants of the overall remittance level. These determinants include:

(1) The number of Salvadoran workers in the United States; (2) the premium between the black market and the official exchange rate; and (3) the average salary of Salvadorans residing in the United States.

Salvadoran authorities can only affect the second determinant and, to a very limited extent, the first one.

We have shown[27] that there will be a demographic constraint reducing Salvadoran migration rates to the United States in future years, that immigration controls in the United States have only a short-term impact, and that illegal employment opportunities and wage levels in the United States are independent from the volume of illegal Salvadoran immigration.[28]

Clearly the most important macroeconomic measure for keeping constant the overall level of remittances and for inducing remittances to go through official channels is the establishment of a realistic unitary (single) rate of exchange for El Salvador. Remittances are notably sensitive to overvaluation and multiple exchange rates, such as preferential exchange rates previously used for remittances. They are difficult to control and their capacity to attract remittances through official channels had proven to be of dubious value in the Salvadoran case.[29] From the senders' point of view, it is almost certain that a generalized and uncontrolled devaluation of the colon can only produce a decline in the overall level of remittances sent, while it is not clear that the black market for dollars will disappear. This market exists sumarily to ration hard currency for imports, a policy that will not disappear in the short term.[30]

The most important policies are those that attract remittances through official channels. We surveyed small business owners' reaction to the implementation of a new law that would forbid the changing of dollars on

TABLE 22

OPINIONS ON EXCHANGE RATES BY TYPE OF NEIGHBORHOOD

	Type of neighborhood					
	Lower-middle class		Poor		Extreme poverty	
	%	(N)	%	(N)	%	(N)
Reaction to a better exchange rate						
Yes	78.2	(68)	73.9	(65)	69.4	(25)
No	5.7	(5)	12.5	(11)	8.3	(3)
No answer	16.1	(14)	13.6	(12)	22.2	(8)
TOTAL	100.0	(87)	100.0	(88)	100.0	(36)
Reaction to dollar banking accounts						
Yes	70.1	(61)	69.3	(61)	52.8	(19)
No	16.1	(14)	15.9	(14)	19.4	(7)
No answer	13.8	(12)	14.8	(13)	27.8	(10)
TOTAL	100.0	(87)	100.0	(88)	100.0	(36)
Reaction to more credit facilities						
Yes	65.5	(57)	55.7	(49)	52.8	(19)
No	32.2	(28)	43.2	(38)	44.4	(16)
No answer	2.3	(2)	1.1	(1)	2.8	(1)
TOTAL	100.0	(87)	100.0	(88)	100.0	(36)

Source: Survey interviews, June 1989.

the street. Their reactions were divided: 37 percent said that they would stop exchanging their dollars on the street, 25 percent said that they would not stop doing it and 38 percent did not know what they would do. We also asked for their reaction to three kinds of banking incentives: a preferential exchange rate, permission for the opening of dollar accounts and credit facilities for regular receivers of remittances.

Table 22 indicates that small business owners in different neighborhoods did not differ substantially in their views on a preferential exchange rate for remittances. More than 70 percent would welcome such a measure, if the bank exchange rate were at least at the same amount as the street rate.

Reaction to the eventual opening of dollar accounts was very similar, with the exception of extremely poor entrepreneurs who received lower monthly remittances and had less access to banking services. The fact that dollar accounts are as welcome as a preferential exchange rate may point to one of their main advantages: they would permit dollar holders to keep their remittances in a safe place. No other remittance intermediary can guarantee this function.

Only 66 percent of lower middle-class entrepreneurs showed a clear interest in more credit facilities. This probably represents those who have had more credit experience in the past.

These results show a need for policy initiatives. We do not favor a law punishing dollar dealers because it would certainly increase premiums as a result of the higher risk associated with those transactions. We also do not favor compulsory remittances through official channels from Salvadorans working in the United States, such as the government of Philippines requires from their construction workers abroad,[31] because the U.S. government would hardly modify its liberal policy for transfers, unless it had reason to do so.[32] A third proposal of compulsory control was discussed in July 1989. José Manzano, vice manager of the International Department at the Central Bank, proposed that all import permits only be approved when the merchandise was already present in the customs area.[33] This would increase both the amount of dollars received by the banking system and also the level of controls placed upon authorized imports.[34] We do not know the outcome of this proposal, but even if it is accepted, we doubt its effectiveness. Luxury imports have always found their way into the country, and we have seen that the amount of imports financed with black market dollars is only a small portion of total remittances. Therefore, such a regulation would only permit the introduction of a small portion of remittances through official channels.

We do believe that bank incentives might give better results than bank controls. These could include the opening of dollar accounts, premium interest rates on dollar deposits in El Salvador relative to interest rates on comparable dollar deposits in the United States and noninterest benefits to holders of minimum dollar deposits in the banking system.

The opening of checking or savings accounts in dollars is not a new idea in El Salvador. Such accounts were authorized by the Central Bank in 1987, but were never put into effect because no interest rate was stipulated on these accounts and only the exchange rate applied to those dollars. Nevertheless, banking authorities were optimistic about the new economic measures that eliminated the exchange rate premium and increased domestic interest rates in July 1989. According to José Manzano, the elimination of the premium was a good incentive for importers to put their dollars into bank accounts, so they could finance imports at no exchange rate loss. José Riva, in charge of external operations at the Banco Cuzcatlán, did not exclude the near future possibility of opening dollar denominated bank accounts, including certificates of term-deposits that would be competitive with foreign certificates at a premium interest rate.

Premium interest rates on dollar deposits in El Salvador, or banks from El Salvador operating in the United States, relative to the interest rates on comparable maturity deposits in the United States, could become a major focus of the proposal to attract remittances through official channels. An important result of the ten-year old civil war has been the increase in profit opportunities for holders, illegal residents in the United States or domestic residents in El Salvador. These dollar deposits might be attractive if the following conditions materialize:

1) a competitive international interest rate; 2) term-deposits are tax-free; 3) dollars on these accounts are partially or totally repatriable (in dollars) to the foreign country (probably the United States) if it is required by its holder; 4) the Central Bank guarantees commercial banks against financial losses by compensating them when the colon is depreciated vis-à-vis the dollar; 5) people have confidence in the safety and liquidity of their financial assets; and 6) holders of a minimum of dollar-deposits (as well as of dollar-checking accounts) are given preference for non-interest benefits.

Non-interest benefits to holders of dollar deposits or checking accounts might be established in a variety of ways. These include:

1) the linkage of a minimum of dollar deposits to credit facilities for housing, land acquisition or small business expansion, which requires the banks to adapt lending procedures to the availability of collateral and to the viability of the projects; 2) the linkage of minimum dollar deposits to import facilities, including luxury items up to some limit; 3) priority in buying bonds from the government issued in foreign currency and with an even higher interest rate than the one applied to dollar deposits; and 4) customs relief on goods imported, provided the money is remitted from outside in hard currency or placed in an account of a bank from El Salvador operating in the United States. To avoid excessive luxury imports, a ceiling should be established for them.

Policies encouraging Salvadoran workers in the United States to put their savings into productive investment in El Salvador have the advantage of creating a solid link between Salvadoran immigrants and their country of origin. Target remitters might thus be transformed into target savers. Housing, land acquisition or small businesses should be stimulated as preferred investments by regular senders or receivers of remittances. Tax-free schemes, low-interest rates on loans, good maturity conditions and credit and technical supervision might be provided in order to promote these policies.

Pastor and Rogers' initiative[35] involves a more complex policy proposal. According to these authors, remittances could be used to increase foreign aid if Salvadoran banks were to transfer a percentage of remittances absorbed by their offices in the United States and El Salvador to a special fund that could be used as government counterpart for international development projects.

We believe that Pastor and Rogers' scheme might be combined with specific projects for the development of particular communities whose populations have almost entirely migrated to the United States. Such is the case with Intipucá, a town in the Department of La Unión whose population has migrated to Washington, D.C., and with Casitas, a town located in the Department of Santa Ana whose population has migrated to Los Angeles. The former inhabitants of Intipucá or Casitas would be more likely to cooperate if their remittances were used to develop their home community. A similar scheme could be used to create a special fund for the development of small businesses that satisfy minimum requirements for profit, employment, debt, etc. Salvadoran workers who send dollars to relatives in El Salvador who own small businesses should be encouraged to participate.

Other migration for development policies should be used to lure skilled Salvadoran workers or small entrepreneurs (target savers) back to El Salvador. Duty exemptions, information about employment opportunities, permits to maintain dollar accounts, credit facilities, repatriation assistance and other return incentives might favor this policy. The lack of good skilled workers was officially recognized as a problem by the new government in July 1989. The repatriation of target savers is a direct way to invest remittances in productive purposes.

The success of any policy depends on both a major change of the functioning of the Salvadoran banking system vis-à-vis remittances and on the government's priorities. The banking system must spread its services not only in urban areas, but also in rural ones, and reorganize its operations to aggressively compete with private agencies to become effective as remittance intermediaries.

The government must give top priority to its final policy package. President Seaga in Jamaica has been the first Latin American president to invite overseas Jamaicans to participate in the reconstruction of his country by investing in a home or in a foreign exchange account.[36] His example can and should be emulated.

VII. CONCLUSION

After ten years of civil war, many Salvadorans have found a solution to one of their most urgent needs, employment. Today, approximately one out of five families in El Salvador has a relative in the United States who sends remittances on a regular basis. A new, privileged social sector has emerged with an extraordinary economic potential based on remittance income that official authorities and most of the academic community have largely ignored.

Efforts devoted to taking advantage of remittance inflows from Salvadorans residing in the United States are almost nonexistent compared to official measures taken to promote nontraditional and cotton export. Nevertheless, if our minimum estimates of the net amount of remittances that effectively enter the economy are correct, in 1986 the $286.3 million inflow would make remittance inflows the third largest source of foreign exchange for the Salvadoran economy. This income trails the $546.8 million provided by coffee and the $315.3 million provided by U.S. economic assistance. In 1988, with the decline of coffee prices that reduced coffee earnings to $345.7 million, the stagnation of U.S. economic aid at $319.3 million and the quick recovery of the historic levels of Salvadoran illegal migration to the United States, (after a temporary decline due to the application of the new immigration law in 1987), remittances were transformed into the main source of foreign exchange in the Salvadoran balance of payments. This unprecedented use of remittances provided a minimum amount of $380.8 million.

Remittances have drawbacks as well. There has been no import-led boom, but that was probably due to the rationing of hard currency that has prevailed during most of this decade in El Salvador. Nor has there been a demand-pull inflation, but this is likely due to the high level of idle capacity of Salvadoran industry. On the other hand, remittances have played a key role in sustaining import capacity and household incomes. They also have a small but positive impact on domestic consumption which probably is more important in the poorest sector of the population, and a seasonal anti-inflationary role related to their impact (with a negative sign) on the price of the black dollar at the end of the year when the premium reaches its lowest level.

Salvadoran remittances, despite their many important positive characteristics, are not widely absorbed in the banking system. Our estimate is that only roughly a quarter of their annual estimated volume in 1988 has been channeled through the banking system. As a result, their contribution to medium-term Salvadoran development is limited. Surprisingly, an average small business owner invests nearly one of every two dollars received as remittance. As a matter of fact, for all small business categories in our survey, average annual remittances are greater than average annual net profits.

The need to use remittances most effectively is even more important if we realize that future flows of remittances are not likely to be reduced, notwithstanding the views of those who believe that the new U.S. immigration law will dramatically cut remittance flows. Future flows of remittances will depend on Salvadoran illegal immigration to the United States. Flows of illegal immigration again flourished in 1988 and 1989, after a short drop in 1987 when the immigration law became effective. Sooner or later, a demographic constraint will likely reduce the growth rate of net emigration to the United States, but at this point, neither immigration flows nor forced repatriation (which also decreased consecutively in 1987 and 1988) seem to suggest that this rate is headed toward zero or negative levels.

We have developed four alternative scenarios to forecast the volume of remittance inflows for 1989–1993.[37] On the basis of those scenarios, we forecast $479.8 million in net remittance inflows for 1993—an amount that might well retain remittances as one of the two most important sources of hard currency in El Salvador. We are assuming that coffee prices will not remain at their current low levels and that U.S. aid will not return to its historically unprecedented levels of just a few years ago. Hence, remittances will likely count as the first or second largest source of hard currency in El Salvador for many years to come.

Small businesses surveyed showed a positive attitude vis-à-vis new initiatives that the banking system might propose regarding remittances. The importance of the volume of remittances creates an urgent need for a program that will increase their overall amount, absorb them through official channels, give them a productive use and combine them with other developmental policies. No isolated policy can be successful in fulfilling these objectives.

While it is true that the free exchange rate regime put into practice in July 1989 has eliminated the premium and in theory will entice dollar receivers to exchange them in the banking system, we express doubt this policy can reduce inflationary expectations or compete with private agencies in the quality of their transmittal services.

We argued that a real unitary rate of exchange for the colon is the optimal measure to be adopted in order to keep constant the overall level of remittances and to attract remittances through official channels. The devaluation of the colon in 1986 supports this policy. Therefore, a crawling-peg system, characterized by periodic mini-depreciations of the colon and a managed unitary exchange rate, should be preferred to the current regime in the near future.

Among other policies designed to attract remittances through official channels, the opening of dollar denominated checking or term-deposit banking accounts, premium interest rates on dollar deposits and non-interest benefits to holders of a minimum amount of dollar deposits in the banking system are only a few of the mechanisms that could be implemented.

But the channeling of remittances into the banking system by itself is not an adequate solution to medium-term development needs. Investments by dollar senders, incliding those in housing, land acquisition, small business expansion, should be given preferential treatment by banking authorities. A more elaborate policy, such as the one suggested by Pastor and Rogers' initiative, that would tie foreign economic assistance to remittances deserves serious attention by Salvadoran authorities. Furthermore, special investment programs supported by remittance funds could be prepared to promote particular communities in El Salvador, such as Casitas and Intipucá, or to promote particular interests such as small business owners. A complement to this program could be incentives designed to attract Salvadoran target savers or skilled workers from the United States. In combination, these strategies promise to assist in small business development in El Salvador.

NOTES

1. Sharon Stanton Russell, "Remittances from International Migration: A Review Perspective," *World Development* Vol. 14, June 1986, pp. 677–696. This definition is based upon Russell, p. 677. Her definition, however, is restricted to earnings of "migrant workers," whereas we would include earnings sent back to their country of origin by those who have permanently migrated to a second country.

2. José Roberto López and Mitchell A. Seligson, "Remittances and Small Business Development in El Salvador." Report prepared for The Commission for the Study of International Migration and Cooperative Economic Development. Center for Latin American Studies, University of Pittsburgh, Pittsburgh, PA, October 15, 1989. Typescript.

3. Gurushri Swamy, *Population and International Migration* (Washington D.C.: Staff Working Paper No.689, 1985).

4. Wayne Cornelius, "Immigration, Mexican Development Policy and the Future of U.S.-Mexican Relations," Working paper in U.S. Mexican Studies, University of California, San Diego, 1981.

5. Cornelius, "Mexican Migration to the United States," Program in U.S.-Mexican Studies, University of California, San Diego, 1981, p. 9.

6. P. Shankman, *Migration and Underdevelopment: The Case of Western Samoa* (Boulder, CO: Westview Press, 1976).

7. See Swamy, *International Migrant Workers Remittances: Issues and Prospects* (Washington, D.C.: World Bank Staff Working Paper No. 481, 1981).

8. See J. Connel, *Remittances and Rural Development: Migration, Dependency and Inequality in the South Pacific* (Canberra: ANU Press, 1980).

9. Russell, 1986.

10. Russell, 1986, p. 678.

11. Robert Pastor and Rosemarie Rogers, "Using Migration to Enhance Economic Development in the Caribbean: Three Set of Proposals," in *Migration and Development in the Caribbean: the Unexplored Connection,* ed. Robert Pastor (Boulder CO: Westview Press, 1985), p. 322.

12. José Roberto López, "The Nationalization of Foreign Trade in El Salvador," Occasional Paper Series, No. 16, Florida International University, 1986.

13. U.S. General Accounting Office (GAO), "Providing Effective Economic Assistance to El Salvador and Honduras: A Formidable Task." GAO/NSIAD-85-82, (Washington, D.C., 1985).

14. Segundo Montes, *Salvadoreños Refugiados en los Estados Unidos* (San Salvador: UCA Editores, 1987).

15. Montes, "La Crisis Salvadoreña y las Consecuencias de una Repatriación Masiva de refugiados en los Estados Unidos." Boletín de Ciencias Económicas de la Universidad Centroamericana, Año X, No.1, (January–February 1987).

16. These definitions are given in INCAE, *Sondea básico sobre la situación del sector informal de El Salvador* (San Salvador: FUSADES, 1987), p. 15.

17. INCAE, 1987, p. 8.

18. Based upon limited census data, we determined three neighborhood types on which to stratify: lower-middle, poor and extremely poor. Lower-middle neighborhoods were defined as those predominantly populated by individuals with monthly family incomes of between U.S. $300 and $500. In most cases these were employed individuals, with high school education and living in modest dwellings. The "poor" stratum was defined as neighborhoods consisting largely of families of between U.S. $200 and $300, also employed with less than high school education and living in government subsidized housing, rented housing or poor quality private housing. Finally, the "extremely poor" stratum consisted of neighborhoods of individuals with family incomes of $100 or less, a maximum of primary education and who inhabit slum neighborhoods.

19. Douglas S. Massey, Rafael Alarcón, Jorge Durand and Humberto González, *Return to Aztlan: The Social Process of International Migration from Western Mexico* (Berkeley: University of California Press, 1987), p. 211.

20. Massey, 1987, p. 212. In the Mexico study, the focus was upon the money earned in the United States by migrants and its use in Mexico upon their return. Hence, the data are not precisely comparable to the El Salvador remittance survey.

21. Russell, 1986, pp. 686–687.

22. Russell, 1986, pp. 686–687.

23. Russell, 1986, p. 687.

24. Russell, 1986, p. 688.

25. Alejandro Portes and Luis E. Guarnizo, "Tropical Capitalists: U.S.-Bound Immigration and Small-Enterprise Development in the Dominican Republic," Chapter 4 of this volume.

26. Massey, Alarcón, Durand and González, pp. 231–236.

27. López and Seligson, 1989, chapter VII.

28. We assume that demand for illegal labor in the United States is inelastic as to the number of Salvadoran illegals. Compared to the supply of Mexican illegal labor, the Salvadoran supply of labor is not as important.

29. Chandavarkar says that the balance of the application of multiple exchange rates in the Middle East and North African countries receiving remittances is split.

Sudan and Turkey tried them but without any success, while Algeria and Morocco retained them successfully for a long period. See Anand Chandavarkar, "Use of Migrants' Remittances in Labor-Exporting Countries." *Finance and Development* 6 (1980), pp. 36–38.

30. A very low level of foreign reserves in the Central Bank was inherited by the new government founded in June 1989.

31. See Chandavarkar, 1980.

32. We did find one very good reason. The approval of temporary working permits could be linked to the voluntary acceptance by Salvadoran workers that a portion of their salary, an estimated average remittance, be automatically deducted and sent through Salvadoran official channels to his/her relatives in El Salvador. The U.S. government would reinforce its control on the higher number of Salvadoran illegals interested in obtaining at least temporary working permits, and would provide hard currency to the Salvadoran economy at a minimum cost, which eventually could lead to the reduction of current levels of economic assistance. Another option suggested by Pastor and Rogers would be to deduct by the U.S. government a portion of the Social Security tax paid by the emigrant and to transfer it to El Salvador by official channels, but again this would require interest from the U.S. government to help legalize, at least in a temporary form, the Salvadoran workers situation. See Pastor and Rogers, "Using Migration."

33. Actually, import permits can be approved before the departure of the merchandise from its country of origin. Since import permits are approved with some delay, importers get hard currency from the black market in order to realize the operation as soon as possible. When the import permit (or hard currency) is obtained they sell it or keep it for another operation.

34. José Manzano, "Regulaciones para los Registros de Importación," (Central Bank Memorandum, 21 July 1989).

35. Pastor and Rogers, 1985.

36. Pastor and Rogers, 1985.

37. López and Seligson, 1989.

About the Editors and Contributors

Wilbert O. Bascom is chief of international banking, Department of Banking and Finance, State Comptroller's Office in Florida. He was visiting professor in international banking (1987–1988) at the Florida International University and adjunct professor in international business (1984–1988) at Florida State University. Currently, he substitutes for the Florida comptroller as chairman of the state's International Banking and Trade Study Commission. He has established banks in Guyana and Dominica, West Indies. From 1970–1978 he was chief executive of the Guyana National Cooperative Bank.

María de la O Martínez Castellanos is currently working toward a degree in history at the Universidad de Guadalajara. During the last five years she has worked with Dr. Escobar Latapí as an associate researcher.

Sergio Díaz-Briquets is with Casals & Associates, a consulting firm in Washington, D.C. He was research director of the Commission for the Study of International Migration and Cooperative Economic Development, created by Congress. Earlier he held appointments with Duquesne University in Pittsburgh and with the Population Reference Bureau in Washington, D.C., and was a program officer with the International Development Research Centre (IDRC) in Ottawa, Canada. Díaz-Briquets has been a consultant to the U.S. Agency for International Development, the World Bank, and other international development agencies. Holder of a Ph.D. from the University of Pennsylvania, Díaz-Briquets is the author of several books on a variety of development-related topics, including *The Health Revolution in Cuba* (1983), and coauthor of *Social Change and Internal Migration* (1977). Most recently he edited *Cuban Internationalism in Sub-Saharan Africa* (1989).

Agustín Escobar Latapí is *Investigador Titular* at Centro de Investigaciones y Estudios Superiores en Antropologia Social (CIESAS) Occidente in Guadalajara, Mexico. He holds a degree in social anthropology from Universidad Iberoamericana, an M.A. in economics, and a Ph.D. from the University of Manchester, Great Britain. He has done extensive work on the labor market and the informal sector and has written extensively on both subjects.

Luis E. Guarnizo received his M.A. in sociology from Johns Hopkins University, where he is currently a Ph.D. candidate. He received his undergraduate degree in architecture at the University of America in Bogota, Colombia. He has conducted research on low-income housing in Third World countries at the Massachusetts Institute of Technology and has published articles in Colombia.

Francisco A. Leguizamón received his Ph.D. in business administration from the Instituto de Estudios Superiores de la Empresa (IESE) University of Navarra, Spain, and has held the position of academic director of the Central American Institute for Business Administration (INCAE) in Managua, Nicaragua, since 1987. He has published widely on issues relating to Central American development with special focus on the development of small- and medium-sized businesses. He is the principal author of *El Extensionista Empresarial, un Vínculo para el Desarrollo* and has published various articles on small business development in Central America.

José Roberto López belongs to what is recognized as the new generation of Central American economists. He has written five books and has served as a consultant to USAID, the Ford Foundation, the European Community, the Canadian International Development Agency (CIDA), and other international agencies. He holds an M.A. in economics from the University of Pittsburgh and is currently a Ph.D. candidate in economics at the Catholic University of Louvian, Belgium.

Alejandro Portes received his Ph.D. in sociology from the University of Wisconsin, Madison. He currently holds the John Dewey Chair of Sociology and International Affairs at Johns Hopkins University. Dr. Portes has published widely in the fields of sociology, development, and international affairs. His major publications include *Latin Journey,* with Robert Bach (1985); *The Informal Economy: Studies in Advanced and Less-Developed Countries,* with Manuel Castells and Lauren Benton (1989); and *Immigrant America: A Portrait,* with Ruben G. Rumbaut (1990).

Rolando Reyes is director of the School of Economy of the Technological Institute of Santo Domingo (*Escuela de Económica del Instituto Tecnólogico de Santo Domingo*—INTEC) and deputy director and researcher, Center for Economic Research, Inc., (*Centro de Investigación Económica*—CIECA).

Mitchell A. Seligson is professor of political science and director of the Center for Latin American Studies of the University of Pittsburgh. His books include *Peasants of Costa Rica and the Development of Agrarian Capitalism* and *Maquiladoras and Migration: Workers in the Mexico-United States Border Industrialization Program,* with Edward J. Williams. He has served as a Peace Corps volunteer in Central America and has consulted throughout Latin America on development projects.

Sidney Weintraub is Dean Rusk Professor and director of the Program for U.S.-Mexico Policy Studies at the Lyndon B. Johnson School of Public Affairs at the University of Texas at Austin. He is also a Distinguished Visiting Scholar at the Center for Strategic and International Studies (CSIS). As a career diplomat (1949–1975), he was an assistant administrator of the Agency for International Development, Deputy Assistant Secretary of State for international finance and development, chief of the AID mission in Chile under the Alliance for Progress, and chief of commercial policy in the State Department. Dr. Weintraub also has authored numerous books and monographs focusing on Mexico–United States relations, including *Mexican Trade Policy and the North American Community*

(1988), *Industrial Strategy and Planning in Mexico and the United States* (Westview, 1986), *Free Trade Between Mexico and the United States?* (1984), and *A Marriage of Convenience: Relations Between Mexico and the United States* (1990). He is coeditor with Luis F. Rubio and Alan D. Jones of *U.S.-Mexican Industrial Integration* (Westview, forthcoming).

For Product Safety Concerns and Information please contact our EU
representative GPSR@taylorandfrancis.com
Taylor & Francis Verlag GmbH, Kaufingerstraße 24, 80331 München, Germany

www.ingramcontent.com/pod-product-compliance
Lightning Source LLC
LaVergne TN
LVHW011128300926
849160LV00008B/565

* 9 7 8 0 3 6 7 1 6 6 5 1 9 *